W9-AXV-690

The Economic Dimensions of Globalization

The Economic Dimensions of Globalization

Dilip K. Das

First published 2004 by
PALGRAVE MACMILLAN
Houndmills, Basingstoke, Hampshire RG21 6XS and
175 Fifth Avenue, New York, N.Y. 10010
Companies and representatives throughout the world

PALGRAVE MACMILLAN is the global academic imprint of the Palgrave Macmillan division of St. Martin's Press, LLC and of Palgrave Macmillan Ltd. Macmillan® is a registered trademark in the United States, United Kingdom and other countries. Palgrave is a registered trademark in the European Union and other countries.

ISBN 1–4039–1895–3

A catalogue record for this book is available from the British Library.

Library of Congress Cataloging-in-Publication Data

Das, Dilip K., 1945-
    The economic dimensions of globalization / Dilip K. Das.
        p. cm.
    Includes bibliographical references and index.
    ISBN 1-4039-1895-3 (cloth)
    1. Globalization–Economic aspects. 2. Globalization–Economic aspects–Developing countries. 3. Globalization–Economic aspects–Europe, Eastern. 4.
    Globalization–Economic aspects–China. 5. International trade.
    6. Economic development.
    I. Title.

HF1379.D373 2003
337–dc21   2003053277

10 9 8 7 6 5 4 3 2 1
13 12 11 10 09 08 07 06 05 04

Printed and bound in Great Britain by
Antony Rowe Ltd, Chippenham and Eastbourne

Epigraph

From an economic point of view, globalization represents a process of increasing international division of labor and growing integration of national economies through trade in goods and services, cross-border corporate investment, and capital flows. This process led average global per capita income to more than triple in the second half of the last century... However, globalization means more than just economic growth. It means the free exchange of thoughts and ideas and greater geographical mobility for people. And it is not simply forced upon us, but rather the result of forces of change that are deeply rooted in human nature... Globalization is neither good nor bad: it offers both opportunities and risks. This means that we must seize the opportunities and, at the same time, limit the risks. The world needs more not less globalization, but it must be a better globalization.

HORST KOHLER
Managing Director, International Monetary Fund

(From a speech given on the occasion of the Award Ceremony of the Konrad Adenauer Foundation, Berlin, November 15, 2002.)

For
Vasanti, Tanushree, Siddharth, Sonika
and Mish-Mish

Contents

Preface

If the desire for material or economic progress is a universal drive and if a desire to exchange on the market is a universal human attribute, economic globalization can, and did, indeed serve a basic human goal. Economic globalization is a complex and dynamic process of creating connections and networks, thereby facilitating the trans-border flow of information, goods and services, including factors of production. It is a continuous process of interaction, transformation, integration and institution building.

The underlying theory of economic globalization is the unleashing of unregulated free-market competition and extending its scope globally. There is little new about the concept of economic globalization. If anything, it is an ancient phenomenon. The fundamental ideas fueling globalization are the same as those that inspired tribes thousands of years ago to trade something of value with another tribe. By breaking through conventional national, cultural, and social boundaries that have divided people throughout history, economic globalization has resulted in the near instantaneous exchange of information, trade in goods and services, and movements in factors of production, thereby integrating economic activities – both at macro and micro levels – around the globe.

Often, globalization is either glorified or vilified as an end in itself. It is wiser to judge it critically on the extent to which it advances our highest aspiration, such as broadly shared global prosperity. The industrial economies that have large capital accumulation, have enormously benefited from globalism and the related economic transformation. Another group called the emerging market economies has either recently integrated globally, or is in the process of doing so, and is benefiting from global economic integration. If it is true that globalization is enhancing global welfare, one can say that the rising tide is raising all boats. But it is not true. Many economies have not globally integrated and their prospects for doing so in the future seem to be remote. Professor Nicholas Stern believes that the growth of global markets is continuing to bypass countries that have a cumulative population of two billion.

Experiences of the past two decades demonstrated that there are some downside effects of globalization. Crises and contagions caused by the onward march of globalization have not only attracted a lot of academic curiosity but also adversely affected the quality of lives in many emerging market economies. To most non-economists and to some economists, the globalization ethic seems to systematically allow exploitation of labor and the environment, coercive monopolistic pricing of goods and services, widening gaps between economic classes, and snuffing out of traditional culture and societies. Often, despite the world being more technologically integrated, many so-called "winners" feel increasingly isolated and disconnected from their immediate communities. In an objective and dispassionate manner, this book analyses the achievements of economic globalization, without ignoring its pernicious long- and short-term effects.

During the contemporary period, as economies and societies around the world are becoming progressively more integrated, academic interest in economic globalization is rising. This book has been written in response to the increasing interest in the integration of the global economy. Interest in this theme is sure to be sustained during the early part of the twenty-first century. The book focuses on the principal economic trends in globalization with a view to highlighting their implications for the immediate future. It provides analysis of trends in economic globalization from the perspectives of the student community, researchers and policy makers.

Economic globalization is multifaceted. It is a complex phenomenon, covers a wide canvas and cannot be adequately analysed in a single normal-sized book. My objective is more humble than to examine all aspects of economic globalization. In a succinct manner, this book covers the principal normative and positive strands with which one needs to be properly familiar in this area. As it is essential for a book on globalization, parts of chapters have been written in a "just-the-facts-jack" style. The selection and rejection of themes for coverage in this book has been carefully done. For instance, technological globalization and variations in global productivity have not been covered in this book. Many scholars have analysed global technology spillover and its impact on productivity through imports and foreign direct investment. Despite being a significant economic issue, it is so large an area in its own right that one needs to write a book on this very issue.

The principal foci of the book are the economic, trade and financial dimensions of globalization. Therefore, it delves into issues such as exchange rate regimes, monetary policy fiscal revenue, migration, labor market, competition, and income convergence. The latest knowledge, the newest concepts and analyses in these areas have been focused on.

Domestic and international deregulation and liberalization, declining domestic distortions and falling tariff and non-tariff barriers have enhanced market access for many economies. The final result is better integrated and more globalized markets. Domestic and multilateral endeavors to liberalize trade and financial markets are studied as well as their impact on global trade and financial patterns.

In this book, the picture of globalization has been painted with a broad brush. The unique feature that distinguishes it from the competition is its succinct coverage of numerous, carefully selected, thematic issues that fall under the rubric of globalization. The book is easy to access for the target readership because of its descriptive analysis style, which stops short of mathematical formulations and econometric modeling. It makes the book accessible to a larger number of readers. Many students and other readers, who have good analytical minds and sound knowledge of economics, feel lost in mathematical formulations. Equations, technicalities and econometric modeling miff many potential readers. They find overly technical works rather discouraging to approach. The target readership for this volume includes graduate students in business, economics, finance, international political economy, and senior level undergraduates as well as researchers, professionals and policy makers. This book is not rigorous and not intended for academic specialists in this area.

Given the significance of the issue, the book gives somewhat greater attention to financial globalization, to which a full and somewhat longish chapter has been devoted. The coverage extends to both contemporary and historic issues in this area. The domestic and international *mese-en-scène* of financial globalization has been surveyed. The analysis includes the impact of financial globalization on domestic financial sector, growth, efficiency, competition, and economic growth as well as strengths and limitations of the global financial system. Again, the latest knowledge, the newest concepts and analyses in these topics have covered. In addition, the global financial architecture, which has a direct bearing on financial globalization and has attracted prominent economists of several periods, has been focused upon. Coverage of financial globalization would be considered incomplete without paying adequate attention to the global financial system.

As regards the structure of the book, it is divided into six chapters. Chapter 1 introduces the concept of globalization. After defining the beast and taxonomical issues, it goes into the benevolent versus malevolent debate, and also deals with the ongoing vitriolic dialogue on the impact of globalization on poverty. Chapter 2 delves into the long- and short-term historical aspects of economic globalization, and traces global economic integration over the second millennium as well as during the contemporary era of globalization. Principal characteristics of economic globalization during various periods and sub-periods have been analysed in this chapter. Analysis in Chapter 3 investigates the multiple links of globalization in a succinct manner. The issues included are currency regimes, monetary and fiscal policies, competition, labor markets and migration and income convergence. Chapter 4 addresses trade and global integration, with focus on the global trading system, trade policy liberalization and the various rounds of multilateral trade negotiations. The last two named issues have contributed to globalization through the trade channel. It also analyses the empirical evidence of globalization that advanced with expansion in trade flows. As noted in the preceding paragraph, financial globalization and global financial architecture are the themes of the Chapters 5 and 6.

I take this opportunity to thank my son, Siddharth, for providing prompt and efficient research assistance and two anonymous referees for providing detailed comments on the manuscript. I am grateful to Amanda Watkins of Palgrave Macmillan Ltd, for handling the publication of this book in an exceedingly efficient manner. I have been in the business of researching, writing and publishing for over three decades now and find that Amanda's level of efficiency is an absolutely rare commodity in the publishing industry. To nurture excellence in any area of human endeavor, credit should be given where it is deserved. One neither needs a sword nor a gun to kill excellence in any society. Ignore and it will wilt away.

Dilip K. Das
Toronto
June 2003

1
Globalization: Introducing the Concept

1. Globalization: vintage twenty-first century

During the past quarter century, the concept of globalization acquired a good deal of currency as well as involvement from various stakeholders. Its relevance and significance extends well beyond economists, to policy makers, politicians and to the general public at large. Therefore, it came to acquire considerable emotive meaning and force. The concept lacked *one* crisp and widely accepted definition. If anything, the term globalization is used as a portmanteau. It has become a cliché, a trite, and a stereotype expression that has lost its ingenuity through long overuse. Often in an imprecise manner, the term is used for description, approval, and disapproval. There has been a strong penchant to put any new idea, notion or change of fundamental nature under the rubric of globalization, and accordingly, the literature surrounding the subject is multidisciplinary at best, confused at worst.

The multidisciplinary and multifaceted nature of globalization is obvious from its economic, financial, business, political, technological, environmental, cultural, educational, international relations and national and international security-related dimensions. They may frequently be mutually reinforcing but they are diverse in their origins and therefore it has become an area of intense academic curiosity. It is well recognized that globalization has large and definitive economic and financial dimensions, albeit in no way is globalization limited to economic variables as it is sometimes made out to be. From an economic point of view, globalization represents a process of increasing international divisions of labor and growing integration of national economies through trade in goods and services, cross-border corporate investment, capital flows and migration of human resources. Like economic growth, it is a complex meta-process. Globalization is known to influence factor prices. The economic dimensions entail the ongoing global trend towards the free flow of trade in goods and services as well as factors of production, namely, capital and labor.[1] These movements have contributed to integration of the international economy.[2] As the integrated world markets expand economic freedom and spur competition, globalization raises productivity in economies that open themselves to the global marketplace.

Those who use the term globalization disagree about its consequences. The concept has both fervent supporters and trenchant critics, although most economists fall in the former category. Its supporters believe that it has lifted or can potentially lift millions out of poverty. Conversely, its critics believe that it has pushed millions into deeper poverty. There are some academic analysts who straddle both of these views.[3] While conceding the welfare effects of globalization, this group of analysts contends that the power structure of national and supranational institutions is such that potential benefits of globalization cannot be realized. It is because of this limitation that globalization has turned into "a perverse malign force hurting millions."

Economic achievements of the East and Southeast Asian economies during the 1970s and the 1980s and the fall of Soviet Union in 1991 and disintegration of the socialist bloc, seriously influenced the minds of the policy makers in the developing world. The fall of the socialist bloc economies was an epoch-making event. It created a new group of transition economies that were eager to make up for their economic mismanagement under the socialist economic system. Their need for progressing towards their growth potential was pressing. They attempted to modernize and adopt the neoclassical economic principles, which in turn put them on the long road to globalization. The Russian

---

[1] Despite technological advances and resulting improvements in modes of transport of labor, the contemporary period of globalization is much less than that during the Pax Britannica (cf. Chapter 3, section 6). The world is decisively less liberal in the area of immigration now than it was during the previous era of globalization. Movements of labor have been restricted for cultural and political reasons. Haider's party in Austria and Le Pen's party in France represent the extreme form of political opposition to liberal global labor movements. A similar observation can be made regarding the advancement in financial globalization during the contemporary period. The contemporary level of financial globalization has not reached the level reached during the earlier phase.

[2] One of the logical outcome of this kind of integration of international economy should be convergence of interest rates, which has not come about.

[3] Nobel Prize winning economist and former Senior Vice President of the World Bank, Professor Joseph E. Stiglitz, is one such famous academic analyst.

Federation and some East European economies have made some progress in this direction. This sub-group has done better than the rest of the transition economies. Disintegration of the socialist economies and the failure of the economic system espoused by them belatedly focused the attention of policy makers in the developing world on the wastefulness and futility of statist policy regimes. The significance of market forces and the market-friendly policy environment was made obvious to anybody willing to see. Watchful policy makers in many developing economies realized which set of policies to reject. The end of statism and the planned economic era encouraged a policy penchant toward global integration.

A conspicuous and much-extolled achievement of globalization was rapid economic growth during the last quarter of the last century in twenty plus developing economies that came to be better integrated with the global economy.[4] This set of developing economies earned the name of emerging market economies. "This process led average global per capita income to more than triple in the second half of the last century."[5] There is serendipity in globalization and several emerging market economies benefited from it during the preceding quarter century. Frequently given examples of globalization include the emergence of the People's Republic of China[6] (hereinafter China) as a potential economic power, the alleviation of abject poverty in three large and populous developing economies (for instance, China, India and Indonesia) and a small number of other developing countries, integration of financial markets, recurring financial and economic crises, and accelerated migration of populations to centers of economic activity.

Those who contend that globalization has exacerbated poverty around the world are wrong (see sections 8.1–8.5 below). A large proportion of the world's poor live in the rural areas of China and India. After globalization began in these two economies, the poor people have discernibly benefited. China recorded an average gross domestic

[4] Refer to Das (1991) and Das (1996) for detailed expositions on policy regimes adopted by the high-growth economies of East and Southeast Asia.
[5] Horst Kohler, Managing Director, International Monetary Fund, *Strengthening the Framework for the Global Economy*, a speech given on the occasion of the Award Ceremony of the Konrad Adenauer Foundation, Berlin, 15 November 2002. Available at <http://www.imf.org/external/np/speeches/2002/ 111502.htm>.
[6] Until 1980, the People's Republic of China was grouped with the poorest countries in the world. It recorded double digit growth over the 1980–2000 period, doubling its per capital income every decade. In 2002, a lean year for the global economy, real GDP in China grew by 8 percent.

product (GDP) growth of 10 percent in real terms during the 1980s and the 1990s, and the proportion of poor fell from 31 percent in 1987 to 4 percent in 2000. Similarly, India also experienced acceleration in real GDP growth rate to close to 6 percent per year since economic liberalization began. The average GDP growth rate for three decades before liberalization began was 3.25 percent in India.[7] The proportion of the poor in the population dropped from an average of 50 percent during the 1950–80 period to an average of 25 percent in 2000 (Srinivasan, 2002).

This coin has a flip side. Globalization also included events such as the spread of diseases including human immunodeficiency virus (HIV) and acquired immuno deficiency syndrome (AIDS), and the so-called 9–11 attack on the World Trade Center. Besides, there exists a country group that failed to benefit from globalization. The majority of the members of this group are located in Sub-Saharan Africa. Not only poverty did not decline in these countries, but also in many cases it increased. The causes include inability to liberalize domestic economic structures and integration with the global economy. Additionally, these countries suffered from deeper problems of political strife, social tensions, ethnic conflicts, and poor government.

Being multifaceted, globalization has resulted in several non-economic benefits. For instance, development of the Internet and the World Wide Web revolutionized the flow of economic, financial, political, educational and cultural information. The world of academics and researchers has been transformed forever. The near global spread of business schools, high respect and market value for the Master of Business Administration (MBA) degree, which was an American invention, reflects globalization of educational trends. The entire Security Council vote for Resolution 1441, which aimed at de-weaponizing Iraq, reflects globalization in geopolitical thinking.[8] Rapid and easy communication and transportation around the world further underpinned globalization. In addition, development and expansion of life-extending medical technologies has contributed to health and physical welfare in many parts of the globe.

---

[7] The People's Republic of China adopted the Deng doctrine or "Open Door" policy in December 1978, while India started its first major economic liberalization program in July 1991. India had earlier tried to unsuccessfully launch liberalization programs in 1984 and 1988.

[8] The UN Security Council Resolution No. 1441 on de-weaponizing Iraq was voted on the 8 November 2002. Even Syria, an Arab neighbor, and a non-permanent member of the Security Council, voted for the Resolution.

Thus viewed, there is no gainsaying the fact that there are both winners and losers from globalization (see section 4 also). The benefits of globalization and heightened competition are limited only to those economies that participate in the ongoing globalization process. Protected sectors of the economy – and firms and workers in them – stand to lose from globalization. Countries and regions that did not participate in the ongoing globalization of the last quarter century have lagged behind. Some of them were unable to do so because they had failed to improve their investment climate and had problems with property rights. Myanmar, Nigeria, and Pakistan are the cases in point. There is a pressing need for these countries to utilize the global market for services to improve their investment climate. Tradable services such as banking, insurance and telecommunications are available in the global marketplace and such economies can benefit from them. Until the domestic services can be strengthened and brought to the par, prudence lies in availing the globally availability of services. This could be a beginning of the movement towards globalization.

2. Definition

Globalism or globalization is built and dependent upon structural changes on the economic, financial, political and sociocultural levels. Put in a simple and direct manner, economic globalism is the process of liberalization and integration of goods and factor markets. Alternatively, it can be stated as integration of goods, capital and labor markets, which have thus far functioned in separation. Markets of goods, services, and factors of production have different characteristics and accordingly their movement and trade follow different sets of rules of the game.

The multifaceted nature of globalism has been referred to in the preceding section. Supranational institutions such as the International Monetary Fund (IMF) and the World Trade Organization (WTO), help transmit and enhance globalization. The vagueness and imprecision of the concept of globalization has been lamented by many scholars.[9] In its vague form this concept refers to the growing dimension of economic interdependence among economies and countries, which in turn has been brought about by the increasing volume and variety of cross-border transactions in goods and services as well as cross-border factor flows. It also entails rapid and widespread diffusion of industrial, health and information technologies.

---

[9] Although "global" implies worldwide, in the strict sense of the term contemporary globalization is not worldwide. Many low-income developing economies are still not integrating with the global economy.

It needs to be emphasized that the contemporary phase of globalization is still in its initial phase, if not infancy (Obstfeld, 2000).

Growing inter-economy interdependence was the crucial characteristics. Therefore, in academic writings of the 1970s and the 1980s, this phenomenon was frequently referred to as "economic and financial interdependence" or simply "interdependence."[10] However, interdependence was a far more limited concept compared to globalism or globalization. As for the query regarding the principal drivers of the process of globalization, a simple answer will have to include international trade, trans-border capital flows and foreign direct investment (FDI), international migration, and advances in international and communication technology (ICT). However, this enumeration of driving forces is not comprehensive because international trade could not have expanded without (i) the adoption of liberalization of domestic policies, and (ii) the growth of an enabling framework at the supranational level. Progress in ICT is one of the two main components of what has become known as the "New Economy."

The process of globalization entails increasing globalism, which in turn stands for network of connections or "multiple relationships". It does not mean a single linkage or a one-point bond. Interdependence, not globalism, would describe the single linkage between two economies or countries. The postwar Japan–United States economic and strategic bond was interdependence, not globalism. The Closer Economic Relationship (CER) agreement between Australia and New Zealand again is an example of economic and trade co-operation and collaboration and therefore interdependence, not globalism. To be sure, such interdependencies are a part of, and contribute to, contemporary globalism.

Many scholars have attempted to define globalization from their own respective perspectives. Consequently, close to one hundred definitions of globalization – some simple while others elaborate – exist. Given the degree of interest in the phenomenon, it is not surprising. Globalization can simply be defined as harmonization, homogenization or integration of the countries and economies. This simple definition is elaborated somewhat by Friedman (1999) as follows, "Globalization is the integration of markets, finance, and technologies in a way that is shrinking the world from size medium to size small and enabling each of us to reach around the world farther and cheaper than ever before."

[10] During this period, until 1989, the Soviet Union, Eastern Europe and Indo-China were still drudging under the socialist system, although the People's Republic of China (PRC) had accepted the Deng doctrine and was meticulously following its "Open Door" policy. Therefore, use of the term "interdependence" instead of globalization was not unappropriate for this period.

While Friedman's concept is limited to economic and financial globalization, Held *et al.* (1999) expand it to other spheres of human activity and define globalization as "a process (or set of processes) which embodies a transformation in the spatial organization of social relations and transactions – assessed in terms of their extensity, intensity, velocity, and impact – generating transcontinental or inter-regional flows and networks of activity, interaction, and the exercise of power."

The official World Bank definition of globalization, as it should, focuses on economic integration brought about by trade and factor mobility. It has been defined as "freedom and ability of individuals and firms to initiate voluntary economic transactions with residents of other countries."[11] Empirically it would translate into integration of world economies with greater mobility of factors of production and through increased trade and foreign investment. The last named variable includes both direct and portfolio investment. The Organization for Economic Co-operation and Development (OECD) defined *economic* globalization as "a process in which the structures of economic markets, technologies, and communication patterns become progressively more international over time."[12] A similar, albeit narrower, definition of globalization was put forth by Srinivasan (2002), who defined it as "the process of the dismantling of state-created barriers to trade, and the economic, social, and political responses to such dismantling."

Globalism can simply and functionally be defined as gradually evolving interaction and integration of economies and societies around the world. Keohane and Nye (2001) defined globalization as "a state of the world involving networks of interdependence at multicontinental distances." These networks need to be spatially extensive. They can interact through the flow of finance, goods, services, information, ideas, and people. They can be environmentally and biologically linked. These networks also include national and international security issues.

Taking this argument a step ahead, mere regional linkages and interdependencies cannot be considered globalism. To be christened global, the network of relationships should be multi-country and multi-continental. Distance, a continuous variable, is one variable that matters most in this respect. Geographical distance can range from adjacency to being at a diametrically opposite part of the globe. Canada and the United States are two closely intertwined adjacent economies, while

---

[11] Cited by Milanovic (2002).
[12] See OECD (1997), Ch. 1. A corollary of this definition is that competition becomes increasingly global-market based rather than national-market based.

Australia and Britain until some time ago had close economic and political ties but are at two opposite sides of the globe. Although adjacent links, short-distance interdependence, long-distance interdependence or regional interdependence can be defined, they will all be arbitrary, and not worth our while. The concept of globalism does not aptly fit any of these networks of interdependencies. While regional networks do not qualify, networks of interdependence involving multi-country and multi-continental distances are considered global. While globalism pertains to shrinkage of distances, the shrinkage should only be on a large scale. It is an antonym of the concepts of localism, nationalism or regionalism. An amber signal is essential here, that is, globalism never goes as far as to imply universality.

Several illustrations can help show where to draw lines in this regard. First, according to the concept of globalization defined above, diffusion of Christianity across the globe is an example of globalization. Similarly, diffusion of Islam across Africa and Asia is an example of globalization, while the spread of Hinduism across the sub-continent of India is not, albeit it spread as far as Cambodia[13] and the islands of Java in Indonesia. Second, the Asia Pacific Economic Co-operation (APEC) forum comprises countries of Asia, Australasia, and North and South America and is an example of multi-continental interdependence. It is a clear instance of globalism. Third, the Association of Southeast Asian Nations (ASEAN) is made up only of ten countries in Southeast Asia, therefore, according to our definition it is a regional body and not a global forum.

The process of globalization impinged upon both, institutions and individuals. It has caused a great deal of anxiety in certain quarters. If global economic integration resulted in supporting poverty alleviation endeavors and creating economic prosperity on the one hand, it caused chaotic uncertainty on the other hand. Economic and financial crises of the 1990s, which had high economic and social costs, are considered one of the consequences of globalization.[14] It was held responsible for the so-called contagion effect. In addition, social thinkers have expressed anxiety regarding the rise in inequality due to globalization. Some of the other non-economic outcomes of globalization were shifting power

---

[13] The famous temples of Angkor Wat are dedicated to the Hindu god, Lord Shiva.
[14] Financial crises were not a novel consequence of contemporary globalization. They occurred during the earlier periods of globalization also. However, when such crises occurred during the gold standard period of the Victorian era, they were resolved in a different manner to which they were resolved during the contemporary period of flexible exchange rate.

bases, undermining cultural uniqueness and creeping cultural uniformities. Little wonder that it became a highly emotive issue in the 1990s. Deepening globalization affected governance of nation-states in the normal and conventional sense of the term. In turn, the governance process of the nation-state affected globalization. This circular relationship had its stresses and strains. Whether globalization should be governed and if so, how, became relevant and difficult questions. Many began asking the basic questions. Is globalization relevant? Has it gone too far? Has the nation-state concept reached obsolescence? An interminable debate was sparked on the favorable and unfavorable consequences of globalization. Despite the presence of "Doubting Thomases," a 2001 poll of 20,000 people in twenty developing and industrial countries revealed that by a margin of two to one, respondents thought that globalization will materially benefit their societies and families (Environics, 2001).

3. Taxonomy of globalization

As set out earlier, economic dimension of globalism has attracted a great deal of scholarly attention. Other, non-economic, forms of globalization are equally significant and older than its economic dimensions. Before delving into different dimensions of globalism, it must be stated that they are inevitably somewhat arbitrary. Also, different dimensions of globalism do not co-vary. They neither ascend nor descend in unison nor did they start around the same period.

Environmental globalization is widely considered the oldest form of globalization. For thousands, if not millions, of years environmental and climatic changes were the decisive determinants of ebb and flow of human populations. There were some favorable consequences of environmental globalism. The New World[15] crops enriched cuisine and nutritional standards in the Old World. Principal among these were maize, potatoes and tomatoes (Crosby, 1972). Biological globalization turned out to be equally significant and has had a great deal of impact over various facets of global life. History has long records of the spread of fatal and non-fatal epidemics from country to country and continent to continent. One of the earliest records is that of spread of smallpox from Egypt to China, Europe, the Americas and eventually to Australia between 1350 BC and AD 1789 (Barquet and Domingo, 1997). Spread of

---

[15] The old expression New World usually refers to Australia, Argentina, Brazil, Canada, and the United States.

plague from Asia to Europe in the fourteenth century and of pathogens from Europe to the New World in the fifteenth and sixteenth centuries are all well recorded in the medical annals. Several of these diseases and epidemics had fatal consequences in the recipient parts of the globe.

Three centuries before Christ, the conquering armies of Alexander the Great were responsible for military globalism. His empire stretched across three continents, from Macedonia to Egypt and way up to the Indus River in modern India, where he won a pyrrhic victory over the local king Porus and was forced to abandon his expedition and retreat. This was probably the first but not the last example of military globalism. It continued until Pax Britannica in the nineteenth century. Alexander's victories were not limited to military supremacy. He was responsible for introducing Western thought, philosophy and scientific knowledge to the East. His victories resulted in the spread of Hellenism to the parts of globe he had conquered. Thus, he became the first global purveyor of ideas and information. Ebb and flow of ideas and information is the most pervasive, if not the most meaningful, form of globalism. As alluded to earlier, over the past two millennia four great religions of the world, namely, Buddhism, Judaism, Christianity, and Islam, have managed to diffuse well over several continents. Hinduism, an older religion, was geographically circumscribed earlier but is spreading to Europe and North America now.

Based on the types of networks, flows and "perceptual connections that occur in spatially extensive networks", Keohane and Nye (2001) identified four principal dimensions of globalism. They distinctly and discreetly fall in the following areas: (i) economic, including financial; (ii) military or strategic; (iii) environmental; and (iv) sociocultural. This typological distinction is far from exhaustive because several other dimensions of globalism can be easily conceived. The first kind, as stated above, includes global flows of goods, services and factors of production. Transfer of information and technology also comes under this category. "Slicing up the value chain" to benefit from comparative advantage of different economies and, therefore, locating different parts of the production process in different countries is the latest development in this kind of globalization. Intra-industry trade and accelerating exports of manufactures and services from a set of high-performing developing economies has also helped in the progress of economic globalization. Transnational corporations (TNCs) and large financial institutions in the matured industrial economies played a proactive role in devising and creating global networks in economic and financial areas (Das 2000; Das 2001a).

The concept of national and international security underwent a radical change during the post-Second World War era. The potential scale and speed of new military conflicts grew rapidly and took enormous dimensions. Long-distance networks of interdependence in the areas of national and international security led to the creation of the second type of globalization, namely, military or strategic globalization. Treaties or promises regarding the use of military force between alliances and threat between adversaries created global networks. The cold war era spawned globe-straddling military alliances of power as well as parallel alliances among the neutrals, the non-aligned countries. Few countries were able to eschew being a part of one kind alliance or the other.

Environmental globalism entails long distance movements of materials, biological substances, and other generic materials that threaten human health through the environment or oceans. Two of the most problematic examples of environmental globalism are ozone layer depletion and global warming, which adversely and directly affect the entire global population, flora and fauna. Spread of the HIV virus from central Africa to the entire globe in a short span of three decades also falls under environmental globalism. Many of these adverse environmental changes were caused by reckless human activity. This is not to deny that some of them occur naturally also, without any human intervention.

Long-distance movement of ideas, images, and information comprises socio-cultural globalism. Diffusion of religion falls under the purview of sociocultural globalism, as does the spread of scientific and other branches of knowledge. Although, the latter are also a part of economic globalism. Since the era of Pax Britannica, one socio culture came to lead the others. The socio cultures that follow the leader, try to replicate its institutions and social practices and mores. This phenomenon is described by the sociological expression "isomorphism". Sociocultural globalism reacts with other kinds of globalism. Generally, there is a relationship between sociocultural globalism on the one hand and economic and military globalism on the other hand. Rule of thumb in this regard is that the former follows the latter two.

Although ideas are a veritable force in themselves, they follow economic and military forces. Together they transform societies. Not only that, sociocultural globalism also affects individuals, their personal identities, their attitude towards culture, politics, and work, and leisure. It determines their definition of individual and social achievement. With the advent of the Internet, the cost of the global flow of communication has plummeted sharply, and, therefore, the flow of ideas and cultural globalization is increasing independent of other forms of globalization. There are other types of globalism, some of which would necessarily be subsets of the principal types named above. For instance, political globalism is a subset of sociocultural globalism. Educational globalism is represented by the popularity of the MBA degree that started in the United States half a century ago. Legal globalism is represented by the spread of legal practices and institutions. Other relatively less dimensions of globalisms are those in entertainment, fashion, and language (Keohane and Nye, 2001).

4. Benevolent debate versus malevolent debate

In Section 1, we noted that globalization has spawned both winner and loser economies. Vociferous debate over whether globalization is a benevolent force or a malevolent force has been on for a while now – sometimes accompanied with motley street theater, other times in a violent manner. While average citizens are worried about globalization, average economists are unconcerned. A degree of globalphobia exists among the average citizenry. The international backlash against globalization is strong. One of the favorite arguments of the opponents of globalization is that globalization is a "destroyer of cultures" and that it is bringing about a global cultural homogenization. It goes as follows: The spread of global consumer culture that is spread by companies such as McDonald's and Coca-Cola is causing cultural homogenization, which is unwarranted. However, if one looks beneath the surface and asks people in different countries where their loyalties lie, how they regard their families, and how they react to authority, there will be enormous differences. When these people examine a culture, their vision is limited to aspects such as the kinds of consumer goods that people buy, which is the most superficial aspect of culture. A culture really consists of deeper moral norms and social mores that affect how people link, live and work together. Thus, this argument of uniformity in consumer culture leading to cultural homogenization is exceedingly superficial and weak.

Many developing economies have not integrated with the global economy and have been left out of the burgeoning trade and financial flows. They turned out to be the losers of globalization (see section 5 for the non-globalizers). Instead of merely denying the failings of globalization, one needs to set them in some sort of context. One needs to attempt to work out what governments and people on the comfortable side of the "red-lacquered gate" can do to solve them (Micklethwait and Wooldridge, 2000). The principal reason why this debate has continued to be so frustrating is that supporters and opponents of globalization rarely listen to each other. There is so much evidence available that each side can go on ad infinitum without even bothering to acknowledge the other.

Some observers of the globalization process opine that it is ruled by the laws of the market applied to suite the well-managed market economies, which happen to be geopolitically powerful nations. Concerns regarding the negative influences have been expressed by a diverse range of individuals, ranging from Pope John Paul II to George Soros.[16] Various global issues have huge political and cultural dimensions, and economics and the law of market often seem out of sync with them, leading to negative consequences for several economies (Micklethwait and Wooldridge, 2000).

To leftist mythology and to diverse citizens' groups, globalization and multilateral institutions, particularly the Bretton Woods twins and the WTO, seem to represent a sinister conspiracy against all that is good. These groups range from environmental groups, to labor unions, to human rights activists, to development lobbyists, all with different penchants and agendas. They have learned the use of media masterfully and have become increasingly powerful at corporate, national, and global levels. On several occasions they succeeded in arousing enough public interest as well as public pressure. During the Earth Summit in Rio de Janeiro in 1992, they had succeeded in pushing through an agreement on control of greenhouse gases, during the World Bank's anniversary meeting in 1994 in forcing a rethink of the Bank's goals and in sinking the Multilateral Agreement on Investment (MAI) in 1998. The MAI was a draft treaty designed to harmonize the rules of foreign investment; the OECD economies and Secretariat had devoted a great deal of time and effort to the MAI.

In November 1999, in Seattle, these groups expressed their displeasure over everything from genetically modified crops to fishing subsidies. They decried the panoply of global ills including deforestation, child labor, overfishing, laws of international banking, and pollution. It made for colorful television reporting. The Third Ministerial of the WTO in Seattle was problem-ridden and the possibilities of starting the next round of multilateral trade negotiations (MTNs) were exceedingly low, even negligible. The street theater of the citizens' groups was

---

[16] As Archbishop of Cracow in Poland, Pope John Paul II was a passionate supporter of globalization. But as the 1990s wore on, the Pope became increasingly uneasy about "unbridled capitalism." He expressed his disapproval in his Apostolic Exhortation to the Catholic Church in the Americas in January 1999 by enumerating the following ill effects of globalization: "...the absolutizing of the economy, unemployment, the reduction and deterioration of public services, the destruction of the environment and natural resources, the growing distance between the rich and the poor, unfair competition which puts poor nations in a situation of ever increasing inferiority..."

heavy handed. Although they were not responsible for the collapse of the Third Ministerial of the WTO, they surely contributed to it (Lindsey, 2000).

Globalization does create serious problems for some economies. The enriching competitive, liberalization process that neoclassical economists laude does indeed exact its costs. The doctrine of comparative advantage, *a la* Michael Porter, has a salutary influence in a globalizing economy if you have the wherewithal with which to be competitive. However, to an economy that has had a history of poorly trained manpower, lackadaisical institutional structure and weak governance in the public and the private sectors, and an ineffective and corrupt government, the concept of globalization has little relevance and applicability. This does *not* imply that some economies have to lose for the others to gain. It is not a zero-sum game, albeit globalization has worsened some people's lives.

Further, rapid growth of capital flows, particularly the short-term flows, has been blamed for creating volatility, crisis and contagion situations in the recipient emerging market economies, even in entire regions. These crises were banking, currency, financial, debt and macroeconomic. Many had elements of more than one kind of crisis. After the 1982 debt crisis of Latin America, which pushed the global banking and financial system to the brink of collapse, several major and minor crises broke out in the global economy. They took place in Venezuela in 1994, in Mexico in 1994–95, in Asia in 1997–98, in the Russian Federation in 1998, in Brazil and Ecuador in 1999, in Turkey in 2001, in Argentina in 2001–02 and in Uruguay in 2002–03. All of these crises had high economic and social costs (Das, 2003).

It is natural that those economies that have been left out and have not benefited from trade and financial flows, or those that have been adversely affected by crises of one kind or an other, view globalization as a malevolent force. Globalization also appears as a malignant force to those who are employed in the uncompetitive, albeit protected, industrial sectors. When tariff barriers and non-tariff barriers (NTBs) are lowered with the onward march of globalization, their industries fail to survive and with that their jobs disappear. Many unemployed workers do not like to be re-skilled. They blame their misery on globalization. Idealistic young people in the prosperous industrial countries share these perceptions and brand globalization a villain.

The maxim that globalization is a benign force is one of the principal strands of liberalism in the classical sense. In free global markets, firms would maximize profits and people would choose the best options from a much wider range. This in turn would lead to socially optimum outcomes and maximize global welfare. However, the liberal tenet presupposed an important, if not adequately forceful, institutional role. That is, national governments and supranational institutions were to ensure provision of public goods, in that they were required to ensure the legal and contractual environment for the efficient functioning of competitive markets. They were also expected to address the issues of externalities and anti-competitive tendencies. The moot question is whether or not these abstract assumptions are fulfilled in a real life situation. If they are, the following question is to what extent they are fulfilled.

Antagonists have put forth several arguments. For one, trade in real world is not free, as the protagonists of globalizations assume. Trade barriers and NTBs applied to export products (or exportables) from the developing countries to the industrial economies are now high and were higher in the past. Farmers and dairy product producers in the industrial economies are highly subsidized, thereby driving the poor unsubsidized producers from the developing economies out of the global markets in these products. Voting in the international financial institutions (IFIs) is weighted, which gives large industrial economies, such as the United States, virtual veto power in the governing boards of the IFIs. Although the WTO members have voting rights, members seldom vote except when they ratify the entry of a new WTO member. Traditionally the WTO decisions are consensus-based. More often than not, interests of the developing countries do not prevail in the consensus-based decision-making mechanism. Therefore, one can say that globalization is unfettered capitalism, which serves the rich countries in making them richer. These arguments are superficial and seem convincing on their face value. However, close scrutiny easily reveals that that while some are highly exaggerated, others are erroneous. Those that are valid, can easily be rectified (see also Chapter 4).

Economists believe that at an aggregate level globalization is a substantial boon. If one sheds polemics and looks at globalization in a pragmatic manner, one finds that it is essentially a benevolent force that creates opportunities for rapid growth and faster poverty alleviation *in the economies that are ready for it*, that is, in those economies in which domestic economic, social and political environment is conducive to underpinning the process of globalization. Many developing economies with endemic corruption, ineffective legal system, and poor property rights, do not provide supportive ambience for globalization to set in motion the virtuous circle or the growth spiral. In such economies, many economic and non-economic barriers to globalization exist. For instance, financial system discourages risk taking. Other major economic barriers are discussed below in section 5. Conflicts with neighbors and civil and sectarian strife do not allow globalization to lay down its roots. Therefore, the primary challenge for these developing economies that are being passed by globalization is to transform their domestic environment and strengthen their institutional framework in such a manner that they become conducive to globalization (Srinivasan, 2002).

5. Non-globalizing economies

The World Bank (2002) has identified a group of 49 developing economies, with a population of 2 billion, which have thus far failed to globalize. The World Bank (2002) has christened this country group the non-globalizing economies. They either did not integrate with the global economy or developed only weak bonds with it. Countries on the continent of Africa and the Former Soviet Union (FSU) dominate this group. This country group suffered external shocks like volatile terms of trade for its exports of primary commodities. Their divergence from the more-globalized economies was nothing short of dramatic.

The basic reason why these weak globlizers lagged behind the more-globalized economies is that they followed poor macroeconomic policies, and failed to harness their comparative advantage in labor-intensive goods and services. There was a strong long-term need for macroeconomic and trade reforms in this group of economies. Other complementary reasons behind their failure were poor infrastructure, inadequate spread of education, rampant corruption and high tariff and non-tariff barriers (NTBs). Whatever cost advantage there was due to abundant cheap labor was more than offset by these disadvantages. Why did this group fail? Is it too late for these countries to attempt to integrate with the global economy? These are some of the important questions looking for answers. A plausible scenario is that if this country group succeeds first in adopting a proper and pragmatic macroeconomic policy package, stays the course and then strengthens its infrastructure and institutions, it should be able to harness its comparative advantage in labor-intensive manufactures and services and eventually integrate with the global economy (World Bank, 2002).

However, this scenario may be a little too simplistic and overly optimistic. There may well be some countries that suffer from the fundamental disadvantage of location. Even in cases where a country does not suffer from economic and social malaise, namely, poor macroeconomic policies, infrastructure and education related inadequacies, rampant corruption, weak and poorly developed institutions and high tariff and non-tariff barriers, if they are land-locked, or sea-locked, or if these countries have a high incidence of malaria or other diseases, it will be difficult for them to take measures to be competitive in labor-intensive manufactures and services. Benefits of reforming policies would be so meager in such an environment that there would be little incentive to take the appropriate policy and institutional measures. In some cases, adverse geography can be greater barrier than the trade policy restructuring can benefit. Locational disadvantage leads to high transport costs. Even if a low tariff rate is added to the high transport cost, together they can become an effective barrier to exporting to an industrial economy. Thus, the real barrier to globalization in such cases is not the trade policy of the industrial country but adverse geographical factors.

Quality of infrastructure also has a decisive effect on the transport cost. African countries trade much less among themselves and with the rest of the world than warranted by a simple gravity model exercise. Essentially, poor quality transport infrastructure is considered responsible for it (Limao and Venables, 2000). It is not limited to substandard ports and airports, but extends to domestic transport infrastructure such as roads, railroads, telecommunications. Collier and Gunning (1999) have provided a detailed account of these inadequacies in Africa and compared them to the better performing developing economies on other parts of the globe, particularly in Asia. They concluded that not only do African countries have much less infrastructural facilities on average, but it is also of questionable quality. The rural roads network is one-sixteenth of that of India, telephone connections are one-tenth of the Asian average and they have three times the level of faults of Asia. Railroad networks in Africa are old-fashioned, based on steam locomotives. Its dieselization or electrification is exceedingly slow. On an average, diesel trains are 40 percent less than in Asia. Use of infrastructure services cost far more in Africa. Collier and Gunning (1999) found that railway freight rates are double that of Asia while airfreight costs four times as much. The same applies to port charges. A container costs $200 in Abidjan, and corresponding costs in Antwerp are $120. This illustrates how bad location and poor infrastructure resulting in high transport costs lead to poor integration with the global economy.

Earlier in this section, it was asked whether it is too late for the non-globalizing 49 economies to attempt to integrate with the global economy. A realistic answer will have to be in the affirmative. Global demand for manufactures and services is currently being balanced by the global supply. It cannot be expected to rise monotonically, or even asymptotically. Besides, due to externalities offered by the agglomeration effect and scale economies, firms have already located themselves in the appropriate clusters. If the cluster they found is satisfactory, they have little economic incentive to move out. This seriously limits opportunities for the non-globalizing economies. To be sure, not all of them have checked into a cul-de-sac. Some of these countries can still reform their macroeconomic policies, strengthen their infrastructures and build their institutions and develop their own successful clusters. If many are able to do so, there will be more well-located sites than new clusters. To that extent the non-globalizing economies have missed out on their opportunity to integrate. Some countries indeed have serious geographical disadvantage and will have great difficulty in industrializing, let alone globally integrating.

6. Globalization and the catch-up endeavors in transition economies

A group of some 30 countries that followed statist or command economy systems began the fundamental transformation of their economic structure after the breakup of the Soviet Union. The majority (27) of these economies were located in the FSU[17] and Eastern Europe[18] and a small number in Asia. These economies devoted the entire decade of the 1990s to their transformation to a market system so that they could improve the performance and usher in competitiveness and efficiency. Their objective was to eventually integrate globally. The institutional transformation they needed was of historic proportions.

From the perspective of globalization, there was a pressing need for a transition in this group of economies. Their economic transformation was an indispensable part of the onward move of globalization. Without it globalization would fall short of its full dimension and dynamism. The transition economies comprise fairly large countries such as the Russian Federation and Ukraine, with a combined population of 200 million, which is half of the population of this group of countries. Besides, many of the smaller countries have a considerable future economic potential.

Everybody in these countries, including policy mandarins, knew that bringing about such a fundamental transformation in their economies would be an exceedingly difficult task.[19] But, as hindsight reveals, they

[17] There were 15 economies, namely, Armenia, Azerbaijan, Belarus, Estonia, Georgia, Kazakhstan, Kyrgyzstan, Latvia, Lithuania, Moldova, the Russian Federation, Tajikistan, Turkmenistan, Ukraine, and Uzbekistan.
[18] The Eastern European countries comprise the following 12 economies: Albania, Bosnia-Herzegovina, Bulgaria, Croatia, Czech Republic, Hungary, Poland, Macedonia, Romania, Slovakia, Slovenia, and Yugoslavia.

had underestimated the magnitude of the difficulties involved. In a majority of these economies the transition recession lasted for a much longer period than initially visualized and economic contraction was much deeper than initially estimated. Several unforeseen developments made the transition period more problematic that what was originally conceived. In the words of Kolodko (2000), the protracted recession became "a Great Transitional Depression." The recovery, when it began, was far from smooth and the original expectations of rapid recovery and robust growth were belied completely.

The principal characteristics of a globalizing world economy have been identified and discussed above. For the transition economies this implies that they not only have to deal with the ongoing structural transformation but also need to address the issues brought forth by globalization. At the beginning of a new century, they need more sound policy responses because there are more issues to deal with than mere structural transformation. Globalization has made their catch-up objective more difficult than before. Because of a decade-long privatization endeavors, the private sector in the transition economies has expanded considerably. It is taking over the role of the old state sector. It is this sector that needs to take the initiative in integrating with the global economy. Thus, in a globalizing world, the role of this sector in the transition economies has become more important than before.

Systemic transition to market economy essentially entails three processes: (i) liberalization-cum-stabilization, (ii) institution building, and (iii) restructuring the industrial capacity (Kolodko, 2000). Some of the transition economies are progressing on all three fronts and are trying to build a full-fledged market economy, while others are still attempting to reform their existing systems and build a half-way house. To be able to integrate financially and economically with the global economy all of the three processes need to be completed.

Although transition economies were not autarkies in the past, their trade partners essentially were the other centrally planned economies and a good deal of their trade was barter. When these economies began to liberalize and open up to the rest of the world, their imports and exports grew faster than the growth rate of their GDP. These economies are now providing easy entry into and exit from their markets for both domestic and global firms, a practice so healthy and essential for their economies. Likewise, capital flows have been liberalized for two-way movements of

---

[19] The only transition economy that succeeded in effecting this transformation in a methodical and phased manner is China (See Das, 2001b, 2001c).

capital. The infant capital markets in some transition economies can participate in the global financial markets and gradually integrate. Global investors are highly active in the financial and utilities sectors of the transition economies, improving the efficiency and quality in these sectors.

Much-needed infrastructure and industrial restructuring took place with the microeconomic reforms and with the entry and expansion of the TNCs in these economies. The entry and presence of TNCs has proved to be a strong channel of globalization (Daianu, 2002). The production and distribution processes in the transition economies are slowly integrating with those of the TNCs. Increasing volume of FDI is stimulating this process. A sustainable inflow of FDI would contribute to better integration of these economies with the global economy. However, concerted endeavors would be needed for sustaining the levels of FDI. Privatization attracted a good deal of FDI in these economies during the 1990s. If the domestic environment continues to be conducive to rapid growth, FDI inflows are likely to continue as well, even after privatization is complete because of financial globalization. These flows are expected to enhance both growth and competitive efficiency in the transition economies (Daianu, 2002).

Whether this country group will be able to catch up will be contingent upon the choice of strategy and the political will to follow it up. In addition, variables such as the endowment of physical and human capital, geographical location, work ethics and culture, efficacy of governance and quality of political leadership will matter in determining the pace of the catch-up process. Several countries are so aptly located that they can benefit from the advantage of proximity to a large market. For instance, Estonia is next door to the Scandinavian countries, the Czech Republic to Germany, Bulgaria to Turkey, Azerbaijan to Iran, and Kyrgyzstan to China.

Several countries in this sub-group have been preparing to join the European Union (EU) and carrying out their institution-building task in earnest. Hungary and Poland fall in this category. The preparation to join the EU has helped these economies in laying down a strong foundation of a market economic system. No doubt their future growth endeavors will be built on this foundation. The advanced candidates for EU membership, namely, Estonia and the Czech Republic, would logically catch up faster than the other countries in this sub-group of countries (Kolodko, 2001). Yet, Daianu (2002) was pessimistic about the prospects of catch-up of these economies. According to him, having "a well-functioning competitive market economy" is not a sufficient guarantee of catching up.

7. Globalization: mercurial and un-global

Both the long- and the short-term history of globalization demonstrated that the process was far from monotonic. Progress with an uneven pace was its hallmark (see also Chapter 2). There were periods when it stalled and there were swaths of time when it made complete reversals. The most recent period of reversal of globalism was the interwar period (1919–39).[20] In addition, the preceding two sections demonstrated that thus far globalization is far from global. Only a sub-group of economies have succeeded in integrating with the global economy.

Often strong criticism and opposition to the spread of globalization is heard in many fora. Given this polemics, one is left wondering whether the contemporary wave of globalization can or will be stopped in its tracks or reversed. Crafts' (2000) answer to this query was negative. During the interwar period several factors coalesced to force a retreat of globalization. Undoubtedly, the *causae causante* was the so-called Great Depression. The other economic and political forces that pulled globalization down included firms and industries that lost from the operation of globalized world markets. They clamored and pressurized their governments to protect them from market competition. Retaliatory trade policies *were* adopted and trade hostilities were real. Similar tendencies have been noticed during the contemporary period as well. There has been a rise in regionalism in trade. All through the decade of the 1990s, apprehensions were expressed by academicians and policy makers alike regarding regionalism turning into a stumbling block rather than a building block for multilateral trade expansion. There were instances when it was felt whether the consensus in favor of free trade and globalization in the large industrial economies is giving way to the problems of sunset industries and high rates of unemployment, particularly among low-skilled workers.

Other focal points of discomfort include the fiscal "termites" and tax competition (see also Chapter 3), which have become a concern of the tax administrations, essentially in the OECD countries. That globalization has increased the risk exposure is apparent from the numerous incidents of financial, banking, currency crises and macroeconomic instability in the globalizing economies. Although evidence on the long-term growth benefits of economic liberalization and openness abounds, TNC operations in economies where domestic income

[20] Most international trade that was conducted in both the First World War and the Second World War was under the control of governments, and the interwar period of 1919–39 saw a significant slow-down in globalization.

inequality is rising may create an obstructive environment for the TNCs and FDI inflows. Sometimes parochial nationalism also leads to the same outcomes.

That being acknowledged, the beginning of the twenty-first century is markedly different from the interwar period in several important respects. Losing domestic firms and industries can now be protected with the help of a large range of policy instruments. Besides, the sunset industries in many industrial countries have their own defensive policy structure to follow. Dynamic corporations plan for their sunset phase. Second, the WTO did not exist then. It exists now with its streamlined trade regulations and bound set of tariffs. Member countries cannot abandon the WTO discipline at whim. Third, the egregious policy errors of the interwar period are well known and were endlessly debated by academicians. Macroeconomic lessons of that period are expected to serve the contemporary period. Fourth, it is believed that problems of unskilled labor in the OECD countries are largely due to "skill-biased technological change rather than factor price equalization through trade" (Slaughter, 1999). Informed economists understand that resolution of this contentious issue has to be at the domestic level, not global. Thus, risks of a reversal of globalization are considerably less now, albeit pressure points continue to exist.

During the interwar period retaliatory trade policies had a great deal of destructive effect over the global economy which contributed to the globalization backlash. The consequences of those policies have been decried universally. It is highly unlikely that during the contemporary period that episode would be repeated. Trade partners are aware that mutual co-operation is mutually benefiting as well as mutually reinforcing. It is likely to be preserved by prospects for future payoffs. The flip side of this coin is that the unequivocal support for free trade during the postwar period has eroded considerable over the last two decades. Progress in the Doha round of MTNs is far from smooth. Circumstances that gave rise to this erosion include changing patterns of comparative advantage in the global economy and a good number of developing economies moving up the catch-up trail. Many of them have become competitive producers of capital- and technology-intensive products. Competition in an increasing number of industries and services has significantly intensified.

Other than competition, as real wages of workers are stagnating in the industrial economies, an increasing number of interest groups, workers' organizations (such as American Federation of Labor-Congress of Industrial Organizations or AFL-CIO) and political parties are shedding their liberal free-trade posture and turning towards protectionism. In the past, representatives of unskilled labor had enormous clout.[21] Although they failed to hinder the formation of the North American Free Trade Area (NAFTA) in the United States, it was not for a lack of effort. They can be expected to continue pushing the US government towards neo-protectionism. Lately, non-tariff barriers (NTBs) such as anti-dumping measures, which are WTO-consistent, came into use in an increasing number by the industrial economies. Several developing economies also started using them.

On the one hand, the demand for social protection of workers in the OECD countries has increased. On the other hand, the ability of governments to finance this from taxes on capital has declined for two reasons. First, the rate of capital taxation has moderately declines during the last two decades. Second, globalization has increased capital mobility substantially and reduced the ability of fiscal authorities to tax it. Therefore, the OECD economies are facing a pincer movement. This may eventually increase the danger of a globalization backlash. However, this argument loses its edge because capital tax revenues have remained stationary in the OECD economies. As these economies are corporatist, high-consensus democracies, social transfers, if anything, have increased.[22] Given these perspectives, the danger of a globalization backlash during the contemporary period is on the low side.

8. Globalization and poverty alleviation

The issue of the impact of globalization on (i) poverty; (ii) domestic income distribution; and (iii) global income disparities has received a great deal of attention.

However, the debate and coverage was somewhat biased towards how globalization is affecting the wage and income inequalities in the industrial economies.[23] These issues have aroused significant academic curiosity and policy debates, and have also drawn a great deal of popular attention in the economic and financial press.

---

[21] The representatives of unskilled labor did wield enough political clout in the United States to succeed in having Fordeney-McCumber Act (1922) and Smoot-Hawley Act (1930) passed through the United States Congress. They were intended to provide relief to labor-intensive industries that produced agriculture-based consumer goods.

[22] For an empirical treatment of this issue, see Rodrik (1997), and Schulze and Ursprung (1999).

[23] See, for instance, Lejour and Tang (1999) and Robertson (2000).

8.1. Can globalization hurt the poor?

Whether or not globalization hurts or benefits those who are in the low-income deciles on the income distribution curve has become a contentious issue in several quarters. For the pro-globalizers, the gut reaction is: how can a phenomenon that has immensely benefited so many economies over time hurt in any manner? But even the most ardent pro-globlizers cannot deny that globalization can hurt the poor in several ways in the short term. For instance, as the reform process takes hold and trade policy reforms advance, there is a distinct possibility of a rise in the short-term unemployment rate, resulting in greater poverty for unskilled and semiskilled labor. Developing economies are known for a high degree of labor market distortions, such as a low degree of wage flexibility, and imperfect labor mobility across sectors as well as geographical regions. Which makes the low-skill or unskilled labor force more vulnerable at the time of trade reforms. Economic liberalization promotes the entry of global firms and TNCs, which intensify competitive pressure on the domestic firms, throwing some of them out of business. In the short term, unemployment is sure to rise because workers cannot easily move across sectors or industries. In the developing economies, reallocation of labor from uncompetitive sectors to competitive sectors and from tradables to non-tradables is either very slow or nonexistent. Also, in many developing economies there are few provisions for re-skilling of the newly unemployed workers.

The new trade theories talk of trade-growth nexus, but such a relationship exists only in the high-technology industries.[24] Many of the developing economies are technologically not highly advanced. Exports of many of these economies, although not all, are concentrated in "non-dynamic," low-tech sectors such as textiles or raw materials. Therefore, the immediate impact of globalization and liberalization is in many cases a fall in the rate of trade expansion and growth rates. Although globalization enables greater private financial flows, these in turn help in the import of higher technology leading to dynamic gains to the economy in the long term. However, this tends to happen after a transition period of an uncertain length. Over this period, globalization may have little affect on growth or poverty eradication.

Globalization and trade liberalization may also lead to diminished demand for low-skilled and unskilled labor, which in turn may worsen

---

[24] The new trade theories give a lot of importance of the contribution of scale economies and learning-by-doing. Once the economy is liberalized, these factors positively impact upon trade and real GDP growth.

poverty and income distribution. The experience of many emerging markets in Latin America demonstrated that during the 1980s and the 1990s, globalization and trade liberalization created high demand for skilled labor. With that the wages of skilled labor rose in relation to those of the unskilled labor, skewing income distribution in favor of the former. Higher technology follows globalization and trade liberalization, which in turn requires a highly skilled labor force. The relative demand for the old-fashioned unskilled or semiskilled labor force declines (Winters, 2002). Thus, there are distinct possibilities of globalization hurting the poor. The lower the skill level, the greater is the probability of getting adversely affected by the onward march of globalization. Closure of businesses and rising rates of unemployment arouses strong emotional responses in some societies.

8.2. Globalization and incidence of poverty

The next questions are: Has globalization hurt those in the low-income deciles? Has it harmed the developing economies by causing too many business closures? An honest answer is that while there are individual instances of its "hurting" the uncompetitive sectors, and the capital and labor deployed in these sectors, there is evidence to show that on the whole it has not hurt the poor segments of populations. As referred to above (in section 1), on average the incidence of poverty in the world has declined. Despite the world population growing by 1 percent a year during the 1990s, and the population of the low-income countries growing by 2 percent a year, the incidence of poverty has fallen. The number of people living in extreme poverty, or below the poverty line, had stopped rising since 1980. The internationally accepted poverty line is defined as a daily income of $1.08 or below in 1993 dollars (WB, 2001). Those who live on or below this poverty line are called the absolute poor. It bears repeating that the number of absolute poor in the large populous economies such as China, India and Indonesia has recorded a decline (section 1).

As Table 1.1 shows, the proportion of people living below the poverty line has been falling globally as well as in many regions. Some regions have been particularly successful in alleviating poverty. The largest declines in absolute poverty have been recorded in East Asia and the Pacific. However, it has been virtually stationary in Sub-Saharan Africa, and has increased in Latin America and the Caribbean. This increase in absolute poverty was largely caused by prior extreme inequalities in educational attainment. In addition, global integration in Latin America and the Caribbean has further widened wage inequalities between the

Table 1.1   Proportions of people living on or below the poverty line (percent)

Region	1987	1998
1. East Asia and the Pacific	26.6	15.3
1.1 Excluding China	23.9	11.3
2. Eastern Europe and Central Asia	0.2	5.1
3. Latin America and the Caribbean	15.3	15.6
4. Middle East and North Africa	4.3	1.9
5. South Asia	44.9	40.0
6. Sub-Saharan Africa	46.6	46.3
7. World	28.3	24.0
7.1 Excluding China	28.5	26.2

Source: World Development Report 2000/2001.

skilled and the unskilled, resulting in an increase in the number of absolute poor. A sharp rise in the number of absolute poor in Eastern Europe and Central Asia reflects the recent fundamental transformation of these economies from a centrally planned to a market economy system (section 6).

Since the late 1960s, a large part of the population of the developing world has experienced faster real income growth than the population in the established industrial economies, albeit there are disparities in this regard. During the contemporary phase of globalization, cross-country income inequality has not been rising. In a small way, the differences have begun to be narrowed (CIE, 2001).

8.3. Globalization and quality of life

Among the trenchant critics of globalization there is an articulate "can-you-eat-GDP?" group, which argues that human well-being is not synonymous with growth. While GDP and per capita income are perhaps the best measures of material well-being, they are important because they help provide nations, societies and individuals the means to improve the other measures of human well-being. According to Goklany (2002), these measures include freedom from hunger, health, mortality rates, child labor, educational levels, access to safe water and sanitation, and life expectancy. With the rise in GDP and per capita income, this set of indicators improves, but there is no linear relationship between the two. At low levels of per capita incomes the improvements are rapid, but they slow down as per capita incomes rise. Improvements in these indicators stop as they reach their practical limits, notwithstanding rising per capita incomes.

In a comprehensive study, Goklany (2002) examined five indicators that measure distinct, although related, aspects of human well-being. Three of the measures were the measures of human misery – (i) availability of food supply; (ii) infant mortality; and (iii) prevalence of child labor. These three reflect negative well-being. The fourth measure was life expectancy at birth, which is a positive measure and perhaps the most important indicator of human well-being. The fifth is the human development index (HDI) computed annually by the United Nations Development Program (UNDP). In response to the recognition of the fact that there is more to development than GDP, the HDI was developed by the UNDP. With the onward march of globalization, Goklany (2002) found that these indicators of human well being improved as per capita incomes rose. The rate of improvements was higher at the lowest levels of per capita incomes. Greater wealth means more resource allocation, both directly and indirectly, to education, health and other human welfare related areas. Better literacy levels and improved education translates into greater technological innovation and diffusion of technology. A prosperous society is better able to use existing technology for improving child welfare (including reducing infant mortality) and life expectancy. The latter can be improved by treating water supply, improving sanitation and basic hygiene. It can also be improved by providing vaccinations, antibiotics, insect and vector control, and pasteurization. Over the past half century, the well-being of a large majority of global population has discernibly improved. The average person lives better and longer now than half a century ago. The average person is also less hungry, healthier, more educated, and is more likely have children in classrooms than in a shoddy workplace.

Several other indicators are available to show that the quality of life around the globe has been improving, although a great deal is yet to be done. Interestingly, the improvement in the quality of life in the developing world are taking place at a faster pace than in the past and faster than in the industrial economies (CIE, 2001). Gross domestic product and per capita incomes and quality of life are directly related. Statistics compiled by Sab and Smith (2001) demonstrate that convergence in human capital is presently afoot. They found that in 1970, 920 million people around the globe were malnourished. Despite population growth, the number of undernourished people dropped to 810 million in 2000. Similarly, average life expectancy improved from 58 years in 1970 to 66 years in 2000. Analysing by region, at 51 years life expectancy improved slowly in Sub-Saharan Africa. The epidemic of Aids has been having a negative effect on life expectancy in this part of the world. As opposed to this, 10 years to 12 years of improvements were observed in life expectancy in

Asia, the Middle East and the developing Europe. Similarly, the infant mortality rate improved by 17 per thousand in the industrial economies over the 1970–2000 period. However, the improvements were much higher in the developing world. It improved by 66 per 1,000 in the Middle East, North Africa and the developing Europe and by 55 per 1,000 in Asia. For the Latin American economies this improvement was by 50 per 1,000, while for sub-Saharan Africa by 43 per 1,000. Like wise, noteworthy gains were made on literacy and education fronts. Presently, 80 percent of the global adult population is literate – a much higher proportion than the 63 percent of 1970. Virtually all (99 percent) of children are now enrolled in primary schools, up from 86 percent in 1970. This set of statistics lead one to the conclusion that with the onward march of globalization, the global quality of life and human well-being have improved over the past three decades will not be incorrect.

8.4. Globalization and poverty alleviation: a non-linear relationship?

In the first two subsections I focused on how globalization can affect the global poor, and whether it has adversely or favorably affected the quality of human capital. We also need to answer how the domestic – or within country – income distribution is influenced by globalization. It is possible that a linear relationship does not exist between globalization and domestic income distribution. Using the newly developed database created in the context of the work on world income distribution and using household survey data, Milanovic (2002) attempted to answer this query. The first advantage of the new database is that it is entirely based on national household surveys around two benchmark years (1982 and 1997), which made income inequalities statistics fully and mutually comparable. The second advantage is that we do not have to deal with one or two income inequality measures such as the Gini coefficient or the Theil index but the actual data on income levels across ten deciles of income distribution are available for providing comprehensive results.

Milanovic (2002) attempted to gauge the effects of globalization on how the overall shape of income distribution changes, that is, the income distribution at decile levels. This exercise concluded that when an economy is at a low income level, it is the rich, or the population in the higher deciles, that benefits from globalization. When the per capita income rises and reaches the levels of countries such as Colombia, Chile and the Czech Republic, the situation changes and the relative income of the poor (bottom deciles) and middle-income (intermediate deciles) people rises more compared to those of the rich. Thus, globalization makes within-country income distribution worse before making it better. Put differently, the effect of globalization "on country's income distribution depends upon a country's initial income level."

Agenor (2002; 2003) reached similar, if not the same, conclusions.[25] His conclusions were based on linear cross-country regressions that linked various measures of real and financial integration to poverty. Using data for the 1980s and the 1990s, regression analysis was performed over a group of 11 low- and middle-income economies. The regressions were controlled for changes and income per capita and output growth rates as well as various other macroeconomic and structural variables. Based on the principle components of the analysis, Agenor (2003) also derived a globalization index and tested it for linear and non-linear effects. His results indicated that there appears to be a robust, non-monotonic, Laffer-type relationship between domestic income distribution and globalization. He concluded that at a low degree of globalization, globalization does hurt the poor. But at higher levels, globalization leads to a decline in poverty and the poor sections of the population benefit from it. Both of these studies stressed the non-linearity involved in the advancing globalization on the one hand and domestic poverty and income distribution on the other hand (Melchior *et al.*, 2000).

8.5. Globalization and income inequality: the case of China

China is the largest developing economy that embarked on economic liberalization and openness to trade and financial flows a quarter century ago. The economic reform and liberalization program, which was launched in 1978, not only stayed the course but also broadened its scope in the subsequent two decades. It led to double digit GDP growth in real terms in China.[26] Its liberalization program helped in globalizing the economy. This benefited large sections of the population and the number of people living below the poverty line, as noted earlier, declined markedly. China has a middle-class whose size was estimated at 18 percent of the population (or approximately 200 million) in 2001 by the Chinese Academy of Social Sciences (*Financial Times*, 2002).[27]

[25] Permission to cite from Agenor (2003), an unpublished paper, was received on 10 January 2003.

[26] Refer to footnote 6.

[27] These estimates were cited in *The Financial Times*, 29 December 2002. Measuring the size of the middle-class is an inexact science. Other commentators are more conservative than the Chinese Academy of Social Sciences in their measure of the Chinese middle class.

Rapid growth and globalization has had a definite impact over income distribution and poverty in China. A case study of China to study this impact is ideal for several reasons. First, China has become one of the most important developing country *per se* during the preceding quarter century. It provides a methodological advantage relative to a typical cross-country study. Second, it is the largest developing economy that adopted economic and trade liberalization over the preceding quarter century. Starting from near autarky, its trade liberalization was nothing short of dramatic in magnitude. Third, due to unequal natural barriers to trade (for instance distance from ports), the effective increase in openness varies widely across different regions in China. Therefore, it is a better economy to be studied as an in-depth case study than many other developing economies. Fourth, as China is a geographically large country it is divided into a large numbers of regions and sub-regions, which in turn provide a large number of regional and sub-regional observations for a statistical study. Fifth, as China has restrictions over movement of population, the internal migration is much lower than that in other developing economies. Although these restrictions have been lowered over time, they made regions and sub-regions within China separate autonomous countries. Therefore, a cross regional study done in China is akin to a cross-country study (Wei and Wu, 2002).

While the economy liberalized with a rapid rate and globalized over the last two decades, Gini coefficient estimates revealed that overall income inequality in China increased. It increased from 38.2 in 1988 to 45.2 in 1995 (Khan and Riskin, 1998; 2001). The World Bank (1997) calculated the Gini coefficients with a different data set and methodology and found that the Gini coefficient rose from 28.8 in 1981 to 38.8 in 1995. The results of Khan and Riskin (1998; 2001) and World Bank (1997) pointed in the same direction. The Gini coefficients calculated by Andrea and Court (2002) revealed that while the growth rate of 1978–84 was accompanied by broadly stable inequality, since 1985 and especially during the 1990s, growth became increasingly less egalitarian. It revealed that conspicuous regional disparities have developed in China. Disparities between the dynamic and prosperous coastal belts, a middle "rust belt" where a large number of obsolete state-owned enterprises exist, and the underdeveloped and underserved western and northern provinces were clearly discernible (Andrea and Court, 2002; see Table 3).[28] From these aggregate

[28] Using data from the State Bureau of Statistics, Government of the People's Republic of China and the World Bank, Table 3 tabulates values of several Gini coefficients for the 1953–98 periods. For instance, it includes the values of overall Gini coefficients for the economy, urban Gini coefficient, rural Gini coefficients, and measure of inter-provincial income gaps.

statistics and results it is obvious that embracing globalization in China has contributed to increase in income inequality.

A study by Wei and Wu (2002) questioned the veracity of results arrived at with the help of Gini coefficients. Their cross-regional study pooled two unique data sets on Chinese regions or provinces to determine the impact of globalization on income disparity.[29] It is an intra-national study that utilized cross-regional variations within a large country in terms of openness and globalization. An important plank of their research was that openness, or increases in it, may be endogenous. Frankel and Romer (1999) pioneered the technique of using geography as an instrument of openness. According to them, geography has an important influence on trade, and is arguably exogenous with respect to economic growth or income inequality. The Frankel-Romer technique was adopted for this in-depth study of China. As it is semi-land-locked country, not all of the regions, sub-regions or cities participate in global trade equally. Their distances from major ports vary considerably. Until recently, the two major ports of Hong Kong and Shanghai handled half of China's total trade. Therefore, China was an apt case for the application of Frankel and Romer technique.

Conclusions arrived at by Wei and Wu (2002) contradict the ones that were arrived at with the help of the Gini coefficient computations. They documented three basic patterns: First, an increase in openness and globalization was found to be associated with a reduction in the urban–rural income inequality in China. Second, an increase in openness and globalization was found to be associated with a modest increase in inequality within urban areas. Third, an increase in openness and globalization was found to be associated with a decline in inequality within rural areas. Putting together these three inferences, they stated that globalization resulted in the reduction of inequality in China. This research project concluded that the results reached with the help of single measures such as the Gini coefficient are sometimes inadequate and unwarranted, and do not provide a complete picture.

These results are in keeping with the Heckscher-Ohlin-Samuelson theory, which stated that openness to trade, which is an important part of

---

[29] The first data set comprised (i) *Urban Statistical Yearbook*, various issues, published by China's State Statistical Bureau; and (ii) *Fifty Years of Cities in New China 1949–1998*, also published by China's State Statistical Bureau. The second data set was the two household surveys conducted in 1988 and 1995. They were designed by a group of international economists and the Economics Institute of the Chinese Academy of Social Sciences. They are described in Khan and Riskin (1998; 2001). The 1988 survey covered 10,258 rural households in 28 provinces and 9,009 urban households in 10 provinces. The 1995 survey covered 7,998 rural households in 10 provinces and 6,931 households in 11 provinces.

globalization, should raise the returns to relatively abundant factor of production relative to the returns to the scarce factors. China is a large labor-abundant developing economy. The impact of openness to trade and globalization should increase the returns to labor, particularly unskilled labor, faster than that of the rest of the population. This should result in a decline in income inequality. However, an amber signal is necessary here. The Heckscher-Ohlin-Samuelson explanation is one of the many explanations available. In a specific-factor model, the impact of openness on inequality, at least in the short run, tends to be ambiguous.

9. Conclusions and summing-up

During the past quarter century, the concept of globalization acquired a good deal of currency as well as involvement from various stakeholders. The multidisciplinary and multifaceted nature of globalization is obvious from its economic, financial, business, political, technological, environmental, cultural, educational, international relations and national and international security related dimensions. Those who use the term globalization disagree about its consequences. The concept has both fervent supporters and trenchant critics, although most economists fall in the former category. A conspicuous and much-extolled achievement of globalization was rapid economic growth during the last quarter of the last century in twenty plus developing economies that came to be better integrated with the global economy. This process led average global per capita income to more than triple in the second half of the last century. There is serendipity in globalization and several emerging market economies benefited from it during the preceding quarter century.

There is no gainsaying the fact that there are both winners and losers from globalization. The benefits of globalization and heightened competition are limited only to those economies that participate in the ongoing globalization process. Protected sectors of the economy – and firms and workers in them – stand to lose from globalization. Globalism or globalization is built and dependent upon structural changes on the economic, financial, political and sociocultural levels. Put in a simple and direct manner, economic globalism is the process of liberalization and integration of goods and factor markets. Alternatively, it can be stated as integration of goods, capital and labor markets, which have thus far functioned in separation. Markets of goods, services, and factors of production have different characteristics and accordingly their movement and trade follow different sets of rules of the game. There are over a hundred definitions of globalizatin. One of them defines it as "a state of the world

involving networks of interdependence at multicontinental distances."
These networks need to be spatially extensive. They can interact through
the flow of finance, goods, services, information, ideas, and people.
Economic dimension of globalism has attracted a great deal of scholarly attention. Other, non-economic, forms of globalization are equally
significant and older than its economic dimensions. Before delving into
different dimensions of globalism, it must be stated that they are
inevitably somewhat arbitrary. Also, different dimensions of globalism
do not co-vary. They neither ascend nor descend in unison nor did they
start around the same period.

Globalization has spawned both winner and loser economies.
A vociferous debate over whether globalization is a benevolent force or
a malevolent one has been on for a while. Economists believe that at an
aggregate level globalization is a substantial boon. If one sheds polemics
and looks at globalization in a pragmatic manner, one finds that it
is essentially a benevolent force that creates opportunities for
rapid growth and faster poverty alleviation *in the economies that are
ready for it.*

The World Bank has identified a group of 49 developing economies,
with a population of 2 billion, which have thus far failed to globalize.
This country group has been named the non-globalizing economies.
They either did not integrate with the global economy or developed
only weak bonds with it. Countries on the continent of Africa and the
Former Soviet Union (FSU) dominate this group. A group of some
30 countries that followed statist or command economy systems began
the fundamental transformation of their economic structure after the
break-up of the Soviet Union. The majority (27) of these economies were
located in the FSU and Eastern Europe and a small number in Asia.
Systemic transition to market economy essentially entails three
processes: (i) liberalization-cum-stabilization; (ii) institution building;
and (iii) restructuring the industrial capacity. Some of the transition
economies are progressing on all three fronts and are trying to build a
full-fledged market economy, while others are still attempting to reform
their existing systems and build a half-way house.

Both the long- and the short-term history of globalization demonstrated that the process was far from monotonic. Progress with an
uneven pace was its hallmark. There were periods when it stalled and
there were swaths of time when it made complete reversals. The most
recent period of reversal of globalism was the interwar period (1919–39).
In addition, thus far globalization is far from global. Only a sub-group of
economies have succeeded in integrating with the global economy. Often

strong criticism and opposition to the spread of globalization is heard in many fora. Given this polemics, one is left wondering whether the contemporary wave of globalization can or will be stopped in its tracks or reversed. An educated answer to this query has to be in the negative.

The issue of the impact of globalization on poverty, domestic income distribution and global income disparities has received a great deal of attention. There are distinct possibilities of globalization hurting the poor. The lower the skill level, the greater is the probability of getting adversely affected by the onward march of globalization. Closure of businesses and rising rates of unemployment arouses strong emotional responses in some societies. But this is a short-term and selected phenomenon.

On the whole it has not hurt the poor segments of populations. On an average the incidence of poverty in the world has declined. Despite the world population growing by 1 percent a year during the 1990s, and the population of the low-income countries growing by 2 percent a year, the incidence of poverty has fallen. The number of people living in extreme poverty, or below the poverty line, had stopped rising since 1980. The internationally accepted poverty line defined as the daily income of $1.08 or below in 1993 dollars. In general, the indicators of human well-being improved as per capita incomes rose. The rate of improvements was higher at the lowest levels of per capita incomes. Greater wealth means more resource allocation, both directly and indirectly, to education, health and other human-welfare-related areas. Globalization makes within country income distribution worse before making it better. Put differently, the effect of globalization on country's income distribution depends upon the country's initial income level. There appears to be a robust, non-monotonic, Laffer-type relationship between domestic income distribution and globalization. Laffer concluded that at a low degree of globalization, globalization does hurt the poor. But at higher levels, globalization leads to a decline in poverty and the poor sections of the population benefit from it. Both of these studies stressed the nonlinearity involved in the advancing globalization on the one hand and domestic poverty and income distribution on the other hand.

A case study of impact of globalization on poverty and income distribution in China revealed that: First, an increase in openness and globalization was found to be associated with a reduction in the urban–rural income inequality in China. Second, an increase in openness and globalization was found to be associated with a modest increase in inequality within urban areas. Third, an increase in openness and globalization was found to be associated with a decline in inequality within rural areas. Putting together these three inferences, they stated that globalization resulted in the reduction of poverty and inequality in China.

References

Agenor, P.R., 2002, "Benefits and Costs of International Financial Integration: Theory and Facts", Washington, DC: World Bank. Policy Research Working Paper No. 2788, February.

Agenor, P.R., 2003, "Does Globalization Hurt the Poor?", January 7 (unpublished paper).

Andrea, G. and J. Court, 2002, "Inequality, Growth and Poverty in the Era of Liberalization and Globalization", Helsinki: United Nations University, World Institute for Development Economic Research, Policy Brief No. 4.

Barquet, N. and P. Domingo, 1997, "Smallpox: The Triumph Over the Most Terrible of the Ministers of Death", *Annals of Internal Medicines*, October 15, 636–8.

Centre for International Economics (CIE), 2001, *Globalization and Poverty: Turning the Corner*, Canberra: CIE.

Collier, P. and J.W. Gunning, 1999, "Explaining African Economic Performance", *Journal of Economic Literature*, Vol. 37, No. 2, 64–111.

Crafts, N.F.R., 2000, "Globalization and Growth in the Twentieth Century", Washington, DC: International Monetary Fund, Working Paper No. WP/00/44, March.

Crosby, A., 1972, *The Columbian Exchange: Biological and Cultural Consequences of 1492*, London: Greenwood Press.

Daianu, D., 2002, "Is Catching-Up Possible in Europe?", Warsaw: Leon Kozminski Academy of Entrepreneurship and Management, Transformation Integration and Globalization Economic Research (TIGER), Working Paper Series No. 19, May.

Das, Dilip K., 1991, *Korean Economic Dynamism*, London: Macmillan.

Das, Dilip K., 1996, *The Asia-Pacific Economy*, London: Macmillan, and New York: St Martin's Press.

Das, Dilip K., 2000, "Portfolio Investment in Emerging Market Economies: Trends, Dimensions and Issues", *Journal of Asset Management*, September, Vol. 3, No. 3, 144–82.

Das, Dilip K., 2001a, "Stimulants to Capital Inflows into Emerging Markets and the Recent Role of Speculators", *Journal of International Development*, January, Vol. 18, No. 1, 32–64.

Das, Dilip K., 2001b, "Liberalization Efforts in China and Accession to the World Trade Organization", *Journal of World Investment* Vol. 2, No. 4, 761–89.

Das, Dilip K., 2001c, *China's Accession to the World Trade Organization: Issues and Implications*, Australian National University. Asia Pacific School of Economics and Management. Canberra. Working Paper No. EA01-1. Available at <http://ncdsnet.anu.edu.au>, July 2001, 41 pp.

Das, Dilip K., 2003, *Financial Globalization and Emerging Market Economies*, London and New York: Routledge.

Environics, 2001, "Poll Findings Suggest Trouble Ahead for Global Agenda: Survey of 20,000", Available at <http://environicsinternational.com>, September.

36   *The Economic Dimensions of Globalization*

Financial Times, 2002, "Middle Classes in China's Long March to Prosperity", December 29, p. 3.

Frankel, J.A. and D. Romer, 1999, "Does Trade Cause Growth?", *American Economic Review*, Vol. 89 No. 2, 379–99.

Friedman, T.L., 1999, "Dueling Globalization: A Debate Between Thomas Friedman and Ignacio Ramonet", *Foreign Policy*, Fall, 110–19.

Goklany, I.M., 2002, "The Globalization of Human Well-Being", Washington, DC: Cato Institute, Policy Analysis Paper No. 447, August 22.

Held, D., A.G. McGrew, D. Goldblatt and J, Perraton, 1999, *Global Transformations: Politics, Economics and Culture*, Stanford: Stanford University Press, p. 16.

Keohane, R.O. and J.S. Nye, 2001, "Introduction", in Keohane and Nye (eds), *Governance in a Globalizing World*, Washington, DC: Brookings Institution Press, pp. 1–41.

Khan, A.R. and C. Riskin, 1998, "Income Inequality in China: Composition, Distribution, and Growth of Household Income, 1988–1995", *China Quarterly*, Vol. 31, No. 2, 221–53.

Khan, A.R. and C. Riskin, 2001, *Inequality and Poverty in China in the Age of Globalization*, New York: Oxford University Press.

Kolodko, G.W., 2000, *"From Shock to Therapy: The Political Economy of Post-Socialist Transformation"*, Oxford: Oxford University Press.

Kolodko, G.W., 2001, "Globalization and Transformation: Illusions and Reality", Paris: OECD Development Center, Technical Paper No. 176, May.

Lejour, A.M. and P.J.G. Tang, 1999, "Globalization and Wage Inequality", Rotterdam: CPB Netherlands Bureau of Economic Policy and Analysis (mimeo).

Limao, N. and A.J. Venables, 2000, *Infrastructure, Geographical Disadvantage and Transport Costs*, Washington, DC: World Bank.

Lindsey, B., 2000, "Globalization in the Streets Again", Washington, DC: Cato Institute, Center for Trade Policy Studies, 27 May. Available at <freetrade.org/pubs/articles/bl-4-15-00.html>.

Melchior, A., K. Telle and H. Wiig, 2000, "Globalization and Inequality: World Income Distribution and Living Standards 1960–98", Oslo: Royal Norwegian Ministry of Foreign Affairs, Studies on Foreign Policy Issues, Report 68, September.

Micklethwait, J. and A. Wooldridge, 2000, *A Future Perfect*, New York: Random House.

Milanovic, B., 2002, "Can We Discern the Effects of Globalization on Income Distribution?", Washington, DC: World Bank. Policy Research Working Paper No. 2876, April.

Obstfeld, M., 2000, "Globalization and Macroeconomics", *NBER Reporter*, Cambridge, MA: National Bureau of Economic Research, Fall, 18–23.

Organization for Economic Co-operation and Development (OECD), 1997, *Economic Globalization and the Environment*, Paris: OECD.

Robertson, R., 2000, "Trade Liberalization and Wage Inequality: Lessons from Mexican Experience", *World Economy*, Vol. 23, No. 6, June, 827–49.

Rodrik, D., 1997, *Has Globalization Gone Too Far?*, Washington, DC: Institute of International Economics.

Sab, R. and S.C. Smith, 2001, "Human Capital Convergence: International Evidence", Washington, DC: International Monetary Fund, Working Paper No. WP/01/32.

Schulze, G.G. and H.W. Ursprung, 1999, "Globalization of Economy and Nation State", *World Economy*, Vol. 22, No. 2, 295–352.

Slaughter, M., 1999, "Globalization and Wages: A Tale of Two Perspectives", *World Economy*, Vol. 22, No. 3, 609–29.

Srinivasan, T.N., 2002, "Globalization: Is it Good or Bad?" Stanford, CA: Stanford Institute for Economic Policy Research, Economic Policy Brief, December 23.

Wei, S.J. and Y. Wu, 2002, "Globalization and Inequality Without Differences in Data Definition, Legal System, and Other Institution", Cambridge, MA: National Bureau of Economic Research, Working Paper No. 8611.

Winters, L.A., 2002, "Trade Policies for Poverty Alleviation", in B. Hoekman, A. Mattoo and P. English (eds), *Trade, Development, and the WTO*, Washington, DC: World Bank.

World Bank, 1997, *Sharing Rising Incomes: Disparities in China*, Washington, DC: World Bank.

World Bank, 2001, *World Development Report 2000/2001*, New York: Oxford University Press.

World Bank, 2002, *Globalization, Growth and Poverty*, New York: Oxford University Press.

2
Globalization: Tracing the Progress

1. Changing gears of globalization

If globalization is taken to mean that certain dimensions of the global economy, finance, polity, culture and environment are interconnected, then it is hardly a new phenomenon. It began centuries ago. In this chapter, an attempt is made to trace the initial phases of global economic integration by way of expansion of global trade and flows of factors of production. To this end, this chapter, *inter alia*, focuses on therecent history of globalization and the trends and developments during the preceding two centuries. Globalization endeavors after the Industrial Revolution in Great Britain is the principal focus of this chapter. In order to establish that globalization is not a recent phenomenon, it also dwells upon the important historic periods, namely, the first and second halves of the second millennium, in particular the period followed by the famous voyages of discovery undertaken by Christopher Columbus[1] and Vasco da Gama.[2]

Both Columbus and da Gama were busy charting the sea route to India, a rich country of their period of history. This was called globalization following the age of exploration, which covered the sixteenth century, and the first half of seventeenth century. The post-Industrial Revolution era of globalization spanned the mid-eighteenth century and the nineteenth century. The nineteenth and the twentieth centuries

[1] In the pivotal year 1492 that obscure Genoese, Christopher Columbus, navigated across the Atlantic. He made his landfall in the Bahamas thinking that he was near India. He is credited with "accidentally" discovering the Americas.
[2] Portuguese navigator who lived between 1460 and 1524 and who discovered the sea route from Portugal to India. He sailed around the Cape of Good Hope to reach India.

were the two other periods that deserve special scholarly and analytical attention.

One clear inference that has emerged is that during the last millennium, globalization neither progressed at an even pace nor was it unidirectional and monotonic. It had had exceedingly slow periods of progress, followed by rapid growth periods such as the nineteenth century. It also suffered reversals. The century preceding the Napoleonic Wars (1796–1815) is a good example of interruptions and stalling.[3] The interwar period of 1919–39 is an excellent example of globalization going into a reverse gear. During the contemporary era, it again made steady progress in two periods. The first was in the aftermath of the Second World War, when the industrial economies integrated well with enormous welfare implications for this sub-group of economies. The second period began around 1980 and continues until the contemporary period. This was the period when a sub-group of dynamic developing economies made a successful foray at integrating with the global economy.

2. Global economic integration in the second millennium

To begin, I focus on the last millennium. During the first half of that millennium, there was significant intra-Asian and intra-European trade in commodities, although little trans-border financial flows. Both People's Republic of China (hereinafter China) and India had emerged as countries with relatively larger populations and significant trade links and trade volumes. China engaged in trade with Southeast Asia, the Islamic world of central Asia, the Middle East and northern Africa, the Mediterranean countries and Europe using both the fabled Silk Road and ocean routes. Likewise, India traded with the Southeast Asian countries, the Islamic world through the ocean routes and the Mediterranean and the European countries through both land and ocean routes. The Baltic trade with Eastern and Northern Europe was also substantial.

The two large centers of population and economically viable systems of the first half of that millennium were the Islamic world extending from the Atlantic to the Himalayas and the Sung Dynasty of China covering a large land mass in its own right. These two economic systems had the largest cities of the contemporary period, considerable manufacturing and commercial activity as well as fairly sophisticated monetary, financial and credit systems. With the exception of relatively

---

[3] The intermittent wars waged by France, principally against England, Prussia, Austria and Russia.

advanced Italian city-states and Flanders, during this period Western Europe was essentially a sprawling agrarian area.[4] The Islamic world and China became both large exporters to and importers of commodities from other parts of the globe. A complex pattern of trade linkages had evolved. During the thirteenth century the Mongol Empire had established itself. Thereafter, the *Pax Mongolica* unified Asia and Europe and not only promoted trade in commodities through the land routes but also transmission of ideas, techniques and migration of labor (Needham, 1954).

In the thirteenth century, the Yuan Dynasty founded by Kublai Khan,[5] succeeded in building up the largest trans-continental empire of this period. Mongol emperor, Kublai Khan, adopted many elements of the Chinese government system and encouraged cross-cultural economic and social exchanges among merchants and traders. Dadu was the capital of the Yuan Dynasty, which received foreign visitors from all parts of the vast Mongol empire. This open-door policy ushered in an unprecedented era of economic growth and prosperity. During the rise and fall of the Yuan Dynasty, Mongols attempted to unite a vast number of countries and peoples in Asia and Europe. In his pursuit for greater access to foreign nations, Kublai Khan planned and implemented a massive transport and communications project. It was regarded as the most advanced physical infrastructure project of his period.

The geographical area covered by the empire boasted an efficient transport and communication infrastructure. The Yuan Dynasty also strengthened the legal infrastructure of this period.[6] Some scholars have

[4] Findlay (1996) and Findlay and O'Rourke (2001), provide more details regarding these developments.
[5] Mongol emperor Kublai Khan was the grandson of Genghis Khan.
[6] It was important for Kublai Khan to ensure economic growth because without economic resources his offensive and defensive military expeditions could not take place. He paid much attention to boosting the Yuan economy, in particular to developing transport and communications infrastructure. He developed a new roads and canal system for transport and a swift mounted courier services. These services were run with the help of 10,000 large post houses, each stabling hundreds of horses. Each post house was approximately 40 kilometers from the next. Some of them were so large that they looked like palaces. This new infrastructure project strengthened the existing infrastructure and facilitated economic transactions (see Marshall, 1993; and Mote, 1999). Kublai Khan also paid a lot of attention to devising and expanding a comprehensive legal and judicial system with the help of legal practitioners. The Yuan Dynasty is credited with the development of a legal code. It was likely that this codified system of law was based on the *yasa* system of the law of the Mongols, which was modified and further developed during the reign of Kublai Khan (Phillips, 1969; Langlois, 1981).

argued that accelerated economic and cultural exchanges between Asia and Europe during the thirteenth and fourteenth centuries were the starting point of the subsequent global explorations endeavors by various European nations.[7] It can be argued that the Mongols of the thirteenth and fourteenth centuries were among the pioneers in initiating globalization.

During this period, shipping and nautical systems and technology were gradually emerging through a complex interplay of several civilizations and economic systems. Who was the leader and who the follower in this respect inspired endless debates, and the last word is not yet in. It was easy to assume that the Europeans led because they are believed to be the first to develop the necessary nautical technology. However, Abu-Lughod (1989) disproved this Eurocentric assumption by providing comprehensive accounts of the voyages of the Ming Dynasty admiral Zheng He in the early decades of the fifteenth century. His massive and highly organized fleets sailed in the Indian Ocean between China and Africa, touching and trading with several countries *en route*. This raised the question about technological capability playing second fiddle to economic incentives.

The motivation of the so-called voyages of discovery, noted in section 1 above, was economic and cultural globalization and formation of a world economy during the latter half of the second millennium. Towards the end of the fifteenth century, the much-vaunted and better-chronicled voyages of discovery started transfer of ideas, merchandise, technology, flora and fauna, and diseases on a substantial scale. These voyages, *inter alia*, provided opportunities "to break the monopoly of the spice trade held by the ruler of Egypt and the Italian city-states, particularly Venice and Genoa" (Findlay and O'Rourke, 2001). This implies that a good deal of global trade existed in the first half of the second millennium to provide economic incentive to undertake the voyages of discovery.

The Renaissance began in the fourteenth century, extending until the seventeenth century, marking the transition from the medieval to the modern period. The two voyages of discovery noted above were a momentous event of this period.[8] Crossing of the Pacific Ocean and

---

Cont.
Development of a system of legal documentation contributed to the growth of legal professionalism, which in turn helped in an effective administration of justice and property rights. All these developments had definitive economic implications.

[7] See the contributions of Marshall (1993) and Rossabi (1983).

[8] Scholarly accounts of post-medieval period economic integration are available. For instance, Das (1986) provides a detailed account of economic, particularly financial, globalization since the beginning of the medieval period. See chapters 1 and 2.

circumnavigation of the globe soon followed. For the first time the ocean routes connected continents that were unconnected before, giving rise to new trade routes, resulting in expansion of trade. Manila was founded in 1571, which according to some scholars, marked the beginning of modern global trade.[9] It was not large in volume because of the high transport costs. It was kept essentially to commodities with a high ratio of value to weight and bulk, such as silk, spices (pepper, cloves, cinnamon, nutmeg), precious metals (in particular silver), wool and woolen cloth, cotton textiles, and porcelain. This laid the foundation of global trade, which grew in volume when transport costs subsequently fell due to technological advancement, and when capital accumulation took place. Although global trade grew during this period, the rate of growth was slow. The noted economic historian Angus Maddison (1995) found that between 1500 and 1800, world trade grew at a little over 1 percent per annum.

That the voyages of discovery had a discernible qualitative and quantitative impact over the European economies is a well-established fact. Global integration brought about by them and the following voyages affected both the core and the periphery countries of this period. They had a definite impact over the globalization trend of this period. Other than the welfare implications, there was a direct impact on the core economies. As transatlantic trade grew, the location of the core per se shifted. The principal locus of economic activity moved from the Mediterranean to the Atlantic. Consequently the economic importance of Antwerp, Amsterdam, Seville, Lisbon and London was enhanced at the expense of Venice and Genoa. In modern parlance, this could be taken as the impact of globalization. Antwerp emerged as one of the largest and most dynamic economic centers during the early sixteenth century. This indicates that intercontinental trade overshadowed the intra-Europe trade.

3. First modern era of globalization

The Industrial Revolution that began in Britain in the late eighteenth century provided further impetus to globalization. It ushered in a new era in the evolution of a global economy. Expanding foreign trade played a role in sustaining the Industrial Revolution in Britain. Globalization, which entailed expansion of trade, established Britain as a dominant industrial power of the post-Industrial Revolution period. International trade as a share of national income grew steadily from

[9] Flynn and Giraldez (1995) date the origin of world trade to 1571 because according to them Manila linked Asia, Europe, the Americas and Africa.

8.4 percent in 1700, to 14.6 percent in 1780 and 15.7 percent in 1801 (Crafts, 1985; Frankel, 2001).

The pace of globalization was neither uniform nor smooth. It was an on-again-off-again process during the post-Industrial Revolution period and was interrupted by numerous wars of national supremacy in Europe. These wars, in particular the Napoleonic wars, promoted import substitution, which required adoption of the strategy of protectionism for protecting domestic industries that could only grow under hothouse conditions. Napoleon abdicated in 1814 and the Napoleonic wars ended in 1815. The 1820s are notable as being known for the dismantling of mercantilism and emergence of the policy of liberalism. Some evidence of international commodity prices convergence is available for this decade (O'Rourke and Williamson, 2000). Since 1820, the rate of growth of world trade accelerated to 3.5 percent and remained high until the end of the nineteenth century (Maddison, 1995).

Since the advent of new shipping technology during the early nineteenth century, transport costs plummeted constantly throughout this century, providing further direct impetus to global economic integration. The new technology was nothing short of revolutionary and entailed screw propellers, the compound engine, bigger size hulls and shorter turn-around time in port. Steamships were first introduced in inland maritime shipping and in the Baltic and the Mediterranean. Transatlantic shipping services were not introduced until the 1830s. Initially steamships carried only high-value goods, the kind presently carried by cargo aircraft.

The Atlantic economy was most powerfully affected by these developments. Lindert and Williamson (2001a) show that declining transport costs accounted for two-thirds of the integration of world commodity markets over the century following 1820, and for all world commodity market integration in the four decades after 1870. The opening of the Suez Canal in 1869 was another important development. In the absence of sufficient coaling stations on the route to the East, trade was still dominated by sail. The Suez Canal halved the distance between Bombay and London. Also, after opening of the Suez Canal steamships could pick up coal at Gibraltar, Malta, and Port Said.[10] Ships that ran on compound engines were fuel-efficient and had lower coal requirements.

---

[10] Fletcher (1958) provides a detailed account of the advent of steam shipping, its economic impact as well as documents the sail tonnage and steam tonnage during this period.

Railroad expansion was the other novel technological advancement of this era, and this opened up many economic opportunities in the form of exploitation of land and extractive industries. The expansion of the railways in the United Kingdom began in 1830, which was rapidly emulated in continental Europe. The expansion of railroad mileage in the United States was phenomenal, which succeeded in integrating the domestic market in the United States, which was an event of major economic significance. In Russia, railroad expansion took-off after 1860. The cost of moving goods declined considerably, consequently exports, particularly commodity exports, received an impetus. Expansion of rail-roads led to convergence in prices. Adoption of the gold standard by many important and large economies of this era, the opening of the Panama Canal, laying of telegraph lines and transoceanic cables were among the most important economic and technological achievements of this era. They contributed to the creation of the first ever global marketplace.

There is large convergence in the view that the first era of serious globalization in the modern period should be taken to begin in 1870, that is, if one risks ignoring the economic integration that took place in fits and starts during the early centuries of the second millennium and the medieval period. Declining transport costs, reduced tariffs as well as the above-mentioned technological achievements, essentially encour-aged this so-called wave of globalization. Declining tariff barriers followed the Anglo-French agreement in this regard. The world trade pattern that emerged was that a group of New World[11] countries exported land-intensive primary commodities and imported manufac-tured goods from the relatively older, industrializing economies of Europe. Global exports as a proportion of global GDP increased from 4 percent to 8 percent between 1870 and 1914 (Maddison, 2001). This period is also regarded as the high-water mark for the trans-global flow of factors of production, namely, capital and labor (see Chapter 5 for capital movements during this period). Rapid globalization during this era affected factor prices.

Land-intensive and extractive economic activities were notoriously labor-intensive. They promoted large-scale labor migration from Europe to the Americas, Australia and other parts of the New World. According to one estimate, during 1870–1914, it was close to 60 million.[12] As there

---

[11] As noted in Chapter 1, the old expression New World refers to Argentina, Australia, Brazil, Canada, and the United States.
[12] This periodization was made by the World Bank (2002).

was enough of newly opened land, incomes were high and fairly equal. Due to outward migration, the pool of available labor in Europe shrank, causing a rise in wages. Outward migration from the less-developed world to the other parts of developed and underdeveloped countries was also as large as that from Europe (Lindert and Williamson, 2001b). Labor migration from densely populated China and India to other parts of Asia as well as to the Americas and Australia was substantial, although it is not so well recorded. While Chinese diaspora was more or less inspired by economics, not all outward migration from India was voluntary.[13] All of these population movements accounted for almost 10 percent of the total global population of the period under consideration (World Bank, 2002).

Land-intensive and extractive production activities and exports cannot take place without adequate capital. Using statistics from different sources, the World Bank (2002) calculated that the foreign capital stock was 9 percent of the older industrial countries' GDP in 1870. By 1914, its level had risen to 32 percent. Britain was the largest exporter of capital during this period and about one half of the total British savings was invested abroad (Das, 1986). The telegraph facilitated the necessary flow of financial information. Using the financial system in Europe and Britain as the prototype, countries in the New World tried to build their own financial systems and consequently global growth accelerated markedly. Global per capita income that was rising at the rate of 0.5 percent per annum during 1820–70, rose at an annual rate of 1.3 percent over the 1870–1914 period (Maddison, 2001). Not all countries participated in this wave of globalization. But many that had fully participated (Argentina, Australia, Canada, New Zealand, the United States) subsequently became some of the advanced industrial economies of the world. They improved their standards of living and became affluent by exporting land-intensive and extractive primary commodities. They were large importers of labor and capital, and improved their institutional structure by imitating that in Europe and Britain – the so-called Old World. With the exception of Argentina, all of these economies are presently highly industrialized, matured economies.

Essentially due to large labor migration, convergence of income was observed among the economies that participated in the globalization

---

[13] Recurrent famines and other natural calamities drove large waves of migration from Eastern India to the Caribbean Islands and Latin American countries. There was a stark choice for these migrants, had to choose between starvation and migration. These immigrants were taken to work on sugar cane and tobacco plantations as indent laborers by the colonial power of that period.

process during this era. Lindert and Williamson (2001b) calculated that outward migration of the labor force resulted in a 32 percent rise in Irish wages, 28 percent in Italian, and 10 percent in Norwegian wages. Conversely, inward migration of labor lowered Argentine wages by 22 percent, Australian by 15 percent, Canadian by 16 percent and American by 8 percent. Thus, immigration played a highly significant role during this globalization period, perhaps more significant that that played by trade and capital flows.

By 1913, the global economy was far more integrated than that in the mid-eighteenth century. As noted earlier in this section, the ratio of world trade to world GDP had doubled in four-and-a-half decades. Also, because of the transport revolution in the nineteenth century, a far broader range of goods was traded. This included commodities with high bulk-to-value ratio. Industrialization had spread to Western and Northern Europe and to its overseas offshoots such as Australia, Canada and the United States. Trade expansion and industrialization had a discernible impact over the global division of labor. This kind of economic development rendered the global economy clearly divided between industrial and primary-producing economies or developed and developing economies. Terms such as "core" and "periphery" subsequently came in use for the two country groups.

According to statistics compiled by Lamartine Yates (1959), primary products accounted for 62 percent to 64 percent of total world exports during the late-nineteenth century. In 1913, their dominance in world trade declined. At this point, food crops accounted for 27 percent of world exports, agricultural raw materials 22.7 percent and minerals 14 percent. The UK and the fast industrializing economies of Western and Northern Europe were the principal importers of foodstuffs, agricultural raw materials and minerals. The same set of economies were the principal exporters of manufactured products. Canada and the United States still predominantly exported primary products, although rapid industrialization was underway in both of the economies. They were laying the foundations of a balanced trade. Other parts of the globe (Africa, Latin America and Oceania) did not export any manufactured products. Only Asian exports included textiles, which came under the category of light manufactures. However, primary products and agricultural raw materials overwhelmingly dominated exports from this part of the world. The new global division of labor that evolved during one hundred and fifty years (from the mid-eighteenth century to 1913) between the core and periphery economies was to become a major issue in the development economics debate later on.

Patterns of land ownership determined the income distribution in the New World. Because as many countries in the New World were colonies, there was an inherent imbalance in land ownership and examples of both of the extremes are available for this period. For instance, in Latin America, where land ownership was concentrated, increased trade led to rising inequality. As opposed to this, in West Africa land ownership was widely dispersed, and therefore primary commodity exports led to lower income inequality. European economies were the principal importers of primary commodities from the New World during this era of globalization. These imports nearly destroyed their landed aristocracy. This was highly conspicuous in Britain (Cannadine, 1990).

Bourguignon and Morrisson (2001) calculated the mean log deviation of world income equality and reported that since 1820 it continuously increased. This deterioration in global income equality continued. However, the unprecedented growth of the 1870–1914 period resulted in a sharp decline of global poverty despite rising income equality. During 1820–70, the incidence of global poverty was almost constant; it recorded a fall of 0.3 percent per annum. However, during the globalization period the rate of decline in the incidence of global poverty more than doubled to 0.8 percent per annum. The 1870–1914 period was an era of rapid and smooth globalization. J.M. Keynes considered it an "extraordinary period in the economic progress of man…" and lamented its culmination with the beginning of the First World War.[14]

4. Dismantling globalization

Progress in globalization need neither be monotonic nor unidirectional. Its movement could be, and was, reversed easily. After 1914, the steadily globalizing world fell apart. The First World War destroyed the liberal economic order that emerged during the nineteenth century. This was a dramatic, if not traumatic, break with the past. Both of the warring sides attempted to disrupt the other's trade through blockades and other hostile means. Trade and shipping activities were brought under central control of governments. Due to the war, quotas on trade and strict controls on allocation of shipping space became the order of the day. High tariff rates were introduced and these further stifled trade.[15] Consequently, global economic integration stopped in its tracks.

[14] See Chapter 5, footnote 9.
[15] Although the declared objective of the McKenna tariffs of 1915 in Britain was to save scarce shipping space, they were explicitly protectionist.

Imports and exports of the European economies involved in the war shrank and were assiduously controlled by their respective governments. The absence of manufactured exports on the world markets stimulated the expansion of industrial capacity in the United States, Japan and the neutral economies of Northern Europe, in particular Sweden. To a lesser extent countries such as Australia, India and the Latin American economies, particularly Argentina, also benefited from it (Kenwood and Lougheed, 1983). After the war, the barriers to trade and financial flows were not eliminated. If anything, they were intensified. The Key Industries Act of 1919 and the Safeguard of Industries Act of 1921 were introduced in Britain to further intensify protection. Although these measures were not severe, they certainly represented Britain's break with its free-trading liberal-minded economic policy stance of the prewar period. Due to currency problems, scarcity of raw materials and in many cases foodstuffs, quantitative restrictions on trade persisted after the war in many European economies. Japan took the lead in introducing anti-dumping legislation in 1920. Australia, New Zealand, the United Kingdom and the United States followed suit in 1921. The US Congress passed the Fordney-McCumber Tariff Act in 1922, and this raised tariff walls substantially higher than those already in existence.[16] These were the long-term impacts of the war on global resource allocation and economic policy.

Appeals to return to the prewar free trade and liberalized financial flows were repeatedly made from various international fora. Notable among them were those made in 1920 by the Supreme Economic Council, in 1922 by the Genoa Conference, and in 1927 and 1933 by the World Economic Conference. But they fell on deaf ears and the global economy continued to recede into the clutches of restrictions and undid the achievements of the prewar period. Failure to heed the appeals to recreate the prewar global economic environment was acknowledged and lamented by the League of Nations in no uncertain terms (Findlay and O'Rourke, 2001).

All of the important trading countries continued to adopt high tariffs and other restrictive policies so that domestic demand could be diverted into their domestic markets. During the Great Depression period the network of global economic integration collapsed completely, which further provided policy makers – both in the core and periphery economies – to adopt illiberal policies. France, Germany, Switzerland and the Netherlands were the prominent core economies in this category. As

---

[16] Kindleberger (1989) and Irwin (1998) provide the exact numerical measures of tariffs and increases in them for various economies during this period.

all of these four economies adhered to the Gold Standard during a major part of the 1930s, their currencies became overvalued, leading to deflation and balance-of-payments difficulties. In an attempt to cope with these difficulties, they adopted restrictive policies and exchange controls. The US Congress raised high tariffs barriers by enacting the Hawley-Smoot Tariff Act in 1930.[17] It brought the US tariff to the highest protective level yet in the history of the United States and protected both industry and agriculture. It turned out to be a highly detrimental measure because other countries soon began to retaliate by raising their own tariffs. The first wave of retaliation came from Canada, France, Italy, Spain and Switzerland. United States foreign trade suffered a sharp decline, and the depression intensified. Between 1930 and 1933, US imports fell by 33 percent. Interestingly, US exports declined by 40 percent during the same period (Mundell, 2000). Rising protectionism led to shrinking global trade and in 1950 its level fell to 5 percent of the global GDP, which was close to its level in 1870. For 80 years freight costs were declining, yet global trade shrank due to the policy-induced barriers to trade (Mundell, 2000). Furthermore, new entry barriers restricted immigration. Pre-1914 share of the immigrant population in the United States was 14.6 per cent on average. During the interwar years the annual average rate fell to 6.9 percent (Lindert and Williamson, 2001a). Thus, the globalized world was dismantled solely by restrictive policy measures.

Thus viewed, economic policy makers retreated into nationalism and economic nationalism became the domineering strategy of the day. Governments in the capital-exporting countries imposed controls over the export of capital and several developing economies, particularly in Latin America, defaulted on their repayments. This was the first set of major sovereign defaults in the twentieth century. Foreign capital stock of the developing countries steadily declined. In 1950, it was a paltry 4 percent of their GDP. This was a far lower level than that in 1870. In addition, the global movement of labor was drastically restricted. One

---

[17] The US Congress passed the Hawley-Smoot Tariff Act in June 1930. President Hoover desired a limited upward revision of tariff rates with general increases on farm products and adjustment of a few industrial rates. A congressional joint committee, however, in compromising the differences between a high Senate tariff bill and a higher House tariff bill, arrived at new high rates by generally adopting the increased rates of the Senate on farm products and those of the House on manufactures. Despite wide protests, the tariff act, called the Hawley-Smoot Tariff Act because of its joint sponsorship by Representative Willis C. Hawley and Senator Reed Smoot, both Republicans, was signed (June 1930) by President Hoover.

example is the restrictions imposed by the United States. Total immigration into the United States was 15 million during the 1870–1914 period. It declined to 6 million for the 1914–50 period. Thus, it is just to say that global integration of the economy was making a backward motion. Trend towards global inequality persisted, and if anything it worsened. Global GDP growth rate declined by about one-third and in 1950, the global economy was far less equal than it was in 1914 (Maddison, 2001). Weakening global GDP growth rate and rising inequality sharply reduced the decline in the incidence of poverty. It returned to the same level as it was during the 1820–70 period. By 1950, the absolute number of poor people rose by 25 percent (Bourguignon and Morrisson, 2001). The global decline was reflected in social variables also.

It is mentioned above that decline in transport costs continued in the twentieth century, but it was less than that observed during the late-nineteenth century. During the interwar period (1919–39) transport cost declined and freight charges fell further by more that 30 percent. It did not have any impact on the globalization process because of the man-made barriers to trade and financial. This period suffered one more serious limitation. At the dawn of the twentieth century, global economic architecture, particularly the monetary system, was working in an efficient manner. It was rendered completely dysfunctional after the First World War.

5. Return to globalization

That the dismantling of globalization had high economic and social costs was obvious to anybody willing to see. The negative consequences of the reversal of trend towards globalization endeared globalism once again to policy makers. Their frame of mind began to change radically. Not wanting to see the repetition of the catastrophes of 1914–45, countries were willing to co-operate and collaborate in economic, financial and political spheres. After the Second World War, globalization resumed, *albeit in a restricted manner*. Only the industrial economies of North America, Western Europe, Japan and Australia and New Zealand participated in this immediate-postwar era of global integration. This left out a large part of the globe, in both the developing and socialist economies. It raised the moot question whether or not it could genuinely be considered and era of globalization when only a small number of economies were integrating. The group of industrial economies that were integrating during this period accounted for 15 percent of the global population, generated 57 percent of the global GDP and were responsible for 76 percent of world exports (Kolodko, 2002). While their dominance over the global economy was overwhelming, could they be regarded as the global economy?[18]

During this era of restricted globalization, industrial economies, led by the United Kingdom and the United States, endeavored to bring the global economy on an even keel. Many of them were willing to bring down the trade barriers erected during the interwar era. Under the sponsorship of the General Agreement on Tariffs and Trade (GATT), tariffs began to come down, albeit selectively in terms of products and countries. Several rounds of the multilateral trade negotiations (MTNs) were sponsored by the GATT. By the time the eighth round MTNs, the Uruguay Round, was launched in Punta des Este (in September 1986), trade in manufactures between industrial economies was substantially free of tariff barriers. However, the global trading system remained skewed against the developing economies. Trade barriers against them were lowered only for non-agricultural goods. Several important lines of developing economies exports (such as textiles and apparel) were kept out of the GATT system. Developing countries continued to erect high trade barriers, the most frequent reasons for which were balance of payments difficulties and infant industry protection (Das, 1990; Das, 2001a).

There was a further fall in transport costs by one-third between 1950 and 1980. In particular, rates of airfreight declined steadily during this period, and somewhat slowly in the 1990s. The decline was the greatest on the North American and Asian routes. There was a more than tenfold increase in the ratio of air-to-ocean shipments between the early 1960s and the mid-1990s (Hummels, 1999). The impact of limited tariff reduction was compounded with falling transport costs, giving impetus to global trade. By the late 1970s, global trade, as a proportion of global GDP, had recovered to the level of the first wave of globalization (World Bank, 2002). In a somewhat different manner, the earlier trade pattern re-emerged. That is, developing economies were exporting land-intensive primary commodities for importing manufactured products. However, during this period globalization in capital flows and the labor market was not restored.

For the industrial economies, the post-Second World War globalization, turned out to be highly significant, although it was different from the

---

[18] According to the periodization of the World Bank (2002), 1950–80 is another era of normal globalization. However, the author disagrees because this globalization was geographically restricted.

pre-1914 era of globalization. Factor migration during this period of globalization was much less impressive, while trade barriers among the industrial economies were lower than that in the earlier period. Strategies adopted during this period were influenced by the policies adopted by the dominant economy of this period – the United States. It had switched from a protectionist country welcoming immigration to a free-trader restricting immigration. Lowering or elimination of trade barriers expanded trade between the industrial economies enormously and this included large intra-industry trade between this sub-group of economies as well as trade generated by "slicing of the value chain." With the expansion of trade, specialization in manufacturing grew considerably, which in turn contributed to agglomeration and realization of scale economies. Consequently, income levels in the industrial economies rose much higher *vis-à-vis* the rest of the world.

The industrial economies began to specialize in niche markets, both in the manufacturing and the service sectors. This mode of production was efficient and enjoyed productivity gains from agglomerations. Thus, trade among the industrial economies was not only based on their respective comparative advantages but also on cost savings resulting from agglomerations and scale economies. Firms either clustered together to produce similar items or their production was vertically integrated. This tendency was observed first among Japanese auto manufacturers. They wanted their part suppliers to be located within the same agglomeration, and short distance from the main plant. Soon it spread to other industries, such as electronics. Large proportions, almost two-thirds, of manufacturing output were sold by one firm to another, as against by a firm to consumers. Networks of manufacturing firms were created resulting in positive externality to each firm in the network. The end result was highly cost-efficient production because of savings on transportation of inputs, production co-ordination, and quality monitoring (Sutton, 2000). Expanding markets and trade further underpinned the ability of networked firms of trade at low cost, which enabled them to specialize even more. Economies of agglomeration have a shady side. A geographical region may be considered uncompetitive only because an adequate number of firms have not decided to be located there. They cannot consider relocating until the production cost at the new location is so low that it would offset the loss of agglomeration economies. However, once the movement of firm starts, it is known to develop momentum of its own.

Developing countries were neither able to develop this mode of efficient production nor did they participate in this so-called second wave of globalization. Industrial economies expanded their trade in manufactures and services substantially. The developing economies stayed out because of export pessimism of the 1950s, generally poor investment climate in these economies, a marked anti-trade bias in their development strategy,[19] and high tariffs for their exports in the industrial economies. They concentrated on the exports of primary commodities. As late as 1980, only 25 percent of their exports were those of labor-intensive manufactured products.

During this period, a new trading structure emerged in global economy. It comprised two parallel trading patterns. The first was trade flows between the industrial economies and the second was the trade flows between developing and industrial economies. The first trading pattern was overwhelmingly dominated by manufactured goods and services, and a substantial part of it was intra-industry trade. The second was predominantly on "primary-goods-exports-for-manufacturing-goods-imports" line of trade. The first had a strong income equalizing effect on the trading partners. There was a discernible long-term income convergence among this group of countries, and lower income industrial economies did a good job of catching up with the higher income economies. During this period, social protection programs were implemented in the industrial economies, therefore, inequalities within the individual countries were also reduced (Martin, 2001). For the Organization for Economic Co-operation and Development (OECD) economies,[20] Clark *et al.* (2001) have empirically demonstrated that a dramatic reduction in both between-country and within-country income inequality occurred during this period. This era of rapid growth with equity in the OECD economies was unprecedented in their economic history. The developing economies were mere onlookers of this spectacular economic performance in the industrial world. Their per capita income growth rates had picked up marginally from the slump during the interwar period. However, due to high population growth rates, the number of absolute poor in the developing economies continued to rise. During this period, the global economy was clearly divided between the rapidly growing OECD economies and the laggards,

---

[19] China was a near autarky and India continued to be a weak trader, having a strong anti-trade bias in its development strategy until the early 1990s.

[20] The Organization for Economic Co-operation and Development (OECD) has 30 members. It is essentially an organization of industrialized countries, but it includes Korea and Turkey. By the mid-1990s, Korea had appeared graduated permanently to the ranks of industrial economies, only to find itself on the brink of bankruptcy in late 1997.

which was almost the rest of the world. Consequently, the globalizing OECD economies left the rest of the global economies behind on their onward march of economic progress.

6. Contemporary era of globalization

The contemporary phase of globalization began around 1980. During this period, a group of developing economies stopped being onlookers from the sidelines and began to participate in the global economy. They harnessed their abundant human resources, produced labor-intensive manufactured goods and services in which they had comparative advantage, and exported them. Several of them handled their exports of labor-intensive goods in a pragmatic manner and succeeded in acquiring important market niches in specific product lines. Beginning from 25 percent in 1980, the percentage of manufactured exports in total exports of developing economies soared to 80 percent in 1998. This was an impressive spectacle of economic transformation in a short period.

Although rather diverse groups of developing economies had moved into cashing in on their comparative advantage in labor-intensive manufactures, several Asian economies turned out to be the most successful in this regard. A stellar performance was that turned in by China, which was a near autarky in 1978, when Deng Xiao Ping adopted the much-vaunted open-door policy.[21] By the early 1990s China had become a middle-income country and by 2000, it was the largest developing country trader and the seventh largest global exporter. Rapid export growth helped in turning China into an important player on the global economic sage. In the 23 years between 1978 and 2000, China's export growth rate was higher than its GDP growth rate during 18 of those years. This implies that during the reform era the Chinese economy has

[21] At the Third Plenary Session of the 11th Central Committee of the Chinese Communist Party (CCP) in December 1978, the People's Republic of China adopted its "open-door policy". This became famous as the Deng doctrine because Deng Xiao Ping was the intellectual father of this liberal economic strategy. This marked a turning point in Chinese economic performance as well as economic history. It grew with a healthy clip through the 1980s and the 1990s. Gross domestic product (GDP) increased by 10 percent per annum in real terms over the 1980–2000 period. In a short span of two decades China economically transformed itself. Between 1978 and 2000, the GDP grew almost fivefold, per capita income quadrupled, and 270 million Chinese were lifted out of absolute poverty (*The Economist*, 2001). In 1990, China's GDP was $378.8 billion and per capita GDP was $341.60. A decade later, in 2000 GDP reached $1,080 billion, while per capita GDP rose to $853.40.

been integrating aggressively with the global economy by way of trade. It has been establishing niche markets for its goods and services globally as well as providing a market for exports from other developing and industrial economies (Das, 2001b).

The collapse of statist economic policy regimes in the socialist economies of the Soviet bloc and the import-substitution regime everywhere enhanced the acceptability of globalization-related notions, policies and concepts. Consequently, policy mandarins in an increasing number of countries became predisposed towards the benefit of economic liberalization. Examples of liberalizing countries such as China (noted above), Chile (mid-1970s), Argentina and Mexico (after the debt crisis of 1982) were followed by developing economies in other parts of the globe. They began opening their economies and welcoming foreign direct investment (FDI). The futility and failure of policies such as governments running public enterprises, administering trade monopolies, applying stringent exchange and price controls, and monopolizing the provision of infrastructure and public services, became increasingly obvious. Such a policy structure began to be seen as an unproductive liability. The policy mandarins adopted liberalization and globalization because of the collapse of alternative visions.

During the decades of the 1980s and the 1990s, some low-income developing countries such as Bangladesh and Sri Lanka not only successfully liberalized their economies but also managed to have large volumes of manufactured exports. Shares of manufactures in their export were larger than the world average of 81 percent. China came in this category, although it had a higher per capita income and cannot be called a low-income developing country. There were others (such as India, Indonesia, Morocco, Turkey) whose share of manufactures were approximately the same as the world average (World Bank, 2002). Another noteworthy feature was that the several developing economies grew into substantial exporters of commercial services. In 1980, industrial economies accounted for 17 percent of global exports of commercial services and the developing countries 9 percent. In 2000, the share of industrial countries rose to 20 percent, while that of developing countries nearly doubled to 17 percent (Martin 2001).

How did a sub-group of developing economies take to globalizing? Due to agglomeration and scale economies effects on the one hand and natural geographic advantages on the other hand, economic activity became highly geographically concentrated. Geographical location of a country became a significant variable. While some newly globalizing countries were helped by their location, others made conscious efforts to integrate with the global economy. A confluence of policy measures was responsible for their strategic transformation. First, developing economies that launched into globalization consciously changed their economic policies. The newly adopted set of policies was pragmatic, result-oriented, market-friendly, and more in line with the neoclassical economic principles. The newly globalizing economies also supported their firms by improving the complimentary infrastructure, skills, and institutions needed for modern production. This helped them in entering the global markets. Second, many of them undertook trade liberalization unilaterally or under the tutelage of the Bretton Woods institutions.

Third, tariffs on manufactured goods continued to decline in the industrial economies and the developing economies benefited from it due to the most-favored-nation clause in the first Articles of Agreement of the GATT and subsequently the World Trade Organization (WTO). Fourth, many developing economies removed restrictions against FDI, and improved their investment climate. Fifth, the newly globalizing economies adopted policy measures to promote macroeconomic stability and improve property rights. Sixth, technological progress in transport and communication helped them in plugging into the ongoing globalization movement. Containerization and the falling cost of airfreight, noted above in section 4, sped up movements of merchandise at a low cost and enabled these economies to become part of regional or global production networks.

To see how much conscious effort was responsible for globalization of the newly globalizing economies during the 1980s and 1990s, WB (2002) ranked developing economies by the extent to which they increased trade relative to income, and compared the top third with the rest of the countries. The first category had 24 developing economies, with close to 3 billion people, and was christened "more globalized" or globalizing economies.[22] Chile, Hong Kong SAR, Korea, Singapore, and Taiwan were exceptions because they had started their globalization process earlier than the 24 developing economies that were called more globalized. They are known as the newly industrialized economies (NIEs). All of the other developing economies once again failed to join

---

[22] The World Bank (2002) identified the following 24 countries as "more globalized" economies: Argentina, Bangladesh, Brazil, China, Colombia, Costa Rica, Cote d'Ivoire, Dominican Republic, Haiti, Hungary, India, Jamaica, Jordan, Malaysia, Mali, Mexico, Nepal, Nicaragua, Paraguay, the Philippines, Rwanda, Thailand, Uruguay, and Zimbabwe. For this study, the following countries were separated out as rich and globalized: the original members of the OECD, Chile, Hong Kong SAR, Korea, Singapore, and Taiwan. The population of these countries totaled 2.9 billion in 1997.

in the march to globalization. In the non-globalizing category, 49 countries were studied because the required statistics were available for them. During the period under consideration, the 24 more globalized economies recorded a larger (104 percent) increase in trade relative to increase in GDP. China recorded the largest increase in trade relative to GDP growth, closely followed by Mexico, Argentina and the Philippines, in that order. For the industrial economies this increase was 71 percent. Regrettably, the remaining two-thirds of the developing economies recorded a decline in trade to GDP ratio during this period. The largest decline was observed for Zambia, followed by Egypt and Nigeria.[23]

For the more-globalized and non-globalizing country groups, the World Bank (2002) identified the following characteristics: (i) although the two country groups had similar educational attainments in 1980, the more-globalized performed significantly better in the spread of basic education during the contemporary era of globalization.[24] A better spread of basic education is known to ameliorate poverty, raise health standards and indirectly helps in raising productivity levels in the economy; (ii) while both the country groups succeeded in bringing inflation down, the more globalized countries were markedly more successful; (iii) an index of property rights and rule of law was made for the two country groups. The more globalized groups were found to be moderately better than the non-globalizing country group; (iv) on average, the more-globalized countries slashed their tariff barriers more (34 percent) than the non-globalizing countries. The latter group brought down its average tariffs only by 11 percent during this period.

Although according to the criterion adopted by the World Bank (2002) study, both India and China have been classified together as more-globalized, from the vantage point of 2003, the two economies appear quite different. Notwithstanding the fact that the two are highly populous emerging-market economies, India is still not an outward-oriented economy in the manner of East and Southeast Asian economies and China. Although the Indian economy has benefited from its partial liberalization (see Chapter 1, section 1), the liberalization program was launched late and progressed at a tardy pace. A gargantuan amount of government interference still causes much inefficiency in the economy. India attracted relatively little FDI, was not affected by the regional crisis of 1997–98, and plays a small role in world trade and world markets. Despite its niche market in software programming, India has not participated in production

[23] Refer to World Bank (2002), Chapter 1.
[24] For a statistical comparison, see World Bank (2002), Table 1.1.

chains that are increasingly an important aspect of regional trade patterns in East and Southeast Asia and China. To an external onlooker, the target of economic growth and development seems to be a low priority of the society and of the government. Conversely, the political constituency for liberalization in China was large and influential, and therefore, after an early start, liberalization endeavors progressed much faster than those in India. China has been playing a large and growing role in world trade, accounting for almost 5 percent of global exports in 2002 – which was seven times larger in value terms than those of India. China is by far the largest link in the East and Southeast Asian production chains. It has continued to remain a dominant recipient of FDI, receiving $55 billion in 2002. The target of economic growth and development seems to have a high priority for the society and government in China (Ziegler, 2003).

Reforming, liberalizing and integrating with the global markets had an obvious impact on the growth performance. When low-income economies start integrating and exporting labor-intensive products, their export earnings could finance more imports, thereby intensifying competition and widening choices. There is some evidence that trade raised not only the level of real income but also the growth rate. However, trade must not be equated with growth. It is not a sufficient condition for growth. The 24 more-globalized economies were able to accelerate their GDP growth rate from an annual average of 2.6 percent through the 1970s to 5.0 percent through the 1990s (Dollar and Kraay, 2001). It appears that in this country group "growth and trade reinforced each other, and the policies of educational expansion, reduced trade barriers, and strategic sectoral reforms reinforced both growth and trade." Although there is little empirical evidence of openness causing growth, if the more globalized economies had faced market restrictions, their growth would have suffered.

Liberalization makes integration with the global markets possible. That market size is one of the important determinants of growth is an age-old axiom of classical economics. Three immediate material benefits of access to larger markets are: new productive and profitable ideas, including technological know-how, more and larger dosages of investment, including investment in large fixed-cost areas of production, and finer division of labor leading to greater specialization of production. In a liberalizing economy, firms can purchase better inputs and machine tools at competitive prices. No autarky is known to have produced world-class products. Furthermore, one of the most significant characteristics of a large market is intensification of competition, leading to efficient production and innovation. Therefore, integration with the global economy is relatively more important for the smaller developing economies than the large economies (Collier and Gunning, 1999). The 1990s witnessed further momentum in globalization endeavors. Continuously declining transportation and communications costs were the reasons behind it. In addition, there was sharp fall in the cost of transmitting information. Increase in the power of information processing led to plummeting costs of computing. During this period, a shift from digital to analog information technologies took place, and this helped in the merger of several segments of the information industry. These technological changes in the area of information and communication technology (ICT) worked towards enhancing the spread of globalization.

6.1 Contemporary globalization and capital flows

After the Second World War, the industrial economies gradually recovered and restructured themselves. As the recovery strengthened, the industrial countries began lifting restrictions on outward capital flows. Britain was one of the last to do so in 1979. At the recipient end, governments in several developing countries grew less hostile towards external capital inflows and liberalized restrictions on them. The new policy environment grew positive towards private foreign investors. The oil shocks of the 1970s had created a glut of private capital in the global capital markets, seeking profitable investment opportunities. This started a flow of private capital towards a group of developing economies.

As for the quantum, capital flows to the emerging market economies were a mere trickle in the 1970s. They averaged less than $28 billion annually during this decade. Since then they went on increasing and, in real terms, they peaked in 1997 at $306 billion (Schmukler and Zoido-Lobaton, 2001). They declined thereafter due to the successive financial crises in five Asian economies (1997–98), Brazil (1998), and sovereign default by the Russian Federation (1998), financial crisis in Ecuador (in 1999) followed by sovereign default by Argentina (2000–02), financial crisis in Turkey (2001–02) and Uruguay (in 2002–03). The composition of capital flows underwent a radical transformation during the 1980s and the 1990s. Official flows had initially dominated the global financial flows to the developing countries in general. During this period they were dwarfed by private capital flows. It must, however, be clarified that the private capital did not go to all developing countries. They had a definitive target. They became the major source of external finance only for the rapidly globalizing group of developing countries, which became known as the emerging-market economies. The more-globalized developing economies were a subset of this larger group.

Furthermore, during the 1980s and the 1990s, the structure of private capital flows underwent a great deal of transformation. FDI was growing during the 1980s, but its rate of increase accelerated dramatically during the 1990s. Mergers and acquisitions (M&As) in the rapidly globalizing group of developing countries were one of the primary reasons behind their rapid growth. A lot of public sector enterprises were privatized during the 1990s, bringing in substantial foreign capital as FDI in the rapidly globalizing developing economies. Although syndicated bank lending was a popular means of finance in the 1970s, it lost its appeal in the 1980s. The debt crisis of 1982 had rung the death knell of syndicated bank lending. Portfolio equity flows to the developing economies were not a popular mode of investment, therefore, and their volume was exceedingly low in the 1970s. Net portfolio flows to the emerging market economies grew from $10 million in the 1970s to $103 billion in 1996, in real terms (Schmukler and Zoido-Lobaton, 2001). Large financial institutions (investment banks, pension funds, and mutual funds) in the industrial economies, in the process of looking for lucrative investment opportunities, globalized their operations and channeled equity flows into the newly liberalized stock markets of the emerging market economies.[25] This issue is discussed at length in Chapter 5.

The volume of private capital flows increased substantially during the 1990s. External capital stock was measured at 22 percent of the developing country's GDP in 1998 (Maddison, 2001). However, this level was much lower than the 32 percent reached in 1914. Private capital was highly unevenly dispersed among the emerging market economies. The top 12 of these, which were all more-globalized economies, accounted for the overwhelming amount of the net inflows (see Chapter 5). Among these, Argentina, Brazil, China, India, Malaysia, Mexico, and Thailand were the most-favored destinations. With regard to the FDI flows, the two most successful economies were Chile and Malaysia. In both, the stock of FDI was approximately $2,000 per capita. In absolute terms, China was and continued to be the largest recipient of FDI.

It is well known that capital flows in the form of FDI bring in additional benefits in the form of advanced technical and managerial know-how, and the wherewithal to access international markets. The

---

[25] The source of statistics in this section is Schmukler and Zoido-Lobaton (2001). See also Rugman (2002) and UNCTAD (2002).

latter is difficult for developing economies; they can only attain it at high cost and after investing a good deal of time and effort. Also, FDI can link developing economies into regional and global production networks. This is common when transnational corporations (TNCs) make an investment. TNCs based in the G-7 economies account for almost 80 percent of the global FDI (UNCTAD, 2002; Rugman, 2002). As FDI comes packaged with other factors of production, it has a highly favorable impact on growth rate. The impact of other forms of external financial flows on growth rate is not so significant (Dollar and Kraay, 2001).

Capital flows to the emerging market economies in general, and the more globalized economies in particular, are only a small part of total global capital flows. Most capital owners in most periods are risk averse. Therefore, a far larger proportion of capital flows are between capital-rich industrial economies than from industrial to emerging market economies. The two top FDI recipients, Chile and Malaysia, are far below any of the industrial economies. Maddison (2001) has noted that per capita FDI in the United States was $3,200, while the corresponding amount for the African economies was $124. This period could be taken as the initial phase of financial globalization. There is a possibility of its intensification and underpinning of economic growth in other parts of the globe.

7. Conclusions and summing-up

Several clear thematic strands have emerged from the above exposition. The first is that globalization is an ancient phenomenon – there is little novel about it. During the second millennium globalization neither progressed at an even pace nor was it unidirectional. It had had exceedingly slow periods of progress, followed by rapid periods of progress such as those of the nineteenth century. It also suffered reversals. The century preceding the Napoleonic wars has good examples of interruptions.

The Industrial Revolution began in Britain in the late-eighteenth century. This can be taken as the first modern era of globalization. It ushered in a new era in the evolution of a global economy. Expanding foreign trade played a role in sustaining the Industrial Revolution in Britain. Globalization, which entailed expansion of trade, established Britain as a dominant industrial power of the post-Industrial Revolution period. International trade as a share of national income grew steadily from 8.4 percent in 1700, to 14.6 percent in 1780 and 15.7 percent in 1801. As in earlier periods of globalization, the pace of globalization was neither uniform nor smooth. It continued to be an on-again-off-again process during the post-Industrial Revolution period and was inter-rupted by numerous wars.

Since the advent of new shipping technology during the early nineteenth century, transport costs plummeted steadily throughout this century, providing further direct impetus to global economic integra-tion. The new technology was nothing short of revolutionary and entailed screw propellers, the compound engine, bigger size hulls and shorter turn-around time in port. Steamships were first introduced in inland maritime shipping and the Baltic and in the Mediterranean. Transatlantic shipping services were not introduced until the 1830s. The Atlantic economy was most powerfully affected by these technological developments, which promoted globalization. There is a large conver-gence in the view that the first era of serious globalization in the modern period should be taken to begin in 1870.

Land-intensive and extractive production activities and exports cannot take place without adequate capital. Therefore, a good deal of trans-border capital flows took place during this period. The foreign capital stock was 9 percent of the older industrial countries' GDP in 1870. By 1914, its level had risen to 32 percent. Britain was the largest exporter of capital during this period. By 1913, the global economy was far more integrated than that in the mid-eighteenth century. The ratio of world trade to world GDP had doubled in four-and-a-half decades between 1870 and 1914. However, world income equality continuously increased after 1820.

The interwar period of 1919–39 is an excellent example of globaliza-tion going into a reversal. Due to the war, quotas on trade and strict con-trols on allocation of shipping space became the order of the day. High tariff rates were introduced and these further stifled trade. Consequently, global economic integration stopped in its tracks. During the interwar period, transport costs declined and freight charges fell further by more that 30 percent. It did not have any impact on the globalization process because of the man-made barriers to trade and finance. This period suf-fered from one more serious limitation. At the dawn of the twentieth century, global economic architecture, particularly the monetary sys-tem, was working in an efficient manner but it was rendered completely dysfunctional after the First World War.

During the contemporary era, globalization again made steady progress in two sub-periods. The first was in the aftermath of the Second World War, when the industrial economies integrated well with enor-mous welfare implications for this sub-group of economies. That dis-mantling of globalization during the interwar period had high economic and social costs was obvious to anybody willing to see. The negative consequences of the reversal of the trend towards globalization endeared globalism once again to policy makers. Their frame of mind began to change radically. Not wanting to see the catastrophes of 1914–45 again, countries were willing to co-operate and collaborate in economic, financial and political spheres. After the Second World War, globalization resumed, *albeit in a restricted manner*. Only the industrial economies of North America, Western Europe, Japan and Australia and New Zealand participated in this immediate-post-war era of global integration. There was a further fall in transport costs by one-third between 1950 and 1980. In particular, rates of airfreight declined steadily during this period, and somewhat slowly in the 1990s. The decline was the greatest on the North American and Asian routes, which underpinned the trend toward globalization.

For the industrial economies, post-Second World War globalization, turned out to be highly significant, although it was different from the pre-1914 era of globalization. Factor migration during this period of globalization was much less impressive, while trade barriers among the industrial economies were lower than that in the earlier period. Developing countries were neither able to develop modes of efficient production nor did they participate in this so-called second wave of globalization. Industrial economies expanded their trade in manufactures and services substantially.

The second postwar period of globalization started around 1980, when a sub-group of dynamic developing economies made a successful foray at integration with the global economy. During this period, a group of developing economies stopped being onlookers from the sidelines and began to participate in the global economy. They harnessed their abundant human resources, produced labor-intensive manufactured goods and services in which they had comparative advantage, and exported them. Several of them handled their exports of labor-intensive goods in a pragmatic manner and succeeded in acquiring important market niches in specific product lines. Beginning from 25 percent in 1980, the percentage of manufactured exports in total exports of developing economies soared to 80 percent in 1998. During the 1980s and the 1990s, some low-income developing countries such as Bangladesh and Sri Lanka not only successfully liberalized their economies but also managed to have large volumes of manufactured exports. Shares of manufactures in their exports were larger than the world average of 81 percent. China came in this category, although it had a higher per capita income and cannot be called a low-income developing country. There were others (such as India, Indonesia, Morocco, Turkey) whose share of manufactures were approximately the same as the world average.

Reforming, liberalizing and integrating with the global markets had an obvious impact on the growth performance. When low-income economies start integrating and exporting labor-intensive products, their export earnings could finance more imports, thereby intensifying competition and widening choices. There is some evidence that trade raised not only the level of real income but also growth rate. However, trade must not be equated with growth. It is not a sufficient condition for growth. The 24 more-globalized economies were able to accelerate their GDP growth rate. As for the quantum, capital flows to the emerging market economies were a mere trickle in the 1970s. They averaged less than $28 billion a year during this decade. Since then they went on increasing and, in real terms, they peaked in 1997 at $306 billion. They declined thereafter due to the successive financial crises in five Asian economies.

Furthermore, during the 1980s and the 1990s, the structure of private capital flows underwent a great deal transformation. FDI was growing during the 1980s, but its rate of increase accelerated dramatically during the 1990s. Mergers and acquisitions (M&As) in the rapidly globalizing group of developing countries were one of the primary reasons behind their rapid growth. A lot of public sector enterprises were privatized during the 1990s, bringing in substantial foreign capital as FDI in the rapidly globalizing developing economies, particularly those of Latin America. Although syndicated bank lending was a popular means of finance in the 1970s, it lost its appeal in the 1980s. The debt crisis of 1982 had rung the death knell of syndicated bank lending. Portfolio equity flows to the developing economies were not a popular mode of investment, therefore, their volume was exceedingly low in the 1970s. Net portfolio flows to the emerging market economies grew from $10 million in the 1970s to $103 billion in 1996, in real terms. Large financial institutions entered and expanded their role in the globalization of financial markets.

References

Abu-Lughod, J., 1989, *Before European Hegemony: The World System AD 1250–1350*, New York: Oxford University Press.

Bourguignon, F. and C. Morrisson, 2001, "Inequality Among World Citizens: 1820–1992", Working Paper No. 2001–25, Paris: THEMA et DELTA.

Cannadine, D., 1990, *Decline and Fall of the British Aristocracy*, New Haven, CT: Yale University Press.

Clark, X., D. Dollar and A. Kraay, 2001, "Decomposing Global Inequality, 1960–99", Washington, DC: World Bank.

Collier, P. and J.W. Gunning, 1999, "Explaining African Economic Performance", *Journal of Economic Literature*, Vol. 37, No. 2, 64–111.

Crafts, N.F.R., 1985, *British Economic Growth During the Industrial Revolution*, Oxford: Clarendon Press.

Das, Dilip K., 1986, *Migration of Financial Resources to Developing Countries*, London: Macmillan.

Das, Dilip K., 1990, *International Trade Policy*, London: Macmillan.

Das, Dilip K., 2001a, *Global Trading System at the Crossroads: A Post-Seattle Perspective*, London and New York: Routledge.

Das, Dilip K., 2001b, "Liberalization Efforts in China and Accession to the World Trade Organization", *Journal of World Investment*, Vol. 2, No. 4, 761–89.

Dollar, D. and A. Kraay, 2001, "Trade, Growth and Poverty", Washington DC: World Bank, Policy Research Working Paper No. 2199.

The Economist, 2001, "Enter the Dragon", March 10, pp. 21–24.

Findlay, R., 1996, "The Emergence of the World Economy: Towards A Historical Perspective", New York: Columbia University, Columbia University Economics Discussion Paper No. 9596, April.

Findlay, R. and K.H. O'Rourke, 2001, "Commodity Market Integration, 1500–2000", paper presented at the NBER Conference on *Globalization in Historical Perspective*, Santa Barbara, CA, May 2002.

Fletcher, M.E., 1958, "The Suez Canal and the World of Shipping; 1869–1914", *Journal of Economic History*, Vol. 18, No. 3, 556–73.

Flynn, D.O. and A. Giraldez, 1995, "Born with a Silver Spoon: The Origin of World Trade in 1571", *Journal of World History*, Vol. 6, No. 2, 201–220.

Frankel, J., 2001, "Globalization and the Economy", in J. Nye and J. Donahue (eds), *Governance in a Globalizing World*, Washington, DC: Brookings Institution Press, pp. 132–58.

Hummels, D., 1999, "Have International Transportation Costs Declined?", Chicago: University of Chicago (mimeo).

Irwin, D.A., 1998, "From Hawley-Smoot to Reciprocal Trade Agreements: Changing the Course of U.S. Trade Policy in the 1930s", in M.D. Boro, C. Goldin and E. White (eds), *The Defining Moment: The Great Depression and the American Economy in the Twentieth Century*, Chicago: University of Chicago Press.

Kenwood, A.G. and A.L. Lougheed, 1983, *The Growth of the International Economy 1820–1980: An Introductory Text*, 2nd edn, London: Unwin Hyman.

Kindleberger, C.P., 1989, "Commercial Policy Between the Wars", in P. Mathias and S. Pollard (eds), *The Cambridge Economic History of Europe*, Vol. III, Cambridge: Cambridge University Press.

Kolodko, G.W., 2002, "Globalization and Catching-Up in Emerging Market Economies", Helsinki: United Nations University, World Institute for Development Economic Research, WIRER Discussion Paper WDP/2002/51, May.

Lamartine Yates, P., 1959, *Forty Years of Foreign Trade*, New York: Macmillan.

Langlois, J.D., 1981, *China Under Mongol Rule*, Princeton, NJ: Princeton University Press.

Lindert, P. and J. Williamson, 2001a, "Does Globalization Make the world More Equal", Cambridge, MA: National Bureau of Economic Research, Working Paper No. 8228.

Lindert, P. and J. Williamson, 2001b, "Globalization: A Long History", paper presented at the annual conference on Development Economics–Europe Conference, Barcelona, World Bank, June 25–27.

Maddison, A., 1995, *Monitoring the World Economy 1820–1992*, Paris: OECD.

Maddison, A., 2001, *The World Economy: A Millennial Perspective*, Paris: OECD.

Marshall, R., 1993, *Storm From the East: From Genghis Khan to Kublai Khan*, Los Angeles: University of California Press.

Martin, W. 2001, *Trade Policies, Developing Countries and Globalization*, Washington, DC: World Bank.

Mote, F.W., 1999, *Imperial China: 900–1800*, Cambridge, MA: Harvard University Press.

Mundell, R.A., 2000, A Reconsideration of the Twentieth Century", *American Economic Review*, Vol. 90, No. 3, 327–40.

Needham, J., 1954, *Science and Civilization in China*, Vol. I, Cambridge: Cambridge University Press.

O'Rourke, K.H. and J.G. Williamson, 2000, "When Did Globalization Begin?", Cambridge, MA: National Bureau of Economic Research, Working Paper No. 7632, April.

Phillips, E.D., 1969, *The Mongols*, New York: Praeger.

Rossabi, M., 1988, *Kublai Khan: His Life and Times*, Los Angeles: University of California Press.

Rugman, A.M., 2002, "New Rules for International Investment: the Case for a Multilateral Agreement on Investment (MAI) at the WTO", in C. Milner and R. Read (eds), *Trade Liberalization, Competition and the WTO*, Cheltenham: Elgar, pp. 176–89.

Schmukler, S. and P. Zoido-Lobaton, 2001, "Financial Globalization: Opportunities and Challenges for Developing Countries", Washington, DC: World Bank.

Sutton, J., 2000, "Rich Trade, Scarce Capabilities: Industrial Development Revisited", Discussion Paper No. E1/28, London: London School of Economics and Political Science, September.

United Nations Conference on Trade and Development (UNCTAD), 2002, *World Investment Report 2001*, Geneva: UNCTAD.

World Bank, 2002, *Globalization, Growth and Poverty*, New York: Oxford University Press.

Ziegler, D., 2003, "The Weakest Link: A Survey of Asian Finance", *The Economist*, February 13, p. 5.

3

Economic Dimensions of Globalization

1. Globalization and exchange rate regimes

As textbooks report, the Mundellian trilemma, or "impossible trinity," or "inconsistent trinity," has three policy strands: (i) free capital mobility; (ii) a fixed or stable nominal exchange rate; and (iii) an autonomous monetary policy – only two of which can coexist at any point in time.[1] During the Bretton Woods period (1945–71) the economic and political *mise-en-scène* was not conducive to rapid trans-border capital flows. Initially, during this period, large and small war-torn economies of Europe were engrossed in postwar recovery and reconstruction endeavors with the help of the United States. They needed the autonomy of monetary policy to achieve their domestic reconstruction objective. As capital flows did not start taking place until quite late during this period, the other policy strand that came to these economies, as a residual, was adoption of the stability in exchange rates. However, the strategic priorities of the post-Bretton Woods era were different from that of the contemporary period. Of the three Mundellian conditions, autonomous monetary policy to achieve domestic objectives and free capital mobility were the choice of this period. Exchange rate stability was given up in favor of capital mobility. As capital mobility received affirmation from the policy makers, financial globalization progressed during the post-Bretton Woods era.

The process of financial globalization, which started late during the Bretton Woods era, caused a spurt in capital mobility and created many exchange rate related problems for the economies that were trying to

---

[1] Obstfeld and Taylor (2002) have tried to interpret the various periods of globalization in terms of the Mundellian "impossible trinity."

integrate with the global economy.[2] Many of these problems emerged because financial markets, both domestic and international, in general are far from perfect. Several classical market-related limitations plagued the financial markets. These market imperfections included incomplete markets, asymmetric information, noise trading, bubbles, herding, multiple equilibria, moral hazard and contagion. Problems such as incomplete markets generally apply more to the domestic financial markets, while asymmetric information, for example, plague the international financial system.

After the Bretton Woods period, while pursuance of autonomy in the domestic monetary policy and free capital mobility worked reasonably well for the industrial economies, the middle-income developing countries that were trying to globalize faced torrid conditions in this arena. They tried to adopt a range of exchange rate arrangements but in most cases it was with only limited success. Consequently, these economies were bruised by crises. Their range covered arrangements such as soft peg, hard peg, crawls, stationary bands, moving banks, flexible exchange rate system, currency boards and dollarization. Of late, several globalizing economies have demonstrated a preference for the flexible exchange rate system. Although the popularity of this arrangement has been on the rise, the emerging market economies that adopted it have displayed an overly cautious attitude in practising it. These economies have shown that even after opting for a flexible exchange rate, they want to restrict the currency value movements in practice. Consequently they are not able to benefit from an autonomous monetary policy (Larrain and Velasco, 2001; Calvo and Reinhart, 2002).

The globalizing economies of the contemporary period not only did not benefit from all the possible advantages of financial globalization but also were bruised by currency, banking and debt crises.[3] The recent crises in Ecuador and Argentina had all three elements (Bordo *et al.*, 2001). Financial globalization of the contemporary period is hardly comparable to that in the nineteenth century (Compare relevant text in

---

[2] See, for instance, Chang and Velasco (2000); Bordo *et al.* (2001); Aghion *et al.* (2001); Calvo (2002); and Calvo and Reinhart (2002).

[3] Several developing economies in their endeavors to globalize have been bruised by crises. Even if we ignore the Latin American debt crisis that started in July 1982 with Mexico declaring a moratorium on its international debt, the current list of crisis-affected economies is unimpressively long. The contemporary crises took place in Venezuela in 1994, in Mexico in 1994–95, in East Asia in 1997–98, in the Russian Federation in 1998, in Brazil and Ecuador in 1999, in Turkey in 2001, in Argentina in 2001–02, and in Uruguay in 2002–03.

Chapter 2). Over the contemporary period, global market financial flows into these economies were far from steady. They were not always able to follow counter-cyclical monetary policy, and could not take advantage of consumption smoothening, deepening and diversification of their domestic financial markets, discernable reduction in the cost of capital, and significant augmentation of capital and domestic investment. Thus, the benefits of financial globalization to economies that have tried to globalize have so far been far from optimal (Mishkin, 2001).

1.1. Options for currency regimes

To achieve the goal of having a stable currency, sound domestic macroeconomic policies and fundamentals in the traditional meaning of the term are necessary but not sufficient under high global capital mobility. Experiences of the past quarter century show that volatility has been one of the most vexing problems in economies that have integrated recently (or are presently trying to integrate) with the global financial markets. In the financially globalizing world of the twenty-first century, which currency regime would be optimally suited for the globalizing economies? Analysts have brooded over it and the view that emerged over the past decade was that when the trans-border capital mobility is so high, either a global move towards greater exchange rate flexibility would be ideal or its opposite extreme, namely, some variety of fixed exchange rate system. The two currency regimes lay at two opposite extremes of the spectrum and cannot by construction be subjected to speculative attacks. According to this view, all of the intermediate regimes would be dysfunctional and therefore unsuitable for the globalizing economies. This view holds that had one of these two systems been in operation, many of the currency crises of the past quarter century and systemic financial problems could have been avoided.

However, the floating or flexible exchange rate regime cannot be considered totally problem-free because it is also fraught with the problems of volatility. This volatility need not necessarily stem from macroeconomic fundamentals. Besides, it can also create occasional asset bubbles and crashes. Becoming a part of a monetary union wards off this much-maligned volatility and stabilizes the currency. A global monetary union cannot be created because it will be too difficult to implement. Such a union is not feasible. The set of next-best options includes establishment of a regional monetary union, currency boards, dollarization or euroization (Fischer, 1999).

If monetary authorities wish to eschew the problems associated with the floating or flexible exchange rate as well as seek credibility of a stable (or fixed) exchange rate regime, they may consider establishment of a currency board. It is established by fixing the value of the currency, and by not allowing creation of high-powered money until it is fully backed by foreign exchange reserves. Under this regime, the law fixes the exchange rate and therefore it is devoid of variability, until the law decides to change it. The reserve requirements under this regime are stringent. Augmentation of a dollar's-worth of foreign exchange reserve backs each dollars-worth of domestic currency created. In running a currency board, a self-correcting balance-of-payments (BOP) mechanism works. A BOP deficit is readily reflected in a reduction of domestic money supply. Thus, a currency board is apparently a disciplined currency regime.

The currency board is an old system and was popular during the 1940s, largely among the British colonies. They used the pound as their reserve currency. During the contemporary period, Hong Kong SAR established a currency board in 1983, when it was a British colony. Since then its currency board has been functioning in a successful manner and the island economy has enjoyed the benefits of a credible and stable currency. Resurgence in its popularity was observed during the 1990s when similar currency boards were introduced in Argentina (1991), Estonia (1992), Lithuania (1994), Bulgaria (1997) and Bosnia-Herzegovina (1998).

A smoothly functioning currency board contributes to credibility of a currency as well as a policy environment. This system keeps a tight rein on fiscal profligacy and the deficits of the government cannot be financed by the creation of money. Therefore, its use has returned and it was recommended for several recent crisis-afflicted economies such as Indonesia (1997–98), the Russian Federation (1998) and Ukraine (1998). Successful operation of a currency board requires laying down of proper institutional foundations. A high level of foreign exchange reserves and adequately supervised and properly regulated financial markets are indispensable for establishing a currency board. A disciplined fiscal environment and rule of law are the other requirements. If the law is such that it can be easily evaded or changed, the credibility of the system would be seriously impaired.

Notwithstanding the high degree of discipline, credibility of a currency board is open to question because the law that it establishes is subject to change. Therefore, countries in Latin America seriously considered adopting the dollar and those in Eastern Europe the euro as their legal tender. This strategy is called dollarizing or euroizing and implies total surrender of monetary independence. As contagion effects of globalization have been bothering many of the economies that have been trying to globalize, the short-term objective of these countries was to keep contagion at bay by dollarizing or euroizing. Loss of control over their monetary policy did not matter to these economies because they were not benefiting from its freedom anyway. In addition, it was believed that such a currency arrangement would provide stability to their economies. Argentina and Mexico took serious interest in considering adoption of the dollar as their currency during the late 1990s and Ecuador adopted the dollar as the country's legal tender in 2000.

The two kinds of currency regimes, that is, the currency board on the one hand and dollarization and euroization on the other hand, are suitable for economies that are small, integrated with the global economy, and have suffered from episodes of high inflationary or hyperinflation. The economies angling for these two currency regimes met these conditions. It is imperative that the economies that adopt the strong currency of another country (the United States or Britain in the past) or the euro[4] must have strong ties with that country or group of economies. A dollarized or euroized currency regime faces the problem of undesirable swings in the bilateral exchange rates. The country whose currency has been adopted would be responsible for these unexpected swings in the bilateral rates, which may sometimes be harmful for the adopting economy.

De la Torre *et al.* (2002) have argued that in the contemporary era of financial globalization, the economies that are attempting to integrate need the "blessed trinity" to ward off the frequently occurring currency crises. Their concept of the blessed trinity includes: (i) a strong international currency; (ii) flexible exchange rate; and (iii) sound monetary and financial institutions. If the "blessed trinity" is achieved, the economies can integrate well with the global capital markets and take advantage of all the potential benefits. The reverse of the "blessed trinity" apparently is having a weak currency, an overly cautious floating system and weak institutions. When this combination exists, economies not only are not able to integrate well with the global financial markets but also become vulnerable to crises.

Of the three characteristics of the blessed trinity, the first is the most onerous and time-consuming to achieve. While a flexible exchange rate having a credible float and sound institutions are achievable in a relatively shorter period by a set of knowledgeable policy makers who know their job, the process of creating a strong currency which has an international

---

[4] The euro is a composite currency.

stature – one that is accepted as a store of value both at home and abroad – takes time and constant endeavors. Credible macroeconomic policies contribute to and support the international stature of a currency. In particular, the fiscal policy of the currency issuing country has to be balanced and devoid of any shade of profligacy, so that the solvency of the issuer is never called into question. A developing economy that has succeeded in achieving the blessed trinity can integrate successfully into imperfect financial markets without difficulties because "the components of the trinity interact in virtuous ways to control the risks of financial globalization while maximizing its benefits."

1.2. Mitigating currency crises

In the area of human health, prevention is considered the better part of the cure. The same applies to currency crisis. Several noted scholars have addressed themselves to important issues such as crisis prediction, crisis management and crisis prevention. These issues can only be mentioned here furtively because they are not the focus of this book. Besides, a large crisis literature exists for those who are interested. When a currency crisis strikes an economy, it is usually never a pure and pristine currency crisis. Its roots may well be embedded in other areas of the economic and financial structure of the crisis-ridden economy. Thus, the currency crisis is usually intertwined with other elements such as banking, financial and macroeconomic. It is usually a composite crisis. Each one of such crises is *sui generis*; there can be few generalizations in this regard. A policy analyst needs to carefully scrutinize its various contributing factors. Having diagnosed the principal elements of the malaise, the next step is to first find how to manage the crisis, second, to determine the short-term cures to mitigate the crisis, and third identify long-term preventive policies for each one of these crisis-engendering elements. The mitigating and preventive policy measures can be logically stratified as unilateral, bilateral, regional and multilateral.[5]

The unilateral and bilateral measures are taken by the crisis-affected economy on its own or in co-ordination and collaboration with a partner economy. It could either be a large trading partner or a large neighboring economy with which the crisis afflicted economy has close ties. During the Mexican crisis of 1994, the United States provided a helping hand to Mexico and helped it in putting its house in order. For Mexico,

---

[5] Wagner (2000a) has provided an analysis of all the four kind of measures. The stratification has been made in the cited paper.

the United States was both a large trading partner and a large neighboring economy. When a crisis strikes an industrial economy, it is relatively easy for it to take the curative and preventive measures because of its matured economic structure. On many an occasion, taking measure to strengthen and maintain its banking and financial sector is adequate in resolving an industrial country crisis. This, however, is not the case for the emerging market economies. In a world of high capital mobility, this set of economies needs to take a large number of concerted policy measures covering several areas of their economic and financial structure.

Both the academic community and multilateral organizations have addressed themselves to the phenomenon of crises. There is little disagreement regarding the measures needed to minimize the incidence of currency and related crises. For instance, in its endeavor to manage a crisis the crisis-stricken economies may have to (i) strengthen banking and financial structure including the capital base of the banks; (ii) improve the supply of information on the economic and financial affairs of the corporations, banks and the government; (iii) improve policy transparency; (iv) strengthen corporate governance in the corporate and financial sectors; (v) improve corporate finance; (vi) establish asset management companies; (vii) enact bankruptcy laws; (viii) upgrade the supervision and regulatory structure to strengthen the weak links in the financial chain; (ix) install measures against capital flight; and (x) rebuild an economic system around sound macroeconomic and exchange rate policies.

Managing a currency crisis is not an easy task for the developing and emerging market economies. They usually find it difficult to go it alone. Therefore, they join other regional economies – crisis-affected or not – in their co-ordinated endeavors to mitigate a currency crisis. This could be done informally or formally under the aegis of a regional monetary union. During the latter half of the 1990s, several serious proposals of creating monetary unions in Asia, Latin America and North America were taken up for debates in various regional and international fora.[6]

Impressive as it is, the example of the European Union (EU) is not easy to replicate in other parts of the world. The creation of such regional arrangements needs a dominant regional economy that is committed to the creation of such a union. The dominant economy is also expected to become the supplier of core currency. To this end, Japan and the

---

[6] Grubel (2000) has discussed the merits of a monetary union of Canada and the United States.

United States have not shown a strong penchant. On their own, Asian and Latin American economies cannot create a regional arrangement basically because they do not have the necessary core currency. Therefore, new regional arrangements are not on the horizon in the short-term. However, many informal or semi-formal arrangements at the regional level can be functional. At the time of the Asian crisis (1997–98), the informal co-operation and collaboration among the regional economies was conducive to taking various preventive measures, which helped and made the Asian crisis less deep than it could have potentially become.

The last stratum is that of multilateral institutions which assist in the resolution of a currency and financial crisis. These institutions, in particular the International Monetary Fund (IMF) and the Bank for International Settlements (BIS) work towards predicting, managing and preventing the crises, including a currency crisis. The role and involvement of the former is more direct than that of the latter institution. The lack of adequate incentives and timely and orderly restructuring of unsustainable debts has remained an important weakness of the system. During the last several years there has been extensive discussions inside the IMF and in the academic community on the need to develop a new approach debt restructuring, including sovereign debt restructuring. After the Asian crisis, Kenneth Rogoff (1999) published a list of reform proposals for the multilateral institutions with an objective to minimize the cost and risks of the currency crises. More recently Anne O. Krueger (2003) addressed this issue with the express objective of "strengthening the architecture of international financial system." The reform process requires proactive involvement of national governments, private sector in the emerging market economies as well as in the industrial economies and the international institutions. All four are the key players of the global financial system.

So far a usual multilateral response to a crisis was a multi-billion dollar rescue package prepared by the IMF. As the financial resources of the IMF are limited, these rescue packages are prepared with contributions from – and in collaboration with – one or more of the large industrial economies. A realistic alternative is badly needed. Debt restructuring, which includes restructuring of sovereign debt, in a pragmatic manner is one alternative. The basic objective of debt restructuring should be to help preserve asset values and protect creditors' rights, while paving the way towards an agreement that helps the debtor economy's return to viability and growth. The debt restructuring mechanism should "strive to create incentives for a debtor with unsustainable debts to approach its creditors promptly – and preferably before it interrupts its payments. But it should also avoid creating incentives for countries with sustainable debts to suspend payments rather than make necessary adjustments to their economic policies." Krueger (2003) was apprehensive about debt restructuring becoming "a measure of first resort."

To this end, loan contracts with the emerging market economies should include both majority voting and sharing clauses. This should work and improve the welfare of both debtor economy and creditors. At the beginning of the loan or bond negotiation process, the creation of an ambience for devising a pragmatic method of restructuring the debt in a flexible manner is indispensable. Collective representation clauses should help in the creation of such an environment.[7] Bond contracts should include these clauses. Legislators and regulators in the United Kingdom and the United States can help in redesign of the bond contracts in such a manner that these clauses can be added. A large proportion of international bonds of the emerging market economies are issued and traded in these two financial centers. Such an approach is far more realistic than making an attempt to create a supranational bankruptcy court. The IMF can play a proactive role in encouraging restructuring of debts. By facilitating the restructuring negotiations, the IMF would enhance its own legitimacy.

Standing committees of creditors are useful at the time of a crisis. They can communicate with the debtor, if crisis seems imminent. Such committees would help in jump-starting negotiations between the two sides. Information asymmetries between the two sides, which set them on a warpath, can be easily avoided with the help of the standing committees. The IMF has a meaningful and constructive role in such a situation. It can continue lending to countries in arrears on their external debt if they fulfill two conditions. First, they have to launch into serious structural adjustment program. Second, they have to continue good-faith negotiations with their creditors. The IMF credit should be given in conjunction with credit lines extended by commercial banks. In a globalizing financial world; the IMF's role should be transformed from being a global financial firefighter to a global financial policeman. The IMF should monitor emerging market economies more closely, particularly their conformance to international norms in financial-market-related matters, particularly their regulatory and supervision commitments as well as compliance to those commitments (Krueger, 2003).

Some governments,[8] the IMF and other multilateral institutions have invested a good deal of resources in devising early warning systems of different kind. The academic community has also made a good deal of

---

[7] For instance, an indentured trustee can be appointed to represent the creditors.
[8] The Government of Australia has made a substantial commitment to this issue, and this is reflected by the research projects it has recently commissioned.

progress in crisis prediction; however, the probability of sharp market moves still exists. That is not to say that these models do not have any utility, but one cannot expect too much from them because, as Barry Eichengreen remarked, "earthquakes and financial crises are products of complex nonlinear systems whose parts interact in unpredictable ways." Reactions to new information, or new interpretation to old information, can still unsettle financial markets in a completely unpredictable manner. Not a great deal can be done about it because this is the nature of the beast. Capricious market behavior can only be controlled by the application of and compliance with the appropriate regulatory norms.

2. Globalization and monetary policy

Inflation is the basic target variable of a monetary policy. The two basic objectives of a successful monetary policy are (i) control over the rate of inflation and prevention of deflation; and (ii) macroeconomic stability with the help of the other policy measures.

Monetary policy is only one of the many policy planks that supports macroeconomic stability. In the business and economic press as well as among the scholars dealing with globalization and macroeconomic issues, a working hypothesis has emerged regarding global integration exerting a systematic pressure on inflation and keeping it at a low level. Expressions such as "death of inflation" and "gunning for zero inflation" came to be used in the popular press. Numerous models have been devised and analysed to the test the hypothesis of globalization reining in the inflationary rate. They do suggest that globalization reduces inflation.[9]

Liberalization and opening-up are the preconditions to global integration. In an open economy incentives to inflate are low because the real benefits of a surprise monetary expansion are limited. Due to the openness associated with globalization, terms of trade tend to deteriorate with sudden expansion of output. Declining terms of trade lead to welfare loss to the economy. Therefore, the equilibrium rate of inflation in a globalizing economy is very low. Lane (1997) applied a different logic. He posited that open economies have a lower equilibrium rate of inflation even without the terms of trade deterioration. It can take place due to imperfect competition and nominal price rigidity in the non-traded goods sector.

---

[9] See, for instance, Clarida *et al.* (1999); Ball (2000); Brash (2000); Buiter (2000); Meyer (2000); Wagner (2000b); and Gamber and Hung (2001).

In a globalized or globalizing economy a rising inflation rate reflects poor macroeconomic management. It can also lead to economic instability, which in turn adversely affects the capital inflows from the global capital markets. Also, most innovative global firms will never plan to locate their production facilities in such an economy. For global firms operating in the developing economy that is trying to globalize, inflation works like taxation. The real effective capital income tax rises with increases in the rate of inflation. A rising rate of inflation can also spur capital flight. Capital is one of the basics of the production process and of economic growth. Departing capital resources have a high cost. They would lead to loss of production, decreasing factor productivity and falling growth rate. The penchant for capital to flee due to poor economic management is stronger when the economy is well integrated with the global economy.

For the reasons given in the preceding paragraph, the cost of rising inflation is higher in a globalized economy than in a non-globalizing economy. That is true even if the issue of capital flight is ignored. Realizing the high costs for the host economy, policy makers, unless they are myopic, emphasize such a monetary policy structure that goes with low inflation rates. In addition, redistributive effects of inflationary monetary policy tend to become less effective and attractive in a global economic environment where factor mobility is increasing. Thus, the overall impact of globalization is enhancement of price stability (Wagner, 2001).

3. Globalization and fiscal revenue

As with the passage of time, globalization is spreading and deepening, and some of the associated structural, institutional and technological changes are affecting tax systems of the globalizing economies. There is strong apprehension of a negative impact on fiscal system and revenues. Recent literature has pointed to various potentially negative effects of globalization, particularly in the Organization for Economic Co-operation and Development (OECD) economies.[10]

Tanzi (2000) referred to these effects as "termites," which cause decay of the fiscal system. A reality check in this regard is necessary. OECD (2002) statistics on aggregate fiscal revenues shows that so far this concern is highly exaggerated and that there is little quantitative evidence of a collapse of the tax structure in the OECD economies. If anything, the reverse is true. The other side of this argument is that while globalization is indeed likely to influence the ability of countries to collect tax

[10] See, for instance, various contributions to Razin and Sadka (1999).

revenue, it is too early for the impact of globalization to be clearly reflected in fiscal statistics because the contemporary wave of globalization is only in its infancy. Once global integration has progressed far enough, its fiscal effects may be magnified and discernible.

For a majority of the 30 OECD countries, tax revenues have continued to rise. By the mid-1990s, they reached their historical peak (OECD, 2002). The *Revenue Statistics* shows that the tax-to-GDP ratio for the OECD economies rose from 26 percent in 1965, to 35 percent in 1985, and to 37 percent in 1997. The tax-to-GDP ratio rose marginally (37.4 percent) until 2000, but declined to 36.1 percent in 2001. Despite widespread cuts in tax rates in this country group, this marginal growth in OECD tax-to-GDP ratios during 1996–2000 illustrates the complex factors that determine tax burdens. Part of the explanation for the tiny rise lay in economic growth, which increased corporate profits and lifted individual incomes into higher tax brackets. This is evidenced by an increase in the OECD average ratio of taxes on incomes and profits as a percentage of GDP from 12.8 percent in 1995 to 13.6 percent in 2000. The recent (2000–02) slow-down in the global economy, by reducing that effect, is likely to result in some of the tax cuts having their expected result of the reduction of the tax-to-GDP ratios.[11]

The value of tax-to-GDP ratios as a basis for comparison between countries is limited by differences in the mix of tax relief measures (which reduce the tax-to-GDP ratio) and cash benefits (which do not) used to pursue social objectives such as assisting families with children. Also, countries differ in the extent to which they tax government-provided social benefits, and so increase their tax-to-GDP ratio without adding to the tax burden on economic activities. The composition of tax revenue has changed considerably. Between 1965 and 1985, there was an increase in the proportion of income tax in the total tax revenues of the OECD economies. This trend reversed during the 1990s and the present share of income tax is close to that of the 1970s. As opposed to this, the proportion of corporate income tax has remained virtually stationary during the entire 1965–2001 period. While the share of social security contributions has increased substantially, that of consumption taxes has recorded a small decline. As the dominance of VAT (value-added tax) grew in the OECD economies, a marked shift was noticed from specific taxes to general taxes.

While there is a distinct possibility that globalization poses a serious challenge for the tax administrations, taking for granted a negative

---

[11] The source of these statistical data is OECD (2002).

impact in this regard is not warranted. It remains to be seen whether globalization can engender new opportunities to use knowledge and technology to raise revenues in an innovative manner. With progress in globalization, new taxes as well as novel methods of tax collection and revenue generation may be devised. Invention of VAT in the 1950s and its subsequent widespread use is a good illustration of a novel idea in taxation. The ultimate result may well be higher fiscal revenue levels to meet public expenditure needs.

That progressing globalization can potentially affect the revenue generation from various taxes was studied by Tanzi (2000), who identified eight "fiscal termites." The first that can gnaw at the tax base is electronic commerce (or e-commerce) and electronic transactions, which have been growing at a rapid pace. With advancing globalization, the Internet may become the principal instrument of business particularly of business among enterprises (the so-called B2B). The volume of e-commerce has been projected to cross $5 trillion by 2005 (*The Economist*, 2002). E-commerce has seriously eroded the sales tax base. In addition, current political ambience of taxing e-commerce is not favorable. The second fiscal termite is electronic money (or e-cash), which is a close cousin of e-commerce. With the passage of time, real money would be gradually supplanted by e-cash. This trend would indeed make it difficult for the individual taxpayer to be taxed, making tax authorities' tasks complex and onerous (King, 1999).

The third fiscal termite is the rapidly growing trade between the subsidiaries of transnational corporations (TNCs). Intra-TNC trade now accounts for over one-half of global trade volume (UNCTAD, 2002; Rugman, 2002). It creates problems for national tax authorities because TNCs tend to abuse the "transfer pricing" mechanism. Tax authorities believe that many TNCs manipulate prices to move profits from high tax rate jurisdictions to where the tax rates are low. The offshore financial markets are the fourth fiscal termite. With growing financial integration, they have become an important channel of global investment. Current estimates of investment channeled through them ranges between $6 trillion and $7 trillion. Income earned from these investments is generally not reported to national tax authorities. Derivatives and hedge funds are the fifth fiscal termite. They largely operate from offshore bases and are not regulated. When they operate from an onshore financial center, they are essentially beyond domestic financial regulation.

The sixth termite is the income derived from highly mobile financial capital. As financial globalization levels increase, skilled traders move financial capital swiftly and efficiently from economy to economy and currency to currency. Tax authorities are unable, even unwilling, to tax income derived from such financial movements. When highly skilled professionals and business people work or conduct their businesses outside of their home countries, their incomes become difficult to tax because of lack of contact and exchange of information between the tax authorities in the two countries. This is the seventh fiscal termite. Foreign earnings of individuals and businesses usually go unreported. The eighth fiscal termite is the shopping of low weight and volume but high value items by foreign travelers. Passenger lounges of a large number of international airports have been turned into luxurious shopping centers. Changi airport in Singapore is the one of best example of this genre of shopping centers.

Concerted action can certainly eradicate some of these fiscal termites. For economies in which they create, or are likely to create, large holes in fiscal revenue they could be problematic. Tax authorities should visualize these situations well in advance and plan for measures to tackle them.

4. Globalization and competition

One of the important benefits of globalization is enhanced competition, both at the micro and macro levels. It is particularly applicable to the ongoing financial globalization process (see Chapter 5, section 2). The final result of heightened competition is improved systemic efficiency. Here we are taking the normal definition of efficiency, that is, producing more with the given resources or producing the same quantum with fewer resources. As globalization is essentially driven by structural changes and technological developments, transaction costs in the globalizing economies have tended to reduce. In the integrating economies, exposure of private agents to global competition has increased. Therefore, efficiency level in both the goods and factor markets has been affected favorably.

Citrin and Fischer (2000) have decomposed the effects of globalization-driven competition into microeconomic and macroeconomic levels. At the microeconomic level, as global integration affects both goods and factor markets, it leads to lower price mark-ups in the goods sector, lower excess wages in the labor markets and less expensive capital due to movement of capital from the capital abundant economies to the capital scare economics. Unwarranted price mark-ups are in general unsustainable. They become more unsustainable in a globalized world economy. So do the wage hikes that are not supported by productivity increases. Thus, global integration nurtures discipline in the market-place as well as promotes it in the place of production. The microeconomic impact of enhanced competition and market discipline is a one-time price decline. At the macroeconomic level, as new economies enter the global market scene the market competition become keener. When the four Asian newly industrialized economies (NIEs)[12] broke into the global market place in the late 1970s and the early 1980s, the OECD Secretariat commissioned a study to delve into the effect of their entry on the erstwhile industrial economies. In the late 1980s, when the People's Republic of China (hereinafter China) entered the global markets, it made its presence felt by exporting a wide range of low- and medium-technology products and textiles and apparel at highly competitive prices. The reaction of the matured industrial economies and that of the early-arriving NIEs was to conduct a close scrutiny of the impact of China's entry on their own production and trade patterns.[13] In 1999, the OECD Secretariat commissioned another study to delve into the effect of the emerging market economies on the OECD countries' global competitiveness. Another variety of competition that has been intensified by globalization is related to infrastructure and regulation. Most globalizing economies now make conscious attempts to improve their physical infrastructure and improve the domestic regulatory framework so as to reduce systemic inefficiencies. Macroeconomic competition of this variety is known to exert continuous downward pressure on prices, as opposed to one-time downward shift.

When an economy provides better physical infrastructure and improved policy and regulatory framework compared to its neighbors, it out-competes them in attracting mobile factors of production, namely, human and financial capital. The latter includes FDI, bank credits and investment in securities. Better infrastructure, macroeconomic policy and regulatory frameworks provide incentives for FDI to come in and the probability of domestic firms keeping their own mobile factors of production from moving outwards increases. Here the term infrastructure

---

[12] Namely, Korea, Hong Kong SAR, Singapore, and Taiwan.
[13] Between 1978, when the Deng doctrine was adopted by China and the present, China has successfully become the manufacturing storehouse of the global economy. In doing so, it turned from a near autarky in 1978 to the sixth largest exporter in the world in 2001. It is also the largest developing country exporter accounting for 4.3 percent of the global exports in 2001. In addition, for well over a decade, China has been pre-empting the largest amount of net FDI among the developing economies.

has wider meaning than usual physical dimensions of industrial and financial infrastructure. For instance, it also includes law and order, property rights, contract enforcement, economic and political stability.

Governments play a definitive role in creating the appropriate infrastructure as well as macroeconomic conditions for attracting global capital, both human and financial. Both of them make a remarkable contribution not only to growth and development but also in stimulating the process of integration with the global economy. In order to attract them, savvy policy makers try to create a sound institutional framework and exercise greater fiscal discipline. To achieve this objective, they need to ensure medium-term financial stability of the economy. Globalization-driven pressure to raise the level of competitiveness in their economies and to reduce the probability of macroeconomic instability also makes them cautious in devising their general macroeconomic policy framework (Limao and Venables, 2000).

5. Globalization and the labor markets

Creation of the North American Free Trade Agreement (NAFTA), impending expansion of the European Union both eastward and southward, high unemployment in the EU economies, and rising unemployment in the United States, have raised concern regarding the impact of globalization on employment. The old controversy between the partisan of free trade and globalization on the one side and promoters of protectionism and anti-globalization on the other has been re-ignited by concern regarding the impact of globalization on employment rate. The two contentious groups have been at it for a long time. The ongoing globalization of the labor markets has added a heightened level of fervor to the age-old dispute. There is a fairly widespread notion, largely among non-economists, that globalization has contributed to deterioration of labor market conditions by depressing wages and raising unemployment levels in the matured industrial economies. These notions had strong political overtones in the past, they continue to do so now.

The members of American Federation of Labor–Congress of Industrial Organizations (AFL–CIO) are convinced that globalization of labor has affected them adversely by causing declines in wages and fostering inequality.[14] The high and persistent two-digit unemployment rates of

---

[14] A visit to the website of the American Federation of Labor–Congress of Industrial Organizations (AFL–CIO) is enough to convince any reader of their convictions.

the large EU economies are essentially blamed by the European labor organizations on globalization of labor markets. The theory that globalization has a negative welfare effect for the labor class is not new. During the Great Depression era the same was thought of free trade. John Hicks (1959) reported that loss of jobs and high unemployment rate of this period were blamed on free trade.[15] Consequently, liberal public opinion in England of that period lost its faith in free trade. During the contemporary period the villain of the piece is not free trade but globalization. On their part, labor force in the developing countries begrudges the expansion of globalization for the same very reasons. They blame it for stifling domestic industries, increasing a migratory trend in the industrial sector, and increasing unemployment rates. During the 1980s and the 1990s, deterioration of relative returns to labor market participation on the part of the unskilled workers took place and is a fact accepted by all serious analysts of labor markets. What is open to dispute is the relationship between this and globalization.

Current debate has gone a step ahead of the old "cost of free trade" argument. There are two basic strands in this debate. First, in a globalized or better-integrated world large corporations, particularly the TNCs, move and relocate their production facilities easily to such low-wage emerging market economies that have now developed enough to provide them with the externalities they are used to in their native matured industrial economies. Numerous emerging market economies in Asia, Eastern Europe and Latin America have benefited from this trend during the preceding two decades. China has been the most successful example in this context.

The second argument follows from the first, that is, relocation of large firms and TNCs creates a *mise-en-scène* for what became popularly known as social dumping. It is believed that the developing and emerging market economies find it profitable to become contestants in "a race to the bottom" for the purpose of attracting FDI. Such hollowing-out of manufacturing activity in the industrial economies, particularly where there are record levels of persistent unemployment, is perceived as a limitation of globalization. So is the related phenomenon of a steady flow of low-skill immigrants from the developing economies to the industrial economies.

In its standardized form, neoclassical trade theory can provide some answers, albeit these answers are not adequate for a globalizing world

---

[15] See John Hicks (1959) *Essays in World Economics*, which deals with the disenchantment with trade liberalization in Britain during and after the Great Depression.

economy. The Stolper-Samuelson theorem, under the rubric of the Heckscher-Ohlin-Samuelson (HOS) theory, recognized that trade liberalization adversely affects the capital abundant economy. The Stolper-Samuelson theorem posited that in a simple two factor, two goods (or 2×2) world an increase in relative price of a good increases the real wages of the factor used intensively in producing that good, and lowers the real wage of the other factor. Therefore, prima facie lobbying for protection from the labor groups in the matured industrial economies stands to reason. In the context of the 2×2 model, in a real life situation a variety of interferences are plausible that break or weaken the link between trade and factor prices. For instance, terms-of-trade effects can seriously interfere with the Stolper-Samuelson logic. Thus, weakening of this link is an essential element in the case against trade as a culprit in the deterioration of labor market returns to unskilled workers.

Although, the neoclassical trade theory is clear about the welfare enhancement implications of free trade, it is less clear about the consequences of relocation of production facilities from a high-wage economy to a low-wage economy. Under the perfect competition assumptions with constant returns to scale, location of firms does not matter. Also, under the perfect competition conditions, TNCs have no reason to exist because factor movements and free trade have the same ultimate consequences. Therefore, it is imperative to quit the neat idealized world of the neoclassical theory to analyse various characteristics of globalization where location of firms does matter because of market imperfections.

When in a globalizing world economy firms relocate to a developing or emerging market economy and serve the domestic market through those production plants, the firms are able to exploit the wage differential abroad. However, there are no free lunches. There are fixed costs associated with relocation. Thus, these costs have to be balanced with the benefits of wage differential. Movements of the firms to low-wage economies have apparent social costs for the home economy. In the short-term these costs tend to be non-negligible, creating a hostile political environment for globalization per se. This is not to deny the long-term consequences of free movement of commodities and factors of production having a favorable impact over the allocation of global resources, ultimately leading to positive welfare implications for the global economy.

Cordell and Grilo (1998) put game theory through its paces and solved for the sub-game perfect equilibria of two-stages in which firms choose whether to relocate or not. For their model, they considered firms that produce vertically differentiated goods for the domestic market. They concluded that in the relocation decision of firms, quality of product matters, although not directly. They found that incentives for relocating production facilities in low-wage countries are higher for the firm that produces a variety of product that would have a larger market share if the goods were sold at their marginal cost. This implies that those firms in the industrial economies that produce high-quality goods are natural candidates for relocation abroad. With regard to the social costs of relocation, their conclusion is tentative. They found that in many situations the efficiency gains due to relocation do not offset the losses imposed upon workers by way of increased unemployment in the home economy. They also proved that welfare costs of relocation are higher, the higher the wages paid in the host economy. Thus the welfare costs of relocation of production facility would be lower in China or other low-wage Asian economies, and higher in relatively higher-wage countries of Eastern or Central Europe.

When an economy embarks on its globalization path, its comparative advantage and pattern of trade undergo a transformation. Also, the globalization process, *inter alia*, entails liberalizing the various sectors and markets of the domestic economy. The labor market needs to start a dynamic adjustment process to adjust to the new scenario. Globalization forces some sectors and firms to contract. These are putatively those sectors that have lost comparative advantage and are no longer competitive in the global market place. Conversely, by the same token, globalization spurs expansion of some firms and industries. Additionally, new firms and industries are created in those sectors in which the globalizing economy finds its new areas comparative advantage.

Using a general equilibrium trade model that explicitly accounts for the dynamic aspects of labor market adjustment, Davidson and Matusz (2001) demonstrated how empirically observable parameters of the labor market determine the rate at which labor is released from the contracting sectors and absorbed into the expanding sectors.[16] Most workers of the contracting firms and sectors who lose their jobs in this process are re-employed at some stage, but there is a period of active job search before new employment is found. To be able to be re-absorbed into the expanding sectors and firms, many workers may have to be

[16] The model used by Davidson and Matusz (2001) is overly simplistic. It includes only a single factor of production and all of the labor market turnover rates are exogenous. The key parameter of their model is labor market turnover rates.

re-skilled and re-tooled. There are always groups of unskilled workers who find relocating to another employment in the globlazed scenario so difficult that they exit the job market. This is the dynamic process of labor market adjustment.

Davidson and Matusz reached several interesting, logical and plausible conclusions. They weighed short-run costs of adjustment in the labor market against any long-run gains that may arise from globalization and changes in the structure of trade and trade policy. They concluded that the short-term costs of adjustment could in no way outweigh the long-term gains from globalization. However, adjustment costs are usually substantial in the short-term. The value of output, net of re-skilling costs, was found to decline by more than 1.5 percent one year after the globalization and liberalization process began. Also, adjustment costs may be so large that they nullify a large part of long-term efficiency gains. The length of dynamic adjustment period in the labor market is likely to be non-trivial. When the economy and the labor market are liberalized, the low-skill labor sector demonstrated Stolper-Samuelson type results. Workers in the low-skill sectors were found to be worse-off after liberalization, while those in the higher-skill end stood to gain from liberalization. Liberalization also provided impetus to workers to switch from the low-skill industries to the high-skill industries, and a significant amount of this kind of skill switch or up-grade took place.

6. Globalization and migration flows

During the 1870–1914 period, a large population relocation, measuring around 10 percent of the global population, took place. Another estimate puts this movement of population at 60 million for the same period (Solimano, 2001). Hatton and Williamson (1998) called this the age of mass migration.[17] This number is for migration of European population to the New World economies. Sharply reduced transport costs, *inter alia*, contributed to this relocation of population. Importantly, this wave of migration made per capita income and factor prices convergence feasible in the "Atlantic Economy."

Why did such large global population relocation take place during the earlier period of the modern era (1870–1914)? Human beings are rational

---

[17] Hatton and Williamson (1998) provide a detailed account of migration of various waves of immigrants during different periods. They also provide the relevant statistics in this regard.

economic agents. If they see a possibility for a better economic life on another part of the globe, they try to relocate, work hard and improve the quality of their lives. This is the *causae causantes* behind population or labor movements. The limiting factors in this regard are barriers to relocation. Immigration policies in most large centers of economic activity are not as liberal now as they were during the earlier periods. According to the World Bank (2002), currently 120 million people, or 2 percent of the global population, live in countries other than those of their birth. This stock of immigrants is evenly divided between developing and industrial countries. However, as the population of the industrial economies is one-fifth that of the developing economies, migrant population forms a larger part of the population of the industrial countries (6 percent) than that of the developing world (1 percent) (World Bank, 2002).

As mentioned in Chapter 2, during the phase of globalization that immediately followed the Second World War, the OECD economies grew much faster than the rest of the world. Widening economic differences and income gap created an intense pressure for international migration from the poor areas and countries to the affluent areas. However, in the period following the Second World War, these pressures were kept under control by stringent restrictive laws against movements of people. Globalization strategies of this period favored the movement of goods and capital across national borders more than the movement of people. The strategies subsequently changed and during the contemporary phase these restrictions were relaxed to a limited, calibrated extent, which in turn had a powerful effect on wages in the developing economies. The direction of migration during the contemporary phase is from the developing to matured industrial economies. Large migration of Russian population to Israel during the first quinquennium of the 1990s was an exception in this regard.

It is noteworthy that during the past two decades, particularly during the fast-growing 1990s, migration to the United States increased significantly. The principal source countries of the migrating population were Mexico, Central American countries and Asia. Migration to the United States from Europe (14 percent) declined sharply, while that from Latin America (46 percent) and Asia (34 percent) soared. During the current period, Mexico, Cuba and the Dominican Republic are the principal Latin American source countries, in that order. The Philippines, China, Korea and India, are the principal Asian source countries, in that order. In the other OECD countries, the proportion of immigrant population to the total has been rising. During 1988–97, sharp increases were observed in Austria, Denmark, and Luxembourg. The proportion of immigrants in the total is the highest on Luxemburg (34.9 percent), followed by Australia (21.1 percent), Switzerland (19.0 percent) and Canada (17.4 percent). At the other end of the spectrum, the OECD countries with less than 3 percent of immigrant population are Japan, Finland, Italy, Portugal and Spain.[18] During the decade of the 1990s, after the collapse of the Union of Soviet Socialist Republics (USSR), the flow of immigrants to from the former socialist republics to Canada, Germany, Switzerland, Sweden and the United Kingdom increased significantly.

Higher wages are not the principal motivating factor for nothing. Wages for the same skill-set differ widely from economy to economy and there is a large chasm between the wage levels in the industrial and developing economies. Refining this argument further, there are conspicuous gaps between the wage levels in the industrial economies and the NIEs on the one hand and the NIEs and the developing economies on the other hand. For instance, hourly compensation in manufacturing in Germany is $30 an hour compared to 30 cents in China and India. This ratio of 1:100 in two locations is an extreme case. Wage differential between the United States and the NIEs such as Malaysia and Thailand is 1:10. A recent study of legal immigrants showed that a Mexican worker, on average, on moving to the United States makes nine times more in a job similar to the one he or she held at home. Likewise, daily wages in Indonesia are 28 cents compared to $2 in neighboring Malaysia (World Bank, 2002: *Economist*, 2002). To be sure, a manufacturing worker in Germany and the United States generally has better education standard and skill set than a typical worker in a developing economy or in an NIE. But skill difference can only explain a small amount of the wage differential. As there are large gains to be made in terms of real wages by immigrating to a more economically developed country, migration pressures are created. However, not everybody who wants to migrate can because of the well laid out immigration policies, laws and entry restrictions in the receiving economies.

A recent study of immigration pressure in Africa found that the differential in real wages and a demographic bulge in the 15–29 age group created a pressing need for outward labor migration. This pressure was engendered by the entry restrictions in the receiving countries (Hatton and Williamson, 2001). United States entry restrictions for Mexican workers are not so strong and there are 7 million legal Mexican migrant workers in the United States. According to various estimates,

---

[18] The source of these statistics is Solimano (2001).

close to one half of this number are undocumented Mexican workers. This means that 10 per cent of the Mexican population lives and works in the United States. Outward labor flow of this dimension should have a great deal of impact on the Mexican labor market and real wages.

Hatton and Williamson (2001) estimated the impact of outward labor flows on African economies and found that the wages moved significantly upwards, particularly for unskilled workers. Higher real wages for those who have not migrated is not the only benefit of migration. It is customary for first generation immigrants to repatriate money, generally in hard currency, for their immediate families and other close relatives. For several developing countries remittances are a large source of capital. As this flow is in hard currency, it fills both the savings gap and foreign exchange gap. India is the largest recipient of repatriated capital. It touched $12 billion in 2000. Mexico, Turkey, Egypt, Lebanon, Morocco, Jordan and Dominican Republic are the other large earners of remittances and earn more than $1 billion annually by way of remittances from abroad (World Bank, 2001).

In an important paper, Robert Mundell analytically demonstrated around half a century ago that trade is a substitute for factor movements, including labor movements. The assumptions in his model included constant returns to scale, perfect competition and absence of distortions in the economy. The principal driving force of his logic was trade-led equalization of factor prices. When factor prices – in this case wages – equalize, people have little incentive to move across national borders. In Mundell's model, the assumptions were important and they took his conclusion in an abstract direction. Therefore, when these assumptions were relaxed and the same exercise was performed under the assumptions of economies of scale, factor endowment, cost of mobility, and normal distortions were included in the model, Mundell's conclusion was reversed (Faini *et al.*, 1999). That is, migration and trade were found to be *complementary, not a substitute* for each other. This outcome does not negate the factor price equalization resulting from trade. Given the large gap between per capita incomes of the developing and industrial countries, it would take decades, even a century, for wages to equalize. In many cases, it many never come about. There is an important policy implication of the Mundellian conclusion of trade being a substitute for migration. That is, industrial economies should promote the dismantling of trade barriers, both tariff and non-tariff, to reduce the current pressure of migration. However, in view of the large per capita income differentials, trade liberalization would not be enough to dampen the current pressures.

Immigration, in the long-term, contributes to growth in the receiving economy. This issue is not so simple as it prima facie seems because the questions regarding causality and its direction have not been clearly answered. Historical evidence exists to show that during the age of mass migration, more rapid growth in the resource-rich New World economies preceded immigration. To be sure, immigration can be linked to growth in the recipient economies. Its contributions are made through the addition of varying levels of skills, both quantitatively and qualitatively, to the host economy's labor and skills reservoir. Their presence moderates the wage hike pressures in the receiving economy. By keeping down labor costs, they raise productivity levels and thereby underpin profitability of investment. They also contribute through macroeconomic channels by boosting investment and savings in the receiving economy. These contributions coalesce to accelerate GDP growth (Solimano, 2001).

Insofar as immigration policies restrict migration, they restrict the movement of labor from lower productivity activities to those of higher productivity (or higher productivity countries). The end result is global welfare loss in terms of foregone world output. As mentioned in the preceding paragraph, the long-term consequence of immigration can be accelerated GDP growth in the recipient country. Restricting immigration is just and logical only during the periods of high or rising unemployment. The impact of migration on the source country would entirely depend upon the existing stock of labor and human resources. If there is a surplus, as is common in many developing economies, outward migration is beneficial in that it would rein-in chronic unemployment and generate foreign exchange for the country by way of repatriated revenues.

So far the focus has been on immigration of individuals and families but there have been instances of mass migration. They have been instrumental in other kinds of global integration, that is, globalization by the development of strong bonds of ideas, trade and investment. The Chinese diaspora of the last two centuries is an outstanding example of this kind of globalization. Large migrations of Chinese population took place to Southeast Asian nations such as Indonesia, Malaysia, the Philippines, Singapore, and Thailand. Presently substantial proportions of populations are of Chinese origin in these countries. They acquired a reputation of being enterprising minorities, with enormous business savvy, in these countries. Chinese family networks, or the so-called "bamboo networks," played a significant role in trade and investment flows among these countries and China. Common language and time-tested business culture played a meaningful role in expanding trade and investment links. A comparable example is that of recent surge in Indian immigration to the United States. These people are largely information technology (IT) and computer professionals, working in high-tech sectors. Their presence became conspicuous in Silicon Valley. This will naturally create flows of capital and technology between India and the United States in the IT and computer industries. It will also support US investment in India. Eventually, a trade and investment network is likely to develop between the two countries.

Why were pressures for population migration kept under control by stringent restrictive laws during the second phase? The reason is that while there is a general consensus on the benefits of a free-trade regime and liberal capital movement, the free movement of population is believed to be governed by different economic laws. Therefore, goods and finance, both man-made objects, are free to move globally; but not people. The reason is that migration is a complex issue and its implications and ramifications extend well beyond the economic arena. There are important political, social and cultural considerations associated with immigration. After the tragic event of September 11, 2001, ethnicity and religious beliefs of potential immigrants became a barring factor. Besides, in the receiving country, at least the first generation of legal immigrants, do not enjoy the same political rights as the nationals of the recipient country and are known to suffer serious discrimination. One of the important reasons for the negative public attitude toward them is that they are regarded as a burden on the welfare state in the receiving country because they become entitled to many social benefits.

7. Globalization and flight of human capital

During the contemporary phase of globalization, movement of human capital has soared dramatically. Here we are defining human capital as people with high levels of skill and education – having at least tertiary level education, if not higher professional degrees in specialized disciplines. A PhD in international finance, a neurosurgeon, a software quality expert would fall in this category. The old fashioned term for this kind of human capital movement is "brain drain."[19] The best illustration of human capital movement during the contemporary period is to

[19] The expression "brain drain" became popular in the 1950s. Its context was immigration of first-rank scientists from countries such as the United Kingdom, Canada and other East and West European countries to the United States. Albert Einstein was one such scientist. Subsequently this expression was generalized to indicate international movement of human capital from the developing to industrial economies.

Silicon Valley in California, which is the global hub of the most technologically advanced firms in information and communication technology (ICT). Close to 40 percent of the highly skilled technical workforce and entrepreneurial talent in the Silicon Valley comes from two developing economies – China and India.[20]

During the 1970s, migration of human capital from the developing to industrial economies raised a lot of passion. It was erroneously assumed that outward migration of highly skilled people was always detrimental to the source country. Some economists from the developing economies argued that when high-skilled people immigrate, they create negative externality for those who are left behind. They naively equated this migration with a zero-sum-game and concluded that human capital movement makes the rich economies richer and the poor poorer. Although earlier debates on this issue were impassioned, these arguments were superficial and could not stand close scrutiny of economic analysis.

According to United Nations statistics on the migratory trend, during the 1961–72 period, 300,000 highly skilled people migrated from the developing economies to the industrial economies. In 1990, the US census revealed that 2.5 million highly skilled immigrants from the developing economies were living in the United States. The International Labour Organization (ILO) made regional estimates of human capital flight. For 1990, the ILO estimated that 15 percent of those who were highly educated emigrated from Central America, 6 percent from Africa and 5 percent form Asia. In the Philippines, 40 percent of those who immigrated had tertiary education.[21] The spurt in the migration of higher quality human capital to the industrial countries during the last two decades was due to "quality selective" immigration policies and processes in most of the OECD countries.

The trend in migration of human capital is largely driven by general trends in global integration. The latter reinforces the natural tendency for human capital to agglomerate where it is already in abundance and where it is rewarded. There are three positive feedback effects of human capital migration for the source economy, namely, remittances, return migration after additional skills have been acquired and the creation of business and trade networks by the immigrant population. Chinese diaspora all over Southeast and East Asia and North America is an excellent

---

[20] According to a Silicon Valley wit, IC stands for Indian and Chinese, not for integrated circuits.

[21] These statistical data have been cited by Rapoport (2001).

illustration. Most countries from where human capital has been migrating in increasing magnitude have benefited from it. An additional point is that prospects of migration tend to increase the expected rate of return to education in the source country and hence foster domestic enrollment in education (Rapoport, 2001).

There are large inter-country wage differentials between developing and industrial countries. Prospects of migration influence the incentive structure of those living in the developing economies when they make their education-related decisions. Even if it is assumed that the wage differential between the developing and industrial economies is a modest 6, and there is 0.2 probability of immigrating to an industrial economy, there is large expected return on human capital movement. Such computations affect domestic enrollment in education in a significant manner. When this kind of incentive structure exists, the source country's stock of human capital is increased significantly. Human capital migration and economic growth have an inverse-U-shaped relationship. That is, too much migration is detrimental to growth, but too little is sub-optimal.[22]

For any developing economy, the optimal human capital migration rate will necessarily be positive. Whether its current rate is above or below the optimal rate will have to be determined empirically for an individual developing economy. Some developing countries obstruct the global movement of their human capital on grounds that the education of the migrating professionals was publicly financed. This policy measure is imprudent and myopic, and in effect depletes the long-term value and level of their human capital.

8. Globalization and income convergence

Notwithstanding the wonders of compound rate of GDP growth, income inequality between countries that have existed for a millennium cannot be reasonably expected to be eradicated in a matter of two or three decades. It is possible that *in absolute terms* income inequality between countries may still rise. However, available empirical evidence has demonstrated that there has been a decline in the global income inequality during the contemporary phase of globalization. Distribution of global income is more equal now than it was three decades ago. Yet, the income convergence process is advancing slowly.

This gradual improvement in the global income inequality appears to be in stark contrast to the earlier periods of globalization, that is, during

---

[22] See, for instance, Beine *et al.* (2001); and Kalaitzidakis (2001).

the latter half of the eighteenth century following the Industrial Revolution as well as in the 1870–1914 period. During these periods, only a small number of countries benefited from productivity improvements made possible by new technologies. These countries, which were concentrated in Western Europe, got an early start and grew much faster than the rest of the world. There is evidence of income convergence in this small group of economies (see below). For almost two centuries, productivity improvements did spread slowly to some countries of the New World but did not spread to the other parts of the world. Consequently, global inequalities widened and the income gap between countries grew at a menacing pace. During the deglobalization period of 1914–45, distribution of global income worsened further. Two World Wars, the so-called Great Depression, breakdown of global financial flows and the adoption of protectionist policies coalesced to cut the average growth rate of the global economy by a third of the pre-First World War level. Protectionist policies never contribute to the narrowing of income inequalities.

Income convergence that had started earlier among the matured industrial economies since the late nineteenth century, continued during the contemporary period. By 1995, inequality between the industrial countries was less than half of what it was in 1960, and considerably less than that in 1980 (Clark *et al.* (2001)). However, this trend towards income convergence among countries reversed into a divergence when income distribution within these countries was considered. Domestic inequality within the industrial economies has demonstrated an increasing trend. Immigration, taxation policies, and social policies unconnected to globalization could be responsible for it (Clark *et al.*, 2001). For the OECD countries, while globalization has definitely led to income convergence, different member countries had, and continue to have, differing levels of domestic inequality. Furthermore, industrial countries that were at the same level of globalization show differing levels of domestic inequality.

A striking divergence of GDP growth rates was reported by the World Bank (2002) between the more globalized and less globalized developing economies during 1980–2000. The more-globalized group of developing economies benefited from their exports of manufactures and services, from financial inflows and from migration, and was successful in reducing poverty and improving income distribution. Like the OECD countries, inter-country income convergence took place among the more-globalizing economies also. It seems that this is a characteristic common to all the open economies, industrial and developing. In those

developing economies that have been integrating with the global economy, since the late 1960s – that is, the NIEs – real GDP growth has been
faster than that of the matured industrial economies. Therefore, growth
in global income inequalities has halted and the differences have started
to narrow. Sustained high levels of growth in populous and poor countries such as China and Indonesia has helped in this regard. Although,
the situation in India improved after 1991, the improvements are not
comparable with the other two populous economies.

The Lorenz curve has been frequently used to measure the income
inequality between countries. This provides a comparison between each
country's share of global income and its share of global population. To
plot a Lorenz curve percentage of income going to the poorest 10 percent
of the population, 20 percent, and so on, are plotted against cumulative
population share of the global income produced. The global Lorenz
curve shows greater income equality in the late 1990s than in the mid-
1960s. Using a Lorenz curve, Melchior *et al.* (2000) concluded that
between 1965 and 1997 global income inequality declined by 10 percent.
The Lorenz curve for the 21 members of the Asia Pacific Economic
Co-operation (APEC) forum shows that income equality among this
country group has narrowed much more than the global average. It
declined by 23 percent.[23]

Was international income convergence that occurred during the contemporary phase of globalization caused by global economic integration? It cannot be taken as a mere coincidence. Studies that have
analysed data for the last two centuries have concluded that the rate of
growth in income inequality between nations has been reduced by globalization for the *countries that have successfully integrated* into the global
economy (Lindert and Williamson, 2001a; 2001b). As the results for the
APEC countries in the preceding paragraph show, the better the integration
the higher the level of income convergence among national incomes.

9. Conclusions and summing-up

This chapter deals with the principal economic aspects of globalization
and their implications. Several clear thematic strands have emerged from
the above exposition. The first relates to the choice of exchange rate

---

[23] The Asia Pacific Economic Co-operation (APEC) forum comprises 21 member
economies: Australia; Brunei Darussalam; Canada; Chile; China; Hong Kong,
China; Indonesia; Japan; Korea; Malaysia; Mexico; New Zealand; Papua New
Guinea; Peru; the Philippines; Russia; Singapore; Chinese Taipei; Thailand; the
United States and Viet Nam.

regime for a globalizing economy. During the Bretton Woods period the economic and political *mise-en-scène* was not conducive to rapid trans-border capital flows. Initially, during this period, large and small war-torn economies of Europe were engrossed in postwar recovery and reconstruction endeavors. They needed the autonomy of monetary policy to achieve their domestic reconstruction objective. Their choice of policy was conditioned by the Mundellian trilemma. As capital flows did not start taking place until quite late during this period, the other policy strand that came to these economies, as a residual, was adoption of the stability in exchange rates. However, the strategic priorities of the post-Bretton Woods era were different from that of the contemporary period. Of the three Mundellian conditions, autonomous monetary policy to achieve domestic objectives and free capital mobility were the choice of this period. Exchange rate stability was given up in favor of capital mobility. As capital mobility received affirmation from the policy makers, financial globalization progressed during the post-Bretton Woods era. The globalizing economies of the contemporary period not only did not benefit from all the possible advantages of financial globalization but also were bruised by currency, banking and debt crises. Over the contemporary period, global market financial flows into these economies were far from steady.

Experiences of the past quarter century show that volatility has been one of the most vexing problems in economies that have integrated recently with the global financial markets. In the financially globalizing world of the twenty-first century, which currency regime would be optimally suited for the globalizing economies? Analysts have brooded over it and the view that emerged over the past decade was that when the trans-border capital mobility is so high, either a global move towards greater exchange rate flexibility would be ideal or its opposite extreme, namely, some variety of fixed exchange rate system. The two currency regimes lay at two opposite extremes of the spectrum and cannot by construction be subjected to speculative attacks. However, the floating or flexible exchange rate regime cannot be considered totally problem-free because it is also has its problems.

When a currency crisis strikes an economy, it is usually never a pure and pristine currency crisis. Its roots may well be embedded in other areas of the economic and financial structure of the crisis-ridden economy. Thus, the currency crisis is usually intertwined with other elements such as banking, financial and macroeconomic. It is usually a composite crisis. Each one of such crises is *sui generis*; there can be few generalizations in this regard. A policy analyst needs to carefully scrutinize its various contributing factors.

So far a usual multilateral response to a crisis was a multi-billion dollar rescue package prepared by the IMF. As the financial resources of the IMF are limited, these rescue packages are prepared with contributions from – and in collaboration with – one or more of the large industrial economies. A realistic alternative is badly needed. Debt restructuring, which includes restructuring of sovereign debt in a pragmatic manner, is one alternative. The basic objective of debt restructuring should be to help preserve asset values and protect creditors' rights, while paving the way towards an agreement that helps the debtor economy's return to viability and growth.

Globalization reins in the inflationary rate. The equilibrium rate of inflation in a globalizing economy is very low. Open economies tend to have a lower equilibrium rate of inflation even without the terms of trade deterioration. It can take place due to imperfect competition and nominal price rigidity in the non-traded goods sector.

There is a strong apprehension of a negative impact of globalization on fiscal system and revenues. Recent literature has pointed to various potentially negative effects of globalization, particularly in the OECD. However, a reality check in this regard shows that on aggregate fiscal revenues show that so far this concern is highly exaggerated and that there is little quantitative evidence of a collapse of the tax structure in the OECD economies. If anything, the reverse is true. The other side of this argument is that while globalization is indeed likely to influence the ability of countries to collect tax revenue, it is too early for the impact of globalization to be clearly reflected in fiscal statistics because the contemporary wave of globalization is only in its infancy. While there is a distinct possibility of globalization posing a serious challenge for the tax administrations in the future, taking a negative impact for granted in this regard is not warranted.

One of the important benefits of globalization is enhanced competition, both at the micro and macro levels. At the microeconomic level, as global integration affects both goods and factor markets. It leads to lower price mark-ups in the goods sector, lower excess wages in the labor markets and less expensive capital due to movement of capital from the capital abundant economies to the capital scare economies. Unwarranted price mark-ups become more unsustainable in a globalized world economy than before and so do the wage hikes that are not supported by productivity increases. At the macroeconomic level, as new economies enter the global market scene the market competition become keener. When the four Asian newly industrialized economies (NIEs) broke into the global market place in the late 1970s and the early

1980s, the OECD secretariat commissioned a study to delve into the effect of their entry on the erstwhile industrial economies. In the late 1980s, when China entered the global markets, the OECD seriously studied its impact on the industrial economies. In 1999, the OECD secretariat commissioned another study to delve into the effect of the emerging market economies on OECD countries' global competitiveness. Another variety of competition that has been intensified by globalization is related to infrastructure and regulation. Most globalizing economies now make conscious attempts to improve their physical infrastructure and improve the domestic regulatory framework so as to reduce systemic inefficiencies. Macroeconomic competition of this variety is known to exert continuous downward pressure on prices, as opposed to one-time downward shift.

The theory that globalization has a negative welfare effect for the labor class is not new. During the Great Depression era the same was thought of free trade. The old controversy between the partisan of free trade and globalization on the one side and promoters of protectionism and anti-globalization on the other has been re-ignited by concern regarding the impact of globalization on employment rate. When an economy embarks on its globalization path, its comparative advantage and pattern of trade undergo a transformation. Also, the globalization process, *inter alia*, entails liberalization of the various sectors and markets of the domestic economy. The labor market needs to start a dynamic adjustment process to adjust to the new scenario. Globalization forces some sectors and firms to contract. These are putatively those sectors that have lost comparative advantage and are no longer competitive in the global market place. Conversely, by the same token, globalization spurs expansion of some firms and industries. Additionally, new firms and industries are created in those sectors in which the globalizing economy finds its new areas comparative advantage.

During the 1870–1914 period, large population relocation, measuring around 10 percent of the global population, took place. The reason for such a large-scale population movement was that people saw the possibility for a better economic life on another part of the globe. They worked hard and improved the quality of their lives. However, after the Second World War the pressures for migration of population were kept under control. Globalization strategies of this period favored the movement of goods and capital across national borders more than the movement of people. The strategies subsequently changes and during the contemporary phase these restrictions were relaxed to a limited, calibrated extent, which in turn had a powerful effect on wages in the developing economies. In important paper, Robert Mundell analytically demonstrated around half a century ago that trade is a substitute for factor movements, including labor movements. However, when Mundell's assumptions were relaxed and the same exercise was performed under the assumptions of economies of scale, factor endowment, cost of mobility, and normal distortions were included in the model, Mundell's conclusion was reversed. That is, migration and trade were found to be *complementary, not a substitute* for each other. Why were pressures for population migration kept under control by stringent restrictive laws during the second phase? The reason is that while there is a general consensus on the benefits of a free-trade regime and liberal capital movement, free movement of population is believed to be governed by different economic laws.

During the contemporary phase of globalization, movement of human capital has soared dramatically. Here we are defining human capital as people with high levels of skill and education – having at least tertiary level education, if not higher professional degrees in specialized disciplines. The trend in migration of human capital is largely driven by general trends in global integration. The latter reinforces the natural tendency for human capital to agglomerate where it is already in abundance and where it is rewarded. There are large inter-country wage differentials between developing and industrial countries. Prospects of migration influence the incentive structure of those living in the developing economies when they make their education-related decisions. For any developing economy, the optimal human capital migration rate will necessarily be positive.

Available empirical evidence has demonstrated that there has been a decline in the global income inequality during the contemporary phase of globalization. Distribution of global income is more equal now than it was three decades ago. Yet, the income convergence process is advancing slowly. This gradual improvement in the global income inequality appears to be in stark contrast to the earlier periods of globalization. Income convergence that had started earlier among the matured industrial economies since the late nineteenth century, continued during the contemporary period. By 1995, inequality between the industrial countries was less than half of what it was in 1960, and considerably less than that in 1980. As in the OECD countries, inter-country income convergence took place among the more-globalizing economies also. It seems that this is a characteristic common to all the open economies – industrial and developing. In those developing economies that have been integrating with the global economy, since the late 1960s – that is, the NIEs – real GDP growth has been faster than that of the matured industrial economies. Studies that have analysed data for the last two centuries have concluded that the rate of growth in income inequality between nations has been reduced by globalization for the *countries that have successfully integrated* into the global economy.

References

Aghion, P., P. Bachetta, and A. Banergee, 2001, "Currency Crises and Monetary Policy in an Economywith Credit Constraints", *European Economic Review*, Vol. 45, No. 7, 1121–50.

Ball, L., 2000, "Policy Rules and External Shocks", Cambridge, MA: National Bureau of Economic Research, Working Paper No. 7910.

Beine, M., F. Docquier and H. Rapoport, 2001, "Brain Drain and Economic Growth: Theory and Evidence", *Journal of Development Economics*, Vol. 64, No. 1, 275–89.

Bordo, M., B. Eichengreen, D. Klingebiel and M.S. Martinez-Peria, 2001, "Financial Crises: Lessons from the Past 120 Years", *Economic Policy*, April, Vol. 45, No. 4, 110–360.

Brash, D.T., 2000, "How Should Monetary Policy Makers Respond to the New Challenges of Global Economic Integration?", paper presented at the symposium on *Global Economic Integration: Opportunities and Challenges*, sponsored by the Federal Reserve Bank of Kansas, at Jackson Hole, Wyoming, August 24–26.

Buiter, W.H., 2000, "The New Economy and Old Monetary Economics", London: Bank of England, discussion paper.

Calvo, G.A., 2002, "Globalization Hazard and Weak Government in Emerging Markets", Washington, DC: Inter-American Development Bank, working paper, February.

Calvo, G.A. and C. Reinhart, 2002, "Fear of Floating", *Quarterly Journal of Economics*, Vol. 117, No. 2, 112–40.

Chang, R. and A. Velasco, 2000, "Liquidity Crises in Emerging Markets: Theory and Policy", Cambridge, MA: National Bureau of Economic Research, Working Paper No. 7272.

Citrin, D. and S. Fischer, 2000, "Meeting the Challenges of Challenges of Globalization in the Advanced Economies", in H. Wagner (ed.), *Globalization and Unemployment*, Berlin: Springer, pp. 19–35.

Clarida, R., J. Gali and M. Gertler, 1999, "The Science of Monetary Policy: A New Keynesian Perspective", *Journal of Economic Literature*, Vol. 37, No. 2, 1661–707.

Clark, X., D. Dollar and A. Kraay, 2001, "Decomposing Global Inequality, 1960–99", Washington, DC: World Bank.

Cordell, T. and I. Grilo, 1998, "Globalization and Relocation in a Vertically Differentiated Industry", Washington, DC: IMF, Working Paper No. WP/98/48, April.

Davidson, C. and S. Matusz, 2001, "Globalization, Employment and Income: Analyzing the Adjustment Process", Nottingham: University of Nottingham,

Leverhulme Centre for Research on Globalization and Economic Policy, Research Paper 2001/04.

De la Torre, A., E.L. Yeyati and S.L. Schmukler, 2002, "Financial Globalization: Unequal Blessings", Washington, DC: World Bank, Policy Research Working Paper No. 2903, October.

The Economist, 2001, "Enter the Dragon", March 10, pp. 21–24.

The Economist, 2002, "Survey on E-Commerce: Shopping Around the Web", February 26.

Faini, R., J. de Melo and K. Zimmermann, 1999, *Migration: The Controversies and the Evidence*, Cambridge: Cambridge University Press.

Fischer, S., 1999, "Reforming the International Financial System", *Economic Journal*, Vol. 109, No. 3, 557–76.

Gamber, E.N. and J.H. Hung, 2001, "Has the Rise in Globalization Reduced US Inflation the 1990s?", *Economic Enquiry*, Vol. 39, No. 1, 58–73.

Grubel, H.G., 2000, "The Merit of a Canada-US Monetary Union", *North American Journal of Economics and Finance*, Vol. 11, No. 19–40.

Hatton, T. and J.G. Williamson, 1998, *The Age of Mass Migration: Causes and Economic Impact*, Oxford: Oxford University Press.

Hatton, T. and J.G. Williamson, 2001, Demographic and Economic Pressure on Immigration Out of Africa", Cambridge, MA: National Bureau of Economic Research, Working Paper No. 8124.

Hicks, J., 1959, *Essays in World Economics*, Oxford: Clarendon Press.

Kalaitzidakis, P., 2001, "Measures of Human Capital and Nonlinearities in Economic Growth", *Journal of Economic Growth*, Vol. 6, No. 3, 229–54.

King, M., 1999, "Challenges for Monetary Policy: New and Old", in *New Challenges for Monetary Policy*, Kansas City, KA: Federal Reserve Bank of Kansas City.

Krueger, A.O., 2003, "Promoting International Financial Stability: Sovereign Debt Restructuring", in Dilip K. Das (ed.), *An International Finance Reader*, London and New York: Routledge, pp. 114–41.

Lane, P.R., 1997, "Inflation in Open Economies", *Journal of International Economics*, Vol. 42, No. 2, 327–47.

Larrain, P. and A. Velasco, 2001, "Exchange Rate Policies in Emerging Market Economies: The Case for Floating", *Essays in International Economics*, No. 224, December.

Limao, N. and A.J. Venables, 2000, "*Infrastructure, Geographical Disadvantage, and Transport Costs*", Washington, DC: World Bank.

Lindert, P. and J. Williamson, 2001a, "Does Globalization Make the world More Equal", Cambridge, MA: National Bureau of Economic Research, Working Paper 8228.

Lindert, P. and J. Williamson, 2001b, "Globalization: A Long History", paper presented at the annual Conference on Development Economics – Europe Conference, Barcelona, World Bank, June 25–27.

Melchior, A., K. Telle and H. Wiig, 2000, "Globalization and Inequality: World Income Distribution and Living Standards 1960–98", Oslo: Royal Norwegian Ministry of Foreign Affairs, Report No. 68, September.

Meyer, L.H, 2000, "Structural Changes and Monetary Policy", presentation made before the Joint Conference of Federal Bank of San Francisco and the Stanford Institute of Economic Policy Research, San Francisco, March 3. Available at <http://www.frbsf. org/economics/conferences/000303/agenda/html>.

Mishkin, F., 2001, "Financial Policies and Prevention of Financial Crises", in M. Feldstein (ed.), *Economic and Financial Crises in Emerging Market Countries*, Chicago, University of Chicago Press, pp. 134–60.

Obstfeld, M. and A.M. Taylor, 2002, "Globalization and Capital Markets", Cambridge, MA: National Bureau of Economic Research, Working Paper No. 8846, March.

Organization for Economic Co-operation and Development (OECD), 2002, *Revenue Statistics*, Paris: OECD, October.

Rapoport, H. 2001, "Who is Afraid of the Brain Drain? Human Capital Flight and Growth in Developing Countries", Stanford, CA: Stanford University, Stanford Institute for Economic Policy Research. Economic Policy Brief.

Razin, A. and E. Sadka (eds), 1999, *The Economics of Globalization*, Cambridge: Cambridge University Press.

Rogoff, K., 1999, "Economic Institutions for Reducing Global Financial Instability", *Journal of Economic Perspectives*. Vol. 13, No. 1, 21–42.

Rugman, A.M., 2002, "New Rules for International Investment: the Case for a Multilateral Agreement on Investment (MAI) at the WTO", in C. Milner and R. Read (eds), *Trade Liberalization, Competition and the WTO*, Cheltenham, Edward Elgar, pp. 176–89.

Solimano, A., 2001, "International Migration and the Global Economic Order: An Overview", Washington, DC: World Bank, Policy Research Working Paper No. 2720, November.

Tanzi, V., 2000, "Globalization, Technological Developments, and the Work of Fiscal Termites", Washington, DC: International Monetary Fund, Working Paper No. WP/00/181.

United Nations Conference on Trade and Development (UNCTAD), 2002, *World Investment Report 2001*, Geneva: UNCTAD.

Wagner, H, 2000a, "Which Exchange Rate Regime in an Era of High Capital Mobility?", *The North American Journal of Economics and Finance*, Vol. 11, No. 1, 191–203.

Wagner, H., 2000b, "Globalization and Inflation", in H. Wagner (ed.), *Globalization and Unemployment*, Berlin: Springer, pp. 345–90.

Wagner., H, 2001, "Implications of Globalization for Monetary Policy", Washington, DC: International Monetary Fund, Working Paper No. WP/01/184, November.

World Bank, 2001, *World Development Indicators*, Washington, DC: World Bank.

World Bank, 2002, *Globalization, Growth and Poverty*, New York: Oxford University Press.

4
Trade and Global Integration

1. Evolving global trading system[1]

At the end of the Second World War, interest, enthusiasm and commitment to trade liberalization was exceedingly high among the major trading countries. Even before the International Trade Organization (ITO) charter[2] was approved, 23 of the 50 participants of the Bretton Woods conference decided, as early as in 1946, to launch negotiations with an objective to reduce tariffs and bind them. These economies were eager to give an impetus to trade liberalization and to "begin correcting the legacy of protectionist measures", which were in place since the early 1930s.

An attempt was made to create an ITO under the Havana Charter, which was negotiated in 1947.[3] It was intended that the ITO would join

---

[1] Multilateral trading system is technically a more correct expression than global trading system because not all countries are members of the World Trade Organization (WTO). In July 2003, its membership was 146 countries, which included almost all of the principal trading nations. In addition, 32 countries had observer status. This category included the Russian Federation and Saudi Arabia.
[2] The ITO Charter was ambitious and extended beyond the world trade disciplines. It included regulations on employment, commodity agreements, restrictive business practices, international investment and trade in services. Although the ITO Charter was finally agreed at a United Nations Conference on Trade and Employment in Havana in March 1948, ratification in some national legislatures proved impossible. The most serious opposition came from the US Congress, although the US government was one of the principal driving forces and was trying to champion the cause of free trade.
[3] See *The Final Act of the United Nations Conference on Trade and Employment*, published by the Economic and Social Council of the United Nations, 1947.

hands with the two Bretton Woods institutions. All of the countries that signed the Havana Charter did not ratify the creation of the ITO as a supranational organization. The US Congress had strong reservations relating to several Articles of Agreement of the ITO. It was perceived by the Congress as an organization having too many teeth. As the ITO was still-born, the General Agreement on Tariffs and Trade (GATT) was created in its place. The Protocol was signed on October 30, 1947 and the GATT entered into force on January 1, 1948. The Protocol of Provisional Application of the GATT was signed by 23 countries. These original "Contracting Parties" (or CPs) were Australia, Belgium, Brazil, Burma, Canada, Ceylon, Chile, People's Republic of China, Cuba, Czechoslovakia, France, India, Lebanon, Luxembourg, Netherlands, New Zealand, Norway, Pakistan, South Africa, Southern Rhodesia, Syria, the United Kingdom, and the United States of America.[4] The GATT expanded with the passage of time and continued to exist and function as a residual organization.[5] It became the only multilateral instrument governing international trade, and performed its duties between 1948 and 1994.[6] It was created as a specialized agency of the United Nations and provided the rules for much of the global trade, albeit for all of those 47 years it remained a provisional agreement and organization.

The GATT worked as a well-established organization and presided over periods that saw some of the highest growth rates in global commerce. Since 1995, the World Trade Organization (WTO) is – as the GATT was during its lifespan – the only multilateral instrument dealing with the rules and regulations of international trade between nations. The Final Act of the Uruguay Round (1986–1994) incorporated several other multilateral agreements on trade in goods, such as the Agreement on Agriculture (AoA), the Agreement on Textiles and Clothing (ATC), and the Agreement on Trade Related Investment Measures (TRIMs) and had proposed the creation of the WTO as a full-fledged international governing institution recognized in international law. In addition, the Agreement on the Application of Sanitary and Phytosanitary Measures

---

[4] As the GATT was an inter-governmental agreement, not an international organization, participants were called Contracting Parties or CPs. It was incorrect to call them members.

[5] At the time of its inception, the GATT was signed by 23 countries, which included 12 industrial and 11 developing economies. Subsequently three developing economies withdrew. As it was an inter-governmental agreement, the GATT was not a legal entity.

[6] The GATT was officially terminated on December 31, 1995, although the World Trade Organization (WTO) was born on January 1, 1995.

covered safety requirements for products for human or animal consumption and the Agreement on Technical Barriers to trade covered technical regulations, standards, testing and certification. The Agreement on the Implementation of GATT 1994 Articles VI and VII covered subsidies and countervailing duties as well as customs valuation respectively.

The most ambitious and putatively most important feature of the Uruguay Round agreement was the creation of the General Agreement on Trade in Services (GATS). It represented a multilateral framework of regulations for trade in services, parallel to the GATT. Although the services sector was dominated by most matured industrial and newly industrialized economies (NIEs), it was not hitherto covered under the GATT. This sector covered a wide range of economic activities, including banking and finance, insurance, telecommunications, advertising, construction, transport, and computer and data-processing. The Office of the United States Trade Representative (USTR) had presented a strong case for initiating negotiations on trade in services with an objective to having a "hard" agreement. This objective could not be achieved because it fell foul of several domestic lobbies in the United States.

The European Union (EU) and Japan were in favor of a "soft" agreement covering trade in services and maintained constant pressure during the Uruguay Round for achieving this objective, while the developing countries *en masse* were against the formation of the GATS. The *causae causante* of their opposition was the realization that they did not have comparative advantage in trade in services. As opposed to this, the industrial economies were perceived by the developing economies as having strong comparative advantage in this area of trade. The industrial economies overwhelmingly dominated global trade in services. Although not all, the majority of the services tended to be technology and human capital intensive. Therefore, dominance of industrial economies in this sector of multilateral trade was natural. However, some developing economies did enjoy comparative advantage in labor-intensive services such as construction and data-processing. They could be expected to gain from trade liberalization under the aegis of the GATS.

In trade economics, the two expressions, namely, the GATT 1947 and the GATT 1994, are frequently used. The difference between the two is that the latter is the revised version of the original GATT Agreement of 1947. The text of the Agreement was significantly revised and amended during the Uruguay Round and the new version was agreed upon in Marrakesh, Morocco. Apparently, the GATT 1994 reflected the outcome of the negotiations on issues relating to the interpretations of specific articles. In its renewed version, the GATT 1994 includes specific understandings with respect to GATT Articles, its obligations and provisions, plus the Marrakesh Protocol of GATT 1994. Although there were numerous changes in the Articles of Agreement, the noteworthy changes included those in Article II regarding tariff schedules, in Article XVII regarding state trading enterprises, in Article XXIV regarding regional trade agreements, in Article XXVIII regarding modifications of tariff schedule, and in the area of balance of payments provisions covered by Articles XII and XVIII. The GATT 1994 has superseded the GATT 1947. While the GATT 1994 was a natural progression of multilateral trade regulations, it also enabled the CPs to bypass the need to formally amend the original GATT 1947. By creating GATT 1994 they agreed to create a single undertaking, applicable to all. This was a pragmatic plan. All of the members of the WTO only had to sign the GATT 1994, in lieu of the GATT 1947 together with all of its subsequent amendments (Milner and Read, 2002).

An unprecedented 124 countries formally adopted the Marrakesh Agreement in 1994.[7] A tangible outcome of signing the Marrakesh Agreement was the birth of the WTO on January 1, 1995.[8] Like the United Nations and the World Bank, it became a key institution of global governance. Its essential functions are (i) administering WTO trade agreements; (ii) providing a forum for multilateral trade negotiations; (iii) handling trade disputes between members; (iv) monitoring national trade policies; (v) providing technical assistance and training for developing countries; and (vi) handling economic co-operation with other international organizations. These six functions have been outline in Article III of the Marrakesh Agreement.[9] They are performed by the Geneva-based WTO secretariat in co-operation and collaboration with the national delegations of the WTO member states. These states determine and make the systemic moves through their delegations. To this end, most member states maintain their permanent missions in Geneva. They are essentially responsible for determining the multilateral rules of trade in goods and services, the agenda for multilateral trade negotiations (MTNs), policy initiatives, decision making, and interpreting the WTO rules. Thus,

---

[7] The Uruguay Round of multilateral trade negotiations was completed in 1994. The formal agreement was signed in Marrakesh, Morocco, on April 15, 1994, and is referred to as the Marrakesh Agreement.

[8] Refer to footnote 6 above.

[9] They are also a permanent feature of the WTO website.

the member states play a pivotal systemic role in the WTO, while the secretariat plays the supporting role as an institutional facilitator.

The WTO oversees three multilateral trading agreements, namely, the Marrakesh Agreement, the GATS and Trade Related Aspects of Intellectual Property Rights (TRIPs). Built on the foundation laid by the GATT, as an institution the WTO has wider responsibilities than its predecessor, which in turn had strengthened the global trading system considerably. As stated above, the Marrakesh Agreement brought agriculture, textiles and apparel and trade in services into the ambit of global trade regulations. With the help of the single undertaking, the Marrakesh Agreement locked all member countries into a set of agreements.

As Sampson (2000) puts it, the WTO is a set of agreements that create legally binding rights and obligations for all of the member states. These agreements are mutually negotiated and signed by the member countries. The schedule of tariffs and other limitations and restrictions on imports of goods and services attached to the respective agreements of a country create similar legally binding rights and obligations for the members. These schedules bind the degree of openness of domestic markets.

The WTO is essentially a member-driven organization. For instance, in the Trade Policy Review Board (TPRB), members review trade policy of other members. They analyse, discuss, and take stock of all the recent developments in the global trading system. Periodically, they negotiate to liberalize tariff barriers, quota restrictions, and non-tariff barriers. They deliberate over the global trading rules and change them whenever they consider it necessary. The last-named exercise is done within the context of formal multilateral rounds of negotiations (Das, 2001a).

The WTO agreements, as rule, are lengthy and complex. They are essentially legal texts covering a wide range of trade and trade-related activities. However, five simple, fundamental principles run throughout these documents. They are that the global trading system should be without discrimination, progressively freer, predictable, competitive, and beneficial to less-developed countries. Non-discrimination, enshrined in Article I of the Articles of Agreement, is the cornerstone of the global trading system. Member governments agree not to discriminate against the trade in goods and services of other members, either between supplying countries or between domestic and foreign suppliers of the same goods and services.[10]

---

[10] For a more detailed account of the evolution of the global trading system, see Hoekman and Kostecki (2001).

2. Trade policy liberalization and globalization

Over the preceding half century, since the genesis of the GATT, the importance of international trade has increased dramatically in the global economy. It has been a significant driving force behind the spread of globalization among the industrial economies first, and subsequently among a sub-group of developing economies. Capital flows are important in their own right but trade in goods and services is an indispensable instrument of globalization. Being one of the two principal channels of economic globalization, it has contributed to enormous benefits that came from mutual interdependence among nations and from integration of the global economy.

Trade liberalization has been an ongoing feature of global economic activity over the past half century. The outward-oriented economic strategy adopted by the high-growth economies of East Asia first, and those of Southeast Asia after them, were noticed and admired by academics and policy makers in many countries. They had also seen the anemic outcome of inward-oriented import-substitution policies in South Asia. Consequently policy makers pragmatically tried to turn towards policies that involved more open trade regimes. In 1978, the People's Republic of China (hereinafter China) adopted the "open door" policy. By the end of the 1980s, virtually all of the centrally planned economies that had ideologically eschewed market-based policies had either collapsed or had started to adopt economic reforms that brought foreign trade and investment into a prominent place in their development programs.

Four trends can be clearly identified in the global trading system during the preceding half century: (i) highly uneven pace of liberalization of markets in goods and services in both developing and industrial economies; (ii) increasing differentiation in treatment for different levels of developing economies by the global trading system; (iii) a growing number of regional trading agreements (RTAs) among both developing and industrial economies; and (iv) expanding scope and strength of RTAs. Against the background of a general decline in direct trade restrictions, global market openness has increased markedly during this period. According to the statistics published by the WTO, during the 52 years between 1948 and 2000, merchandise trade in real terms grew much more rapidly than global GDP. Merchandise trade increased by 6 percent annually, or 22 fold, *vis-à-vis* global output growth of 4 percent per annum, or seven fold. Global trade growth outpaced global GDP growth by a significant margin. World trade grew more rapidly than world GDP in all but a few years of cyclical downturns. During the 1990s, trade grew much more rapidly than GDP. On average growth rate of world trade was more than twice that of the GDP growth rate. Measured in constant 1987 dollars, the ratio of global trade in goods and services to global GDP increased from 8 percent in 1950 to 29.5 percent in 2000 (WTO, 2001).

There were exceptions to the trade liberalization process. Many exceptions were made for domestic price support systems in agriculture, and therefore, trade in agricultural effectively escaped multilateral discipline. During the 1960s and the 1970s, trade in textiles and apparel was put under a system of quotas by the importing industrial economies. This was clear discrimination of trading and against the fundamental principle of the GATT, or Article I of the Articles of Agreement. In addition, a large area of global trade, namely trade in services, had eluded multilateral trade discipline until the creation of the General Agreement on Trade in Services (GATS) in 1995. This was the first step towards the creation of a comprehensive framework to regulate trade in services.

During the recent period, 1994 was the watershed point for trade policy liberalization and globalization. The Marrakesh Agreement was signed and the concept of the WTO was agreed upon by the 124 countries that participated in the Uruguay Round. During the same year, 21 members of Asia-Pacific Economic Co-operation (APEC) forum, which includes Japan and the United States, signed the Bogor Agreement. Together, the APEC group accounts for more than half of the global GDP. They gave themselves a target of freeing trade completely by 2010 for the industrial countries and by 2020 for the developing member countries. Many analysts took a triumphalist view of these developments and thought that free trade and ever-closer global economic integration have now become an increasingly achievable goal. The process of globalization entails interdependence between the decisions of policy makers. They need to think in unison and reinforce mutual decisions, while advancing towards the common goal. If some major global traders turn away from world markets, it would surely thwart those economies that would like to continue to be a part of the global integration process. This had happened during the 1930s when a downward spiral in world trade was set in motion in this manner.

The discipline of economics has had an enduring debate on trade liberalization and openness. Adam Smith extolled the virtues of trade liberalization, openness and competition in his magnum opus, *The Wealth of Nations*. Other than global integration, the liberalizing process underpins growth. Essentially there are three sources of economic growth – growth in inputs, improvement in efficiency of allocation, and innovation. The process of opening up to trade and investment contributes to each of the three sources of growth. Many scholarly studies have contrasted the growth performance of East Asia at one extreme and South Asian and Sub-Saharan Africa at the other. The contrast was stark and striking. East Asian economies were not only the growth champions but also they integrated with the global economy faster than the 24 "more-globalized" or newly globalizing economies (World Bank, 2002). Any significant degree of relaxation of trade restrictions results in gains, unless there are other policies thwarting their impact. Trade liberalization undertaken from a period of declining growth rates, or even falling real GDP growth rate, can lead to a period of growth above the rates previously realized (Krueger, 2000).

There are important microeconomic implications of trade liberalization and relaxation of restrictions, which lead to spread of economic activities. Fujita *et al.* (1999) posited a spatial theory of trade liberalization.[11] According to them trade liberalization triggers a chain reaction that catalyzes the growth of secondary and tertiary economic activities in a city, a region and beyond. Consequently costs falls and output rises, attracting more firms in the same or related areas. A chain reaction is set in motion, with one stage of development reinforcing the next stage. As more firms are set up or move in, an agglomeration of economic activities is created. As exports rise, these agglomerations become more successful. Average costs for the firms in the agglomeration further decline and profits rise, providing further impetus to expansion. Output expands further, stimulating expansion of agglomeration. Responding to the needs of end products producers, intermediate input producers and non-tradable services producers set up new businesses, giving greater impetus to the process of agglomeration expansion (WDR, 2000). New intermediate inputs make production more efficient in the agglomeration, lower the costs of production and enhance the profitability of the end product producers. They also raise quality standards. This cycle continues until it covers the region and then goes beyond and more businesses are attracted until the agglomeration becomes saturated or congested. The expansion cycle stops when the infrastructure becomes a constraint and costs begin to rise. When a successful agglomeration stops its growth in this manner, it provides an impetus to another in the same region.

3. Facets of trade liberalization

As stated in the preceding section, trade policy liberalization was neither uniform, nor smooth, nor continuous. It was a spasmodic process at

---

[11] See to Chapters 14 and 15 in particular. See also Chapter 17, which describes a "seamless world economy", although the real world is anything but seamless.

best. During the 1950s, the 1960s and the early 1970s, industrial economies increasingly adopted the maxim of trade liberalization. They largely followed the US lead, which was to champion the cause of free and liberal global trade during this period. The GATT provided this country group with an institutional framework for a co-ordinated multilateral liberalization of trade. Its essential focus was reciprocal exchange of "concessions" on market access. Successive GATT rounds of MTNs helped in dramatically reducing tariffs on trade in manufactures. Thus, during this era the GATT became instrumental in underpinning globalization for one set of economies.

Industrial economies, that took the lead in globalizing during the post-Second World War era, are substantial trading economies. Merchandise trade, as a share of merchandise value-added, is very high in these countries. It has increased at a fast clip during 1913–90. According to the calculations made by Feenstra (1998), the ratio of merchandise trade to merchandise value-added increased from 13.2 percent to 35.8 percent for the United States during this period. For Canada this increase was from 39.4 percent to 69.8 percent, for Denmark from 66.2 percent to 85.9 percent, for France from 23.3 percent to 53.5 percent, for Germany from 29.2 percent to 57.8 percent and for Italy from 21.9 percent to 43.9 percent.

In contrast to the industrial economies, during the 1950s and the 1960s developing economies shunned liberalization and pursued inward-oriented strategies. During this period agricultural commodities overwhelmingly dominated their exports. In 1965, this category accounted for 50 percent of exports from the developing economies, while manufactures accounted for a paltry 15 percent. The orthodoxy of import-substitution strategy found ready converts among policy makers. As an integral part of this strategy, tariffs, quantitative restrictions (QRs), and foreign exchange and payment restrictions were made more stringent. The assumption among the policy makers was that industrialization was essential for economic growth and industries could be developed behind protective barriers. Much has been written about the "dependency theory" and the apprehension of secular decline in the terms of trade of the developing countries. Furthermore, vested-interest groups in developing economies strongly supported this strategy because of access to rents created by tariffs and non-tariff barriers (NTBs).[12] Over these decades, developing economies did not participate in the principal activities of the GATT.

---

[12] All barriers other than tariffs that in some manner impede trade or raise the cost of trading are called non-tariff barriers (NTBs).

An illiberal trade strategy is anathema to global integration. This is also called inward-orientation of the policy regime. Developing economies that adopted such a strategy, use instruments such as import substitution. To implement the import-substitution strategy, developing countries frequently created import and export monopolies. Sometime monopoly powers, or monopsony powers were granted to a particular firm or to a state-owned monopoly or monopsony was created[13] (Das, 1991).

In addition, the import-substitution, or inward-oriented strategy always needs the support of a widespread network of trade barriers, which created problems of managing trade policy and for the quality of corporate governance in general. Licenses and permits of different kinds therefore, became scarce, valuable commodities. This encouraged wasteful rent-seeking behavior in the economy. Krueger (1980) found that under import substitution regimes import quotas generate large quota rents, so large that they could be a substantial part of the GDP of the developing country using this policy instrument. Economic distortions created by quotas, licenses and other NTBs were further reinforced and worsened by distortions in foreign exchange markets. In sum, in many developing economies, the pre-1980s trade and foreign exchange regime was "profoundly distorted" (Martin 2001). In such a policy climate, it was difficult to know what kind of reforms or policy package could be welfare improving. Developing economies that remained wedded to the strategy of import-substitution turned out to be poor all-around performers, including in the areas of economic growth, and industrial development. Progress on the social front was also tardy and these indicators remained sluggish for a considerable period. This group of developing economies completely failed to integrate globally.

4. Multilateral trade negotiations under the GATT and WTO regimes

In all, eight rounds of MTNs were conducted under the sponsorship of the GATT. All of them brought down tariff barriers and influenced the

---

[13] State-owned monopolies of monopsonies for the purpose of international trade were used by the industrial economies during their early phases of development. During the early postwar decades, Japan made laudable use of its *Sogo Shosa*, the gigantic and efficiently run trading houses, which made their presence felt almost globally. While developing economies were highly impressed by the Japanese experience and therefore they tried to emulate it, few succeeded in replicating these institutions. A large majority of them failed to run their trading monopolies and monopsonies in an efficient manner and ended up creating distortions in their domestic economies, which had high welfare costs.

global trading environment in a significant manner. Numerous quantitative estimates of declining tariff barriers in both developing and industrial economies are available (Abreu, 1996; WTO, 1994; Martin and Winters, 1996; WTO, 1998; Das, 2001a). Trade in manufactures was the principal focus of the GATT action and in this one area tariff barriers were reduced dramatically. Tariffs on manufactures in the industrial economies in the late 1940s were around 50 percent or above. They fell to 4.1 percent in 1988. Following the Doha Ministerial in November 2001, the first WTO round of MTNs was launched. Some rounds of MTNs also tried to dismantle the NTBs, and consequently coverage of NTBs fell as well.

Developing economies failed to benefit from the earlier rounds of MTNs. As they were wedded to the strategy of import-substitution in their domestic economies, their limited interest in the GATT was to obtain unreciprocated access to industrial country markets by making use of privileges such as "special and differential treatment." Exchange of "concessions" on market access was the principal activity during the MTNs and the developing economies generally kept off it. Some developing countries received preferential market access due to geopolitical reasons and they managed to expand their exports as well as improve their terms of trade. However, in general, policy makers in the developing economies failed to see the shortcomings of the stand taken by them. By following this strategy they abandoned the possibility of negotiating with the industrial economies for market access in products of their interest.

Second, lack of reciprocation encouraged industrial counties to introduce barriers in important areas of interest to developing economies, namely, agriculture and textiles and apparel. Given their background of strong affinity to the import-substitution strategy, this should not have been a surprise to the developing economies. Third, as quid pro quo was not part of the equation, adoption of import-substitution strategy also discouraged exporters to lobby for dismantling tariffs and NTBs at home so that they can secure market access in the industrial countries. Fourth, as expected, the import-substitution strategy worked against the process of global integration. Developing economies following this strategy were emaciating their bond with the global economy and distancing themselves from it.

The history of the last half-century suggests that both in developing and industrial economies there are some forces in the domestic political opposition that generally block moves towards economic and trade liberalization. The latter is a politically sensitive issue and politicians tend to inflate short-term gains, while ignoring long-term losses, which are enormous compared to the short-term gains. Mercantilist hesitation and discomfiture among policy mandarins persists. Entrenched interests fight hard and frequently succeed in maintaining their protected positions for prolonged periods. Consequently, erroneous economic and trade policies as well as distortions continue to harm the economy for decades.[14]

One frequent argument given in support of adopting protectionist policies is, "others are doing so." As Frederic Bastiat put it, it makes no more sense to be protectionist because other countries have tariffs than it would to block up harbors because other countries have rocky coasts.[15] Policy mandarins are often reluctant to implement liberalization measures owing to fears of excessive adjustment costs. There are some misperceptions regarding the adjustment costs. A survey of 50 studies established that adjustment costs are much smaller than the benefits of trade liberalization (Matusz and Tarr, 2000).

The NTBs are another anathema to globalization. Their use was not limited to developing economies. Given the enthusiasm of governments to protect domestic producers, the range of NTBs grew large both in the industrial economies and the developing economies. NTBs used by the members of the Quad[16] had particularly serious repercussions on their trading partners. Individual members of the Quad are the largest or second largest trading partners of the rest of the global economies. Use of NTBs by the members of the Quad can lead to welfare losses, not just domestically but on a global scale. Although the Tokyo Round had addressed NTBs, the Uruguay Round launched a broadside against them. Few imported products in the Quad will be subject to "core" NTBs[17] after the recommendations of the Uruguay Round are completely implemented. Comparatively, the reduction in NTBs is much less in Japan than in other Quad members. The value of imports affected by NTBs should also drop considerably, albeit by much more in the European

---

[14] The Indian economy is one of the best illustrations of this kind of erroneous economic and trade policies, which has continuing for decades. The economy remained wedded to the import-substitution strategy. When liberalization was stared in July 1991, it was much too late; slow, problem-ridden and then not completed. Consequently the economy not only could not realize its potential but also kept lurching from disaster to disaster.

[15] Cited by Krugman (1997).

[16] The European Union, Canada, Japan, and the United States are the four members of the Quad.

[17] Core NTBs consist of two broad kinds of measure: quantitative restrictions (QRs) and price control mechanism.

Union, Canada and the United States than in Japan (Daly and Kuwahara, 1998). This marked decline in the pervasiveness of NTBs is partly due to the elimination of voluntary export restraints (VERs) as well as to the phasing out of the multifiber agreement (MFA). Developing economies also applied a profusion of NTBs. A review of 61 trade policy country reviews revealed that protection through NTBs was greater in low-income developing economies than in the middle- and high-income developing economies (Das, 2001a).

Although the GATT's success during the early 1960s and the early 1970s was well admired, progress in the negotiations during the Tokyo Round of MTN (1973–79) was erratic. It was launched with the intentions of making substantial tariff cuts in the global economy; however, doubts were cast on the possibilities of its success. During the mid-1980s, leading trade experts began to call the GATT a "moribund" organization in a "state of breakdown." The Uruguay Round, launched in September 1986, seemed doomed to failure as, *inter alia*, the European Union and the United States found themselves locked in a politically complex struggle over agricultural pricing and subsidies. This round collapsed and had to be pulled back to its feet by the extraordinary perseverance and diplomatic skills of Arthur Dunkel, the erstwhile Director-General of the GATT. International trade continues to be an important area of global policy debate.

Protection in goods and services has declined markedly during the 1990s and the early 2000s, but still there are substantial protectionist barriers in the industrial and developing countries. Laird (2002a) believed that "they are loaded against developing countries." Despite progress made during the Uruguay Round, trade in agriculture, textiles and apparel and services persistently faces many barriers and they have not been dismantled in accordance with the agreements in the Uruguay Round. Anti-dumping measures, licensing procedures, local content rules, and technical barriers to trade are still thwarting trade flows. Tariff barriers continue to be high on transport equipment in both developing and industrial economies. Tariff peaks (or spikes) and tariff escalation exist and are being addressed in the conventional market access negotiations in the current Doha Round.

The Uruguay Round ended in April 1994 and by 2000 a large part of its recommendations, with a few exceptions, were implemented. Average tariffs on manufactures in industrial countries declined from 6.4 percent to 4.0 percent (Hoekman and Kostecki, 2001). According to one estimate, after the implementation of the Uruguay Round recommendations, bound tariffs across all countries and products is to decline to 6.5 percent, while the applied rate is to be 4.3 percent. In general, bound rates in developing economies were to be higher than those in the industrial economies. The region that is going to have the highest bound (50.8 percent) and applied tariff (30.4 percent) rates is South Asia. The binding coverage, which has increased substantially for all regions after the Uruguay Round agreement, is to be lower for the developing economies outside Latin America (Laird, 2002a). The higher tariff rates and lower binding coverage in some developing economies seem to be a throwback to the import-substitution era mentality and are detrimental to the progress of globalization.

Although MTNs are the most important mechanisms of trade liberalization and globalization through trade, RTAs are considered another important channel. They resolve the interest group problem by widening the policy formulation and decision-making process. Policy reforms and liberalization acquire greater credibility when they are achieved through international treaty commitments than they are when done in an autonomous manner. Contemporary regionalism is almost half-a-century old. Many regional initiatives began in the 1950s and the 1960s. This is the so-called "old regionalism." They accomplished little, except in Western Europe. The relationship of this European integration to multilateral trade liberalization was regarded as benign, largely because of the success of the Kennedy Round (1964–67).

Two quiet decades followed the period of old regionalism. The Single European Market was launched in 1985 and completed in January 1993, and this triggered the second wave of RTAs. In the late 1980s, a new bout of regional integration began, and this is still continuing. This is the so-called "new regionalism." In the 1990s, over ninety RTAs came into force (Das, 2001a). The RTAs that came into being during that decade covered not only trade in goods but also trade in services, investment regimes, and regulatory practices. They have substantially increased not only intra-regional trade but also intra-regional investment flows (Frankel, 1997). Supporters of RTAs contend that these agreements have enabled member countries to liberalize trade and investment barriers far more than MTNs. In addition, RTAs have generated welfare gains for participants with little possibility of negative spillovers into the rest of the world (Baldwin and Venables, 1995; Fernandez and Portes, 1998).

Sectoral trade agreements are another alternative mechanism of trade liberalization, which in turn contributes to globalization. After the Uruguay Round was completed, trade liberalization agreements were negotiated in the information technology sector (March 1997), in telecommunications services and products (February 1998), and in financial services (March 1999). This was done under the aegis of the WTO. These sectoral agreements were the first set of multilateral negotiations under the WTO.

Although sectoral agreements offer a means of achieving additional trade liberalization, they carry the risk of limiting the sort of productive trade-offs that are possible in larger trade negotiations. The broader the array of sectors subject to negotiation, the greater the potential for securing agreements with larger economic gains that are in every participating economy's interest. The sectoral agreements were widely considered remarkable success because they were made without cross-sectoral trade-offs of concessions. They are considered necessary for making reforms acceptable to a sufficiently large number of participating countries. This was a difficult process and soon lost momentum. An attempt was made to make a sectoral trade agreement to liberalize maritime services. It remained unsuccessful.

5. Declining distortions and enhancing market access

Over the past two decades, there has been a radical change in thinking about trade policy in the developing economies, particularly in the middle- and higher-income economies. In many of them, macroeconomic and trade policy changes are being used to address the problems related to current account imbalances. Policy makers in many developing economies now perceive that there is a need to project an image of stable and credible trade policy. Developing economies that instituted reform programs and made policy changes – no matter what the motivating factors – have succeeded in making their economies more stable. Therefore, they are being seen as secure trading partners by the large trading economies.

One pragmatic and effective method of instituting trade policy reforms is by locking them through multilateral commitments. Those developing countries that have succeeded in demonstrating that they have installed a stable and credible trade-policy regime also succeeded in stimulating domestic and foreign investment, which in turn has led to more rapid productivity gains than ever in the past in these economies (Laird, 2002b; Stiglitz, 1998). These developments have enhanced the competitiveness of this set of developing economies, making it feasible for them to capture niche markets in the global trade arena, and in the process augment their trade volumes and integrate with the global economy. Thus, a disciplined trade policy and related regime is logically seen as one that promotes global integration through trade.

The important reason behind the change in thinking about trade policy was the staler economic performance of the East Asian economies in the 1970s, followed by those in Southeast Asia. It attracted a great deal of global attention. This evidence, coupled with the critical assessment of the import substitution strategy, contributed to a gradual evolution of interest in the developing economies in outward-oriented strategy. The debt crisis of 1982 further affected the policy thinking and the trade policy stance of the developing economies underwent a greater transformation in the mid-1980s. Since the early 1980s, as alluded to in earlier chapters, a good number of developing economies began liberalizing their economies in general, and trade and related policies in particular, in a consistent and planned manner.

The change in the mindset of the policy makers was reflected in "the wave of unilateral trade reforms that swept" in the developing economies (Martin, 2001). This was the most profound and far reaching manifestation of their interest in participation in global trade. Consequently, trade policy in these developing economies became increasingly more liberal and neutral between sectors. This was felt more or less in all the regions and affected all types of policy distortions. Reflecting a strategic move towards open economy, China instituted major tariff reforms in 1985. It was a calculated move because in mid-1986 China made a formal move to accede to the GATT.[18] Deep unilateral slashing of tariff lines was accelerated in the 1990, 1993 and 1996 in China (Das, 2001b).

The average levels of tariffs were slashed from 30 percent in 1980 to 15 percent in the late 1990s (World Bank, 2001a). To be sure, there were differences among developing economies in their commitment to the strategy of liberalization. As stated above, some developing economies took the initiative to liberalize unilaterally and many developing economies instituted comprehensive macroeconomic and structural reform programs. This trend gained momentum in the 1990s. Other developing economies took to liberalizing under various structural adjustment programs of the International Monetary Fund (IMF) and the World Bank (WB). These two institutions still have considerable policy leverage, although it has declined over the years. A World Bank study argued that conditionality imposed on unwilling governments has a poor record of success (World Bank, 1998). The programs devised by the Bretton Woods twins were of differing depths. Available evidence suggests that several high- and middle-income developing economies did

[18] Although China was one of the original 23 signatories of the GATT in 1947, it had withdrawn in 1950.

a laudable task of liberalization and reform. Also, during the post-1980 period, tariff reduction was particularly large in the South Asian economies and in Latin America and the Caribbean countries. As opposed to them, tariff reduction in Sub-Saharan Africa, Middle East and the Central Asian Republics was of moderate order. The coverage of QRs and foreign exchange restrictions also fell noticeably in the developing economies after 1980.

The declines in tariff barriers, alluded to above, must not be seen in absolute terms. They need to be carefully examined for their impact because it is possible that declining tariffs are supplanted by NTBs. Frequency of total core NTBs was measured for 1989–98 period (World Bank, 2001b). The results show a sharp decline in NTBs, including state trading monopolies, in all of the regions except South Asia, where they have increased marginally. Two more areas of substantive reforms were foreign exchange restrictions on current account and average foreign exchange premiums. The application of foreign exchange restrictions by developing countries has fallen dramatically (World Bank, 2001b). For a sample of 41 developing countries foreign exchange premiums were calculated and compared for the 1980–97 period. The average decline was from 82.0 percent to 20.3 percent during the period under review. In the Middle East they declined from 165.6 percent to 46.5 percent, in Latin America from 47.8 percent to 4.4 percent, in South Asia from 40.8 percent to 10.1 percent and in Africa from 116.5 percent to 32.2 percent. Thus, average foreign market distortions declined markedly during the 1980s and the 1990s (World Bank, 2001b).

Liberalization programs that were bold and implemented vigorously proved more durable than those that took a hesitant approach. On-again-off-again kind of liberalization programs continued for decades, often with little impact on the economy. Past experience in this regard shows that if liberalization of restrictive tariffs and NTBs was undertaken along with broader structural reforms on a sustained basis – for six or seven years – the consequences were indeed far reaching. For high credibility among economic agents the liberalization program must be announced in advance. The element of surprise in the policy structure must be completely eliminated. Mussa (1998) found that poor macroeconomic management was generally responsible for poor results, and even reversal of liberalization programs. Particularly, fiscal prudence was found to be an important precondition for a successful liberalization program.

During the Uruguay Round, the change in the mindset of the policy mandarins in the developing economies was clearly manifested and they turned from passive onlookers in the MTNs to active players. For the first time, they began exchanging market access concessions in a serious manner, that is, for the first time they became true participants in the global trading system. The coverage of tariff bindings was greatly enhanced in developing economies, and tariff bindings were cut substantially in both developing and industrial economies. Negotiators from the developing economies offered to bind their tariffs on *all* of the agricultural products and over 60 percent of the manufactured exports (Abreau, 1996).

Achievements of the Uruguay Round extended to NTBs. Changes in regulations ameliorated the impact of NTBs such as the voluntary export restraints (VERs), which had escaped being addressed during the earlier MTNs. In a clairvoyant manner, developing economies participated in the so-called "grand bargain," which included agreement on protection of intellectual property rights that the industrial economies wanted for a long time in return for dismantling the grotesquely distorted quota regime of the MFA and ensuring that trade in agricultural commodities returns to the global trading discipline. After several accidents, the Uruguay Round turned out to be highly successful in liberalizing trade, *inter alia*, trade in manufactures, and integrating the global economy ever closer (WTO, 1999).

6. Changing trade patterns and growing integration

During the 1950–73 period, an unprecedented acceleration took place in world merchandise trade, and this exceeded 8 percent a year in real terms. The large beneficiaries of this trade expansion were the industrial economies. Six rounds of MTNs under the aegis of the GATT had contributed to this brisk growth.[19] The next decade-and-a-half (1973–90) saw two oil shocks, high inflation rates plaguing the industrial economies, and the debt crisis of 1982–84. Although the Tokyo Round (1973–79) of MTNs was launched and completed during this period, and the Uruguay Round was launched (September 1986), growth rate of world trade decelerated to 4 percent per annum. During the decade of 1991–2000, it again recovered to 6.5 percent per annum.

Prior to the 1980s, developing economies predominantly exported primary commodities, which exposed them to volatility in commodity

---

[19] These six rounds of MTNs were in Geneva (1947), Annecy (1949), Torquay (1951), Geneva (1956), Geneva (1960–61), called the Dillon Round, and Geneva (1964–67), called the Kennedy Round.

prices resulting in terms-of-trade deteriorations. It also raised concerns regarding the development of dependency on manufactured imports. A consequence of post-1980 liberalization endeavors was a large increase in imports and exports from other developing economies as well as dramatic changes in their composition. During the post-1980 globalization era, as noted above, exports of manufactures from the developing economies increased significantly. Their exports to other developing countries have continued to soar. Furthermore, exports of services have become much more important to a group of developing countries than they ever were in the past.

In 1980, manufactured exports were merely 25 percent of their total exports of the developing economies as a group. By 1998, this proportion soared to 80 percent. The proportion of manufactured exports increased monotonically, without any interruptions, except for a transient decline in 1997. This was caused by the Asian economic and financial crisis. Two important characteristics of trade in manufactures are, first, the prevalence of intra-trade and, second, increasing trade in components. A corollary of rising trade in manufactures was a consistent decline in the share of agricultural products. By 1998, its proportion declined to 10 percent of total developing country exports. High rates of capital accumulation in several high- and middle-income developing countries on the one hand, and technological growth and imports on the other hand, contributed to strong shift toward manufacturing activity and exports of manufactures. The fact that a sub-group of developing countries – such as Sub-Saharan Africa – was left behind cannot be ignored. They continued to be exporters of commodities, and remained sensitive to fluctuations in commodity agricultural prices (WTO, 1999).

Another important development was in the direction of exports. During the pre-1980 era, less than 17 percent of exports from developing countries were destined for other developing countries.[20] By 1997, this proportion had reached 42 percent – a significant increase in less than two decades (WB, 2001b). This increase in the importance of intra-developing trade resulted not only from trade liberalization in the developing economies but also was due to an increase in the share of GDP of developing countries in the global economy. The rising level of intra-developing country trade can partly be explained by supply-side factors. Developing countries became more important as markets for each other's goods and services. With 42 percent of the developing country

---

[20] Although there was a slow rise and in 1980, their proportion had reached 17 percent of the total developing country exports.

trade being intra-trade, the barriers that these countries face among each other are clearly more important than they were in the past. If globalization has to progress, tariff barriers against manufactures in the developing countries need to come down further. Hertel and Martin (2001) computed that over 70 percent of the tariff barriers faced by manufactured exports from developing economies are now imposed by other developing economies. Results of a GTAP exercise[21] conducted by Anderson *et al.* (2001) demonstrated that the benefits of developing countries from abolishing their own protection are 50 percent larger ($65.1 billion in 1995 dollars) than those obtainable from abolishing industrial country protection ($43.1 billion in 1995 dollars). These estimates are extremely conservative in that they ignore the gains from the elimination of anti-dumping duties and other similar forms of protection.

Although it started from a low level, trade in commercial services from developing countries increased substantially over the past two decades. The proportion of export of services from high-income developing economies in global exports of services increased from 17 percent to 20 percent between 1980 and 1997. For low- and middle-income developing economies it increased from 7 percent to 17 percent (Martin, 2001). Two important inferences have emerged from this new trend. First, a significant group of developing economies has succeeded in making a structural shift to capital- and technology-intensive exports by the promotion of capital accumulation and raising the skill level of their workforce. Second, the striking recent developments in the export pattern of developing economies have significant ramifications. The most important is the reduction in the volatility of export revenues.

As supply-side improvements became standard features, the developing economies, particularly the emerging market economies,

---

[21] Global Trade Analysis Project (GTAP) is a modeling framework that is designed to facilitate quantitative analysis of policy issues. Developed from the GTAP project established in 1992, it has been widely used to examine such issues as the impact of the Uruguay Round and future pattern of global trade. GTAP captures linkages within and among economies by modeling the economic behavior and interaction of producers, consumers and governments. It is therefore possible to trace implications of a policy change such as tariff cuts to other parts of the economy as well as other regions and economies in the model. Within GTAP consumers are assumed to maximize utility and producers to maximize profits. Markets are assumed to be perfectly competitive. There are constant returns to scale. Different regions and economies are linked in the model through trade. Some of these assumptions mean that the gains from trade liberalization will typically be understated. One such assumption is constant returns to scale.

gradually increased their exports to industrial economies. The GATT framework and discipline helped the NIEs and other emerging market economies in this endeavor. Consequently, many industrial economies in the European Union and in the United States found that their merchandise imports exceeded their merchandise output (Das, 2001a; Feenstra, 1998). This led to increased competition in merchandise product markets in the industrial economies. The composition of exports from the NIEs underwent a rapid transformation. They became exporters of engineering and medium-technology goods in the 1980s. India and the NIEs from Latin America fell in this category. By 1990, China also became a successful and large exporter of medium-technology products to the developing and industrial economies. The production of high-technology products such as electronics, electrical goods and information technology (IT)-related products from the NIEs in East and Southeast Asia increased substantially during the 1980s and 1990s. These NIEs acquired comparative advantage and an impressive competitive edge in high-technology products and, therefore, became competitive in several product lines in the industrial economy markets.

Globalization was a tangible benefit of (i) liberalization and (ii) supply-side economic improvements for a sub-group of developing countries. Many low-income developing economies failed to participate in growth-inducing and potentially poverty-reducing benefits of trade liberalization, and also were not able to integrate with the global economy at all. Research into the pace of integration with the global economy came up with interesting results. A sample of 93 developing countries was divided into rapid, moderate and slow or weak integrators with the global economy. Results show that only one out of twenty-eight so-called least developed countries in the sample fell in the rapid integrator category, while only seven more were moderate integrator. Thus, the majority of the poorest countries – those most in need of the spur to growth that trade and global integration can provide – were left behind in the race towards effective participation in the global markets. Their share in the global trade declined steadily, from 0.8 percent to 0.4 percent between 1980 and 1997 (World Bank, 2000). This sub-group of economies is not only non globalizing but is making a retrograde motion. Contrary to the performance of this group, high- and middle-income developing economies did a laudable task of integration with the global economy. This phenomenon is discussed at length in Chapter 3.

7. Trade and globalization

The kaleidoscope of the global trading system turned several times and international trade has enormously expanded over the preceding half century (see section 6 above), which in turn contributed substantially to global integration through trade, albeit in a selective manner. Immediately after the Second World War, industrial economies expanded their trade, which in turn supported their integration and globalization. As stated above, they received institutional support from the GATT in this endeavor.

It has been noted above that while 11 developing countries were among the 23 founding members of the GATT in 1947 (see section 1), developing countries did not participate in GATT operations. Until the Dillon Round (1960–61), they remained more or less passive onlookers and accepted little role in the GATT rounds of MTNs, although their participation began during the Kennedy Round (1964–67), with some 35 of them attending the launching meeting. However, during the Round they still continued to be essentially passive. In the Tokyo Round (1973–79) a larger number of them attended the launch and their participation in the proceedings of the MTNs took a serious, although marginal, form.

The developing economies chose to articulate their grievances against the global trading system in and through the United Nations Conference on Trade and Development (UNCTAD), which had no role in formulating global trade rules and policies. The developing economies demanded special and differential treatment (SDT) in world trade and they received it. To this end, Part IV was added to the Articles of Agreement of the GATT. Although a case could be made for the benefits of SDT and for trade preferences through the Generalized System of Preferences (GSP), as the developing economies had opted out of the rule making process, they could not possibly have any influence over the formulation of the rules of the global trading system.

As the developing economies had painted themselves into a corner and could not prevent the industrial economies from taking trade in textiles and apparel out of the GATT system. Once outside of the GATT regulations, the industrial countries were free to use quotas to restrict imports of textiles and apparel into their markets. Similarly, trade in agriculture was kept out of the ambit of the GATT until the Uruguay Round (1986–94). Being small trading countries in terms of volume of trade, the developing countries found that they just had to put up with the trade regulations that were skewed against their exportables. The developing economies bore a large share of responsibility for the world trading system being tilted against them (Srinivasan, 2002).

Therefore, integration of developing economies into the global trading system was slow and did not really begun until the mid-1970s, when a group of them emerged as competitive exporters in several product markets. As noted in section 6 above, this group comprised the NIEs. The success of the NIEs on the trade and globalization fronts had a good deal of demonstration effect. Before commencing their globalization the developing economies had to move up the industrial curve and acquire comparative advantage first in labor-intensive goods and then capital- and technology-intensive products. There was a sea change in the attitudes in several developing countries after 1980. As set out in section 5, during this period, a larger group, which began to be known as the emerging market economies, succeeded in liberalizing domestically and integrating with the global economy. When economies export goods and services in which they have comparative advantage, they not only integrate with the global economy but also enhance global welfare.

As alluded to in Chapter 1, and explained above, domestic support and subsidization of agriculture has continued to be high in the industrial economies. Developing economies' response to such policies need not be the creation of trade barriers of their own or stalling their unilateral trade liberalization moves. Instead they should vigorously participate in the on going Doha Round (2001–05) of MTNs and hold the industrial economies to their commitments to eliminate agricultural subsidies. This should help those developing economies that have comparative advantage in agricultural and food products and are, or can become, exporters in this line of products. However, this situation is complicated because there is a small group of developing economies that have historically benefited from cheap and subsidized agricultural products. The majority of these economies are in Sub-Saharan Africa. As the current scenario indicates, reduction in subsidies will take a good deal of time and effort from the developing economies, because the industrial economies have taken a well-entrenched stand on this issue. But it is well worth their while because it will surely help them in the medium term to enhance their exports in areas where they have comparative advantage and in their desire to globalize.

7.1. Empirical evidence of globalization in trade

Some analysts have drawn attention to the fact that despite advances in technology and lowering of trade barriers, there is little empirical evidence of globalization in trade. Obstfeld and Rogoff (2001) have referred to this as an "interesting riddle in international macroeconomics." A large empirical literature in international macroeconomics that uses the gravity model concluded that there is no evidence of a contemporary wave of globalization leading to a decline in the cost of trade over time.[22] The cost of trade was defined broadly to include transportation cost, communication cost, search cost, information cost, and the like. For analysis in the area of international trade, use of empirical gravity models has become so widespread that these models have earned the sobriquet of "workhorse of international trade." While gravity models explain cross-country trading patterns exceedingly well, they reveal no evidence that globalization causes a decline in the costs of trade. Such results are odd, counterintuitive and highly implausible.

The results of various gravity model exercises that estimated distance coefficient yielded stable distance coefficients over time. As noted above, this does not seem plausible because distance between two trading economies is taken as a proxy for all of the trade related costs in the traditionally estimated gravity models. These costs have putatively declined to a great extent over the last quarter century. If the globe is shrinking because trade related costs are declining, this should be reflected in the results and the estimated distance coefficients should fall in value. Although attempts have been made to explain this oddity in results, explanations do not seem convincing.

One explanation for the stable distance coefficient is the continual transformation in the pattern of global trade. This includes the entry of new products in the global marketplace and the shift towards trade in differentiated products. Also, over time some previously non-traded goods may have become tradable because of technological advances and declining transport costs. It is likely that the previously non-traded goods were not captured in the gravity equation estimate of the first period. In addition, totally new products, which did not exist in the past, could be added to the list of tradables. If this is true, the estimated coefficient on distance could remain stable. There is also a possibility of increase in the estimated coefficient of distance if the trade costs of the

---

[22] The gravity model has been extensively used in empirical trade research. Its foundation lies in Newtonian physics. It comprises a single equation, postulating that the amount of trade between two countries depends positively on economic mass and negatively on resistance. In its simple form, the gravity model relates bilateral trade between countries during a given time period to the economic mass of the two countries and the distance between them. Over time, the gravity model of trade has been elaborated to incorporate a wide variety of other factors. It reveals that countries that are closer to each other (less distance) and more similar in terms of historical and cultural factors are better integrated through trade in goods and services.

newly entered products are higher than the trade costs of goods traded in the first and the second periods.

Leaving the explanations aside, Anderson and van Wincoop (2001) spotted a major flaw in gravity model computations. They found that most of the analyses did not comply with the specifications of the theoretical model. They said that most of the empirical exercises lacked "gravitas" and that the users did not pay attention to the theoretical foundations of the model, hence the counterintuitive results such as stability in distance coefficients were obtained. According to them, those who used the gravity model made an error in the choice of variables. While there are two relative costs that are important for bilateral trade, most users of the gravity model pick the absolute cost for their computations.

As opposed to the above results, Coe *et al.* (2002) found clear empirical evidence of globalization in world trade as well as evidence of the declining significance of geography. They used both cross-section and panel data. The evidence was found to be clearly discernible in the cross-section regressions done for each year from 1975 to 2000, and in panel estimates over the same period. Their estimates are different from what was seen in the general gravity model exercises for two reasons. First, they estimated a non-linear version of the gravity model, and second, they used an additive error term rather than the standard log-linear version. They believed that the non-linear version is superior on theoretical and empirical grounds and better explains the data.

Coe *et al.* (2002) modified the empirical procedure because they believed that "the non-linear specification utilizes the information in the observations where bilateral trade is zero. The log-linear specification discards this information which may lead to biased or inconsistent parameter estimates." In their non-linear specification of the gravity model, coefficient estimates on various measures of geography clearly declined over time. Their measures of geography were distance, remoteness, and size. Their estimates indicated that there was a declining importance of geography, which in turn stood for a spurt in globalization for the 1990s decade. The diminishing importance of geography is logically consistent with the phenomenon of globalization.

7.2. Empirical evidence of globalization in goods markets

Measuring integration in goods market is a relatively easy exercise and has been attempted by several scholars.[23] It is easy because long-term

---

[23] For instance, refer to, Engel and Rogers (2001); Rogers (2002); Hufbauer *et al.* (2002).

time series statistical data are readily available from the IMF publication *Direction of Trade Statistics*. In this empirical exercise bilateral trade flows are used as an indicator of goods market integration, apparently larger flows implying greater market integration. In these exercises, the level of goods markets integration is determined in the traditional manner, using the gravity model.

Parsley and Wei (2001) improved upon the gravity model analysis. In order to ascertain the robustness of the trade-flow-based approach, it is a good idea to look at the prices of goods across markets. Smaller price differentials stand for greater goods market integration. Parsley and Wei (2001) used price dispersion to measure goods price integration. The empirical exercise conducted by them selected 95 tradable goods and 83 cities across the globe. The study was conducted for the data for the decade between 1990 and 2000. They selected disaggregated goods that were standardized by weight and volume. Their sample included goods such as light bulbs, frozen chicken, toilet paper, tonic water and similar items. For ensuring comparability, data were compiled from the same source–the Economic Intelligence Unit (EIU).

The next step was to compute the standard deviation of the of the price differences of the selected goods for every pair of cities for each year. Falling values of standard deviation in this empirical analysis should represent greater market integration and movement towards globalization through trade. The final step was to use the standard deviation in econometric analysis of the factors underlying goods market integration, including transport costs, tariffs and currency arrangements.

Both the price-based analysis and the trade-flow-based analysis or the gravity model computations, led to similar results regarding pattern and determinants of goods market integration and globalization. Inferences that emerged from both the approaches are

(i) Goods market integration increased considerably over the 1990–2000 period. Downward trends were observed in standard deviation of price differences for two-city pairs.

(ii) Higher distance, proxied by higher transport costs, contributed to lower goods market integration. In the trade-flow-based gravity model analysis, bilateral distance always had a negative coefficient, signifying that the greater the distance between countries the smaller the trade between them. As opposed to this, in the price-based approach the distance variable consistently had a positive coefficient signifying that the price dispersion for identical products – which stands for lack of market integration – tends to increase with distance.

(iii) Some regional trading arrangements (RTAs), particularly the North American Free Trade Agreement (NAFTA) and the EU, were found to have a significant effect on the goods market integration.

(iv) Institutionalized currency arrangements such as a currency union or a currency board increase goods market integration among the members (IMF, 2002).

7.3. Regional differences in trade integration

While it is acknowledged that a group of developing economies has become well integrated into the global trading system since 1980, there is a noteworthy unevenness and disparity in the degree of integration.[24] In order to analyse which countries or regions are well integrated into the global trading system and which are laggards, IMF (2002) developed a measure of expected trade across different regions and compared it with the actual trade volume. The rationale was that the difference between expected trade volume and actual trade volume represented a measure of artificial barriers to trade as well as the institutional and policy environment. To establish the expected trade volume benchmark, the versatile gravity model was utilized.

A country or a region was considered as "undertrading" if actual bilateral trade volume, on average, was substantially below the level predicted by the gravity model without explicit policy variables. Conversely, a country or a region was considered as "overtrading" if actual bilateral trade volume, on average, was substantially above the level predicted by the gravity model without explicit policy variables. Rose (2002) posited that as the gravity model is based on natural causes of trade, that is, it determines the volume of trade that should take place without trade policy and other institutional impediments, undertrading and overtrading must represent above- or below-average levels of impediments. This methodology captures the overall impact of a country's trade policies and institutional environment. Bilateral trade flow data for 131 developing and industrial economies were taken by Rose (2002) for the 1995–99 period for the analysis of undertrading and overtrading. The data source is *Direction of Trade Statistics* published by the IMF.

[24] This section draws on IMF (2002). For more detail on this issue, refer to Chapter 3 above.

The upshot of this analysis was that a great deal of undertrading took place in several regions. This group of economies were either not integrating with the global trading system or integrating in an inadequate manner. The cause of this was policy and institutional distortions in trade and macroeconomic regimes and institutional environment. Three regions demonstrated a large degree of undertrading – the Middle East, North Africa and South Asia. As opposed to this, the degree of undertrading was small in Latin America. The Sub-Saharan economies traded a little more than the benchmark set by the gravity model. Countries in East and Southeast Asia turned out to be strong traders and overtraded. They do seem to be better integrated with the global trading system than the other regions. Another interesting revelation was that undertrading was less pervasive in intra-regional trade than in extra-regional trade. One possible reason for this conclusion was that the RTAs such as MERCOSUR and APEC were active in various regions.

During 1980–2000, some undertrading regions turned from weak to weaker traders. This group of economies was the non-globalizing economies. This observation applies to Sub-Saharan Africa and the Middle East. However, North Africa turned from slight overtrading to slight undertrading over this period. Other regions that improved their trade performance included East and Southeast Asia, South Asia, South America, and especially the Caribbean and Central America. The first named country group showed maximum gains. The most important conclusion of this exercise is that in three regions (the Middle east, North Africa and South Asia) undertrading remained a serious problem. These three country groups have not been able to remove the above-average level of artificial barriers to trade in their policy and institutional environment, and consequently they have been able to manage only a weak integration with the global trading system.

8. Conclusions and summing-up

After the end of the Second World War, interest, enthusiasm and commitment to trade liberalization was exceedingly high among the major trading countries. Even before the International Trade Organization (ITO) charter was approved, 23 of the 50 participants of the Bretton Woods conference decided to launch negotiations with an objective to reduce tariffs and bind them. An attempt was made to create an ITO under the Havana Charter, which was negotiated in 1947. All of the countries that signed the Havana Charter did not ratify the creation of the ITO as a supranational organization. In particular, the US Congress was against ratifying it. The GATT was created in lieu of the ITO, and this worked as a well-established organization and presided over periods that saw some of the highest growth rates in global commerce. An unprecedented 124 countries formally adopted the Marrakesh Agreement in 1994, and a tangible outcome of this agreement was the birth of World Trade Organization (WTO) on January 1, 1995. Since 1995, the WTO is the only multilateral organization dealing with the rules and regulations of international trade between nations and is a set of agreements that create legally binding rights and obligations for all of its member states. These agreements are mutually negotiated and signed by the member countries. In addition, the GATS was created during the Uruguay Round of MTNs. The GATS was the most ambitious and putatively most important feature of the Uruguay Round agreement.

Since the genesis of the GATT, the importance of international trade in the global economy increased dramatically. It has been a significant driving force behind the spread of globalization among the industrial economies first, and subsequently among a sub-group of developing economies. Trade liberalization has been an ongoing feature of global economic activity over the past half century. The outward-oriented economic strategy adopted by the high-growth economies of East Asia first, and those of Southeast Asia after them, were noticed and admired by academics and policy makers in many countries. This strategy had a good deal of demonstration effect globally.

Although global trade was being liberalized, there were exceptions to the trade liberalization process. There are important macro- and micro-economic implications of trade liberalization and relaxation of restrictions, which lead to the spread of economic activities. Many exceptions were made due to domestic price support systems in agriculture. Trade in agricultural effectively escaped multilateral discipline. During the 1960s and the 1970s, trade in textiles and apparel was put under a system of quotas by the importing industrial economies. It also escaped multilateral discipline.

During the 1950s, the 1960s and the early 1970s, industrial economies increasingly adopted the maxim of trade liberalization. They largely followed the US lead, which was championing the cause of free and liberal global trade during this period. In contrast to the industrial economies, the developing economies shunned liberalization and pursued inward-oriented strategies during this period. Agricultural commodities overwhelmingly dominated their exports. The developing economies adopted an illiberal or inward-oriented trade policy regime which required a widespread network of trade barriers. These barriers and distortions created numerous problems of managing trade policy and for the quality of corporate governance in general. Licenses and permits of different kinds became scarce, therefore, valuable commodities. An illiberal trade strategy is anathema to global integration.

In all, eight rounds of MTNs were conducted under the sponsorship of the GATT. All of them brought down tariff barriers and influenced the global trading environment in a significant manner. Developing economies failed to benefit from the earlier rounds of MTNs because they were wedded to the strategy of inward-oriented import-substitution in their domestic economies. Their limited interest in the GATT was to obtain unreciprocated access to industrial country markets by making use of the privileges such as "special and differential treatment." A lack of reciprocation encouraged industrial counties to introduce barriers in important areas of interest to developing economies, namely, agriculture and textiles and apparel. The history of the past half-century suggests that both in developing and industrial economies there are some forces in the domestic political opposition that generally block moves towards economic and trade liberalization. This made the adoption of liberalization difficult. Protection in goods and services has declined markedly during the 1990s and the early 2000s, but still there are substantial protectionist barriers in the industrial and developing countries. Trade scholars believe that these barriers are loaded against developing countries.

Since the 1980s, there has been a radical change in thinking about trade policy in the developing economies, particularly in the middle- and higher-income economies. In many of them, macroeconomic and trade policy changes are being used to address the problems related to current account imbalances. The change in the mindset of the policy makers was reflected in the wave of unilateral trade reforms that swept the developing economies. This was the most profound and far-reaching manifestation of their interest in participation in global trade. The average levels of tariffs were slashed from 30 percent in 1980 to 15 percent in the late 1990s. To be sure, there were differences among developing economies in their commitment to the strategy of liberalization. The declines in tariff barriers, alluded to above, must not be seen in absolute terms. They need to be carefully examined for their impact because it is possible that declining tariffs are supplanted by NTBs. Frequency of total core NTBs was measured for 1989–98. The results show a sharp decline in NTBs, including state trading monopolies, in all of the regions except South Asia.

The change in the mindset of policy makers in the developing economies was clearly manifested during the Uruguay Round. The developing economies turned from passive onlookers in the MTNs to active players. During 1950–73, an unprecedented acceleration took place in world merchandise trade, exceeding 8 percent a year in real terms. The large beneficiaries of this trade expansion were the industrial economies. Six rounds of MTN under the aegis of the GATT had contributed to this brisk growth. Prior to the 1980s, developing economies predominantly exported primary commodities. In 1980, manufactured exports were merely 25 percent of their total exports; by 1998, this proportion had soared to 80 percent. The proportion of manufactured exports increased monotonically, without any interruptions, except for a transient decline in 1997. Another important development was in the direction of exports. During the pre-1980 era, less than 17 percent of exports from developing countries were destined for the other developing countries. By 1997, this proportion had reached 42 percent. This increase in the importance of intra-developing trade resulted not only from trade liberalization in the developing economies but also was due to an increase in the share of GDP of developing countries in the global economy. Although it started from a low level, trade in commercial services from developing countries increased substantially over the past two decades. As supply-side improvements became standard features of their economies, the developing economies, particularly the emerging market economies, gradually increased their exports to industrial economies. Globalization was a tangible benefit of (i) liberalization and, (ii) supply-side economic improvements for a sub-group of developing countries. Many low-income developing economies failed to participate in growth-inducing and potentially poverty-reducing benefits of trade liberalization, and also were not able to integrate with the global economy at all.

The kaleidoscope of global trading system turned several times and international trade has enormously expanded over the preceding half century, which in turn contributed substantially to global integration through trade, albeit in a selective manner. While 11 developing countries were among the 23 founding members of the GATT in 1947, developing countries did not participate in GATT operations. Until the Dillon Round (1960–61), they remained more or less passive onlookers and accepted little role in the GATT rounds of MTNs. Although their participation began during the Kennedy Round (1964–67), it was marginal. Instead they stressed the demand for special and differential treatment (SDT) in world trade and they received it. To this end, Part IV was added to the Articles of Agreement of the GATT. Trade in textiles and apparel was not covered by the GATT discipline. Once they were outside of the GATT regulations, the industrial countries were free to use quotas to restrict imports of textiles and apparel into their markets. Similarly, trade in agriculture was kept out of the ambit of the GATT until the Uruguay Round. Therefore, integration of the developing economies into the global trading system was slow and did not really begun until the mid-1970s when a group emerged as competitive exporters in several product markets.

Some trade analysts have drawn attention to the "interesting riddle in international macroeconomics," that is, despite advances in technology and lowering of trade barriers, there is little empirical evidence of globalization in trade. A large empirical literature in international macroeconomics that uses the gravity model concluded that there is no evidence of a contemporary wave of globalization leading to a decline in the cost of trade over time. However, the stable distance coefficient could be explained by continual transformation in the pattern of global trade. Besides, some empirical exercises found clear empirical evidence of globalization in world trade as well as evidence of declining significance of geography. Their estimates indicated the declining importance of geography, which stood for a spurt in globalization for the 1990s. The diminishing importance of geography is logically consistent with the phenomenon of globalization. Exercises that focused on the prices of goods across markets concluded that goods market integration increased considerably during 1990–2000. Downward trends were observed in the standard deviation of price differences for two-city pairs. Also, higher distance, proxied by higher transport costs, contributed to lower goods market integration. The greater the distance between countries the smaller the trade between them. As opposed to this, in the price-based approach the distance variable consistently had a positive coefficient signifying that the price dispersion for identical products – which stands for lack of market integration – tends to increase with distance.

References

Abreu, M., 1996, "Trade in Manufactures: the Outcome of the Uruguay Round and Developing Country Interests", in W. Martin and L.A. Winters (eds), *The Uruguay Round and the Developing Countries*, Cambridge: Cambridge University Press.

Anderson, K., J. Francois, T. Hertel, B. Hoekman and W. Martin, 2001, Potential Gains from Trade Reforms in the New Millennium", Washington, DC: World Bank.

Anderson, J.E. and E. van Wincoop, 2001, "Gravity with Gravitas: A Solution to the Border Puzzle", Cambridge, MA: National Bureau of Economic Research, Working Paper No. 8079. Revised version available at <www.virginia.edu./~econ/vanwincoopx.htm>.

Baldwin, R.E. and A.J. Venables, 1995, "Regional Economic Integration", in G. Grossman and K. Rogoff (eds), *Handbook of International Economics*, Amsterdam: Elsevier Science, pp. 1597–1634.

Coe, T.D., A. Subramanian and N.T. Tamirisa, 2002,"The Missing Globalization Puzzle", Washington, DC: International Monetary Fund, Working Paper No. WP/02/171.

Daly, M. and H. Kuwahara, 1998, "The Impact of the Uruguay Round on Tariff and Non-Tariff Barriers to Trade in the Quad", *World Economy*, Vol. 21, No. 2, 207–34.

Das, Dilip K., 1991, *Import Canalisation*, London: sage.

Das, Dilip K., 2001a, *Global Trading System at the Crossroads: A Post-Seattle Perspective*, London and New York: Routledge.

Das, Dilip K., 2001b, "Liberalization Efforts in China and Accession to the World Trade Organization", *Journal of World Investment*, Vol. 2, No. 4, 761–89.

Engel, C. and J.H. Rogers, 2001, "Deviations from Purchasing Power Parity: Causes and Welfare Costs", *Journal of International Economics*, Vol. 55, No. 10, 29–57.

Feenstra, R.C.,1998, "Integration of Trade and Disintegration of Production in the Global Economy", *Journal of Economic Perspective*, Vol. 12, No. 4, 31–50.

Fernandez, R. and J. Portes, 1998, "Returns to Regionalism: An Analysis of Non-Traditional Gains from Regional Trade Agreements", *World Bank Economic Review*, Vol. 12, No. 2, 197–200.

Frankel, J., 1997, *Regional Trading Blocs in the World Economic System*, Washington, DC: Institute of International Economics.

Fujita, M., P.R. Krugman and A.J. Venables, 1999, *The Spatial Economy: Cities, Regions and International Trade*, Cambridge, MA: MIT Press.

Hertel, T. and W. Martin, 2001, "Liberalizing Agriculture and Manufactures in a Millennium Round: Implications for Developing Countries", in B. Hoekman and W. Martin (eds), *Developing Countries and the WTO: A Pro-Active Agenda*, Oxford: Blackwell, pp. 110–42.

Hoekman, B.M. and M.M. Kostecki, 2001, *The Political Economy of the World Trading System*, Oxford: Oxford University Press.

Hufbauer, G., E. Wada and T. Warren, 2002, *The Benefits of Price Convergence: Speculative Calculations*, Washington, DC: Institute for International Economics, Policy Analysis in Economics, Paper No. 65.

International Monetary Fund, 2002, *World Economic Outlook*, Washington, DC: IMF, October.

Krueger, A.O., 1980, "Trade Policy as an Input to Development", *American Economic Review*, Vol. 70, No. 2, 288–92.

Krueger, A.O., 2000, "Factors Affecting Export Growth and Performance", in Dilip K. Das (ed.), *Asian Exports*, Oxford: Oxford University Press, pp. 25–74.

Krugman, P., 1997, "What Should Trade Negotiators Negotiate About", *Journal of Economic Literature*, Vol. 35, March, 113–20.

Laird, S., 2002a, "Multilateral Market Access Negotiations in Goods and Services", in C. Milner and R. Read (eds), *Trade Liberalization, Competition and the WTO*, Cheltenham: Edward Elgar, pp. 23–58.

Laird, S., 2002b, "The WTO Agenda and the Developing Countries", in C. Milner and R. Read (eds), *Trade Liberalization, Competition and the WTO*, Cheltenham: Edward Elgar, pp. 227–52.

Martin, W., 2001, *Trade Policies, Developing Countries and Globalization*, Washington, DC: World Bank.

Martin, W. and L.A. Winters, 1996, "The Uruguay Round: A Milestone for the Developing Countries", in W. Martin and L.A. Winters (eds), *The Uruguay Round and the Developing Countries*, Cambridge: Cambridge University Press, pp. 1–29.

Matusz, S.J. and D. Tarr, 2000,"Adjusting to Trade Policy Reforms", in A.O. Krueger (ed.), *Economic Policy Reform: The Second Stage*, Chicago: University of Chicago Press, pp. 130–64.

Milner, C. and R. Read., 2002, "Introduction: The GATT Uruguay Round, Trade Liberalization and the WTO", in C. Milner and R. Read (eds), *Trade Liberalization, Competition and the WTO*, Cheltenham: Edward Elgar, pp. 1–22.

Mussa, M., 1998, "Trade Liberalization", in Z. Iqbal and M.S. Khan (eds), *Trade Reform and Regional Integration in Africa*, Washington, DC: International Monetary Fund, pp. 19–65.

Obstfeld, M. and K. Rogoff, 2001, "The Six Major Puzzles in International Macroeconomics: Is There a Common Cause?", Cambridge, MA: National Bureau of Economic Research, Working Paper No. 7777.

Parsley, D.C. and S.J. Wei, 2001, "Limiting Currency Volatility to Stimulate Goods Market Integration: A Price-Based Approach", Cambridge, MA: National Bureau of Economic research, Working Paper No. 8468.

Rogers, J.H., 2002, "Price Level Convergence, Relative Prices, and Inflation in Europe", Washington, DC: Board of Governors of the Federal Reserve System, International Finance Discussion Paper No. 699.

Rose, A.K., 2002, "Estimating Protectionism from the Gravity Model", Washington, DC: International Monetary Fund (mimeo).

Sampson, G.P., 2000, *Trade, Environment and the WTO: the Post-Seattle Agenda*, Baltimore, MD: Johns Hopkins University Press.

Srinivasan, T.N., 2002, "Globalization: Is it Good or Bad?", Stanford, CA: Stanford Institute for Economic Policy Research, Economic Policy Brief, December 23.

Stiglitz, J., 1998, "Towards a New Paradigm for Development: Strategies, Policies, and Processes", Raul Prebisch Lecture, delivered at the UNCTAD Secretariat, Geneva, October 19.

World Bank, 1998, *Assessing Aid: What Works? What Doesn't and Why?*, New York: Oxford University Press for World Bank.

World Bank, 2000, *Global Economic Prospects and Developing Countries*, Washington, DC: World Bank.

World Bank, 2001a, *World Development Indicators*, Washington, DC: World Bank.

World Bank, 2001b, *Global Economic Prospects and the Developing Economies*, Washington, DC: World Bank.

World Bank, 2002, *Globalization, Growth and Poverty*, New York: Oxford University Press.

World Development Report, 2000, Washington, DC: Oxford University Press for World Bank.

World Trade Organization (WTO), 1994,"Developing Countries and the Uruguay round: An Overview", Geneva: Committee on Trade and Development, 77th Session, November 25.

World Trade Organization (WTO), 1998, "Tariffs: More Binding and Closer to Zero", available at <http://www.wto.org/about/agmnts2.htm>.

World Trade Organization (WTO), 1999, *The Legal Texts: the Results of the Uruguay Round of Multilateral Trade Negotiations*, Cambridge: Cambridge University Press.

World Trade Organization (WTO), 2001, "Doha WTO Ministerial: Briefing Notes: 52 Years of GATT/WTO", Geneva: available at <http://www-heva.wto-ministerial.org/english/the WTO, wto_e/minist_e/min01_e/brief_e/brief21_e.htm>.

5

Financial Flows and Global Integration

1. Novelty of financial globalization

Like technological advancement or long-run economic growth, evolution of global financial integration was not "a record of ever-more-perfectly-functioning markets with ever lower transaction costs and ever expanding scope" (Obstfeld and Taylor, 2002). Long-term growth of global financial markets was far from linear. Vicissitudes in the volume of financial flows were more common than uncommon. There were periods of slow growth in global financial integration, followed by those of rapid growth as well as periods of virtual standstill and reversals. There were periods when global financial integration was limited among a small number of countries, which were grouped in two or three categories and there were epochs when this integration expanded much more widely geographically. Liberalized markets did not enjoy high political popularity. Several periods witnessed strong reactions against market trends, in particular the financial markets. In the recent past, in the middle of the twentieth century and towards its end, such cynicism was easy to notice. Reacting to downsides of financial globalization, anti-market and anti-globalization voices became particularly strident towards the end of the last century.

Neither the concept nor the phenomenon of financial globalization can be considered novel. Cross-country capital movements have a long and well-documented history. As for answer to the question when and where the international banks were born, some of the earliest among them were born in Venice. The Medici family of Venice was among the first wealthy families to successfully venture into international banking in a big way during the Renaissance period.[1] Italian banks developed instruments to methodically finance trade and governments around the Mediterranean. Although global financial flows took place during the Renaissance, geographically they were limited among a small number of source and recipient countries and were far from globalized in their movement. With expansion of trade, international financial systems expanded to other parts of Western and Northern Europe and grew more innovative. Instruments such as letters of credit are known to have been working at the Champagne fairs during this era.

From Italy, international banking expanded to the northern port cities of Bruges and Antwerp, and then to Amsterdam and London, essentially in that order. The last two named financial centers grew enormously and became the two most important hubs of international finance. Currencies and financial instruments developed and used in these two centers were considered the most credible and valuable by the market players of this period. As the Industrial Revolution spread out of Britain, the international financial markets expanded *pari passu*. With the expansion of economic activity following the Industrial Revolution, use and significance of the financial instruments created during this period increased between both kinds of market players, public and private.[2]

As economic activity expanded to the so-called New World offshoots of Western Europe, international financial transactions supported it and international financial centers developed in those parts of the New World where the governments were not averse to them and followed supportive strategies. Boston, Baltimore, Philadelphia and Chicago developed as financial centers in the United States, which subsequently gave way to New York. Over the years it dominated them and grew to be the domineering financial center of global significance. Towards the end of the nineteenth century, France and Germany succeeded in developing Paris and Berlin as major international financial centers during this period, and there were well integrated into the global economy. In other parts of Europe and the New World similar financial markets began to grow, although unlike France and Germany they began from a low level of initial development. Financial markets in Buenos Aires and Melbourne were born during this period (Davis and Gallman, 2001). As

[1] Lorenzo de Medici took Michelangelo Buonarroti under his wing when Michelangelo was a little boy and provided the right artistic ambience to him to nurture his genius.

[2] For the birth and expansion of international banking and finance, see Das (1986); Neal (1990); and Cameron (1993).

an increasing number of countries actively adopted the gold standard after 1870, development of international finance as well as financial centers were accelerated. A stable exchange rate contributes to the successful development of international financial markets. The technological advancements of this era buttressed their progress.

Using different measures and indicators, several analysts tried to establish that a greater degree of financial globalization existed in the previous epochs of globalization than in the contemporary period.[3] One important distinction between financial globalization in the past and that in the contemporary period is that in the past a limited number of countries, and a small number of sectors, participated in the financial globalization process. Not the same can be said about the contemporary period. Also, in general, capital followed the migration of population and it was, *inter alia*, utilized in supporting trade flows. Long-term bonds of varying maturity were the most popular financial instruments in the past. Financial activity was highly concentrated in the hands of a small number of freestanding companies, which dominated the arena of global finance and, similarly, a small number of wealthy family groups and their banks dominated financial intermediation in the past.

As shown by the statistical analysis in section 3, this system was functioning smoothly, if at a somewhat slow pace, until the eve of the First World War. The Great Depression of the 1930s and the Second World War added to crises and instability in the global economy. This was a period of economic and financial reverses. Consequently, after the Second World War, policy makers switched their stance and instead of recreating the smoothly-functioning globalized financial markets of the pre-First World War era, they began making policy moves in the opposite direction by imposing capital controls to regain monetary policy autonomy. Policy makers in positions of responsibility were faced with, what the textbooks call, the Mundellian trilemma, or "impossible trinity," or "inconsistent trinity," noted in Chapter 3.[4] An open capital market deprives an economy of the ability to target its exchange rate and to use monetary policy in pursuit of other economic objectives. However, the inconsistent trinity or the policy "trilemma" is only to be taken as

---

[3] Baldwin and Martin (1999) have reviewed the related literature in detail. Several important empirical studies have analysed this issue. For instance, refer to Obstfeld and Taylor (1998); and Taylor (1998).

[4] To repeat what was mentioned in Chapter 3, section 1, macroeconomic policy regime at best can accommodate only two elements of the following three policy objectives: (i) fixed exchange rates; (ii) autonomous monetary policy oriented toward domestic objectives; and (iii) free cross-border capital mobility.

an approximation. Economic policy coalesces with the sociopolitical forces to decide which of the three policy strands will dominate policy formulation in a particular period.

2. Agents of financial globalization

Economic agents that propel economies towards financial integration include governments, borrowers, investors, and financial institutions. Governments are responsible for domestic macroeconomic and financial policy and their policy support is indispensable for financial globalization. By creating an enabling policy framework, they make financial globalization feasible. Two policy actions are considered a precondition of financial globalization. The first is liberalization and deregulation of the domestic financial sector, and second, liberalization of the capital account of the balance of payments (BOP). Regulation of the domestic financial sector and application of various controls used to be a popular practice in the past. This is discussed at length in section 7.

Controls and regulation of the domestic financial sector applied to most economies but they applied *a fortiori* to the developing economies where governments conventionally controlled credit allocation and surveillance over its disbursement through control on prices and quantities. Policy structures and their restrictiveness varied from country group to country group. In the developing economies, governments used a large number of instruments in different policy areas to restrict capital account transactions. These areas are foreign exchange transactions, derivative transactions, lending and borrowing activities by banks and corporations, and participation of foreign investors in the domestic financial system.

During the contemporary wave of globalization, policy structure in the above-mentioned areas started changing. Again, the rate of change varied from country group to country group. The change in policy structure occurred in a sequential manner. Since the 1970s, the traditional controls and restrictive regulations over the domestic financial sector and capital account noted above began to be loosened in many industrial economies. The newly industrialized economies[5] (NIEs) and the emerging market economies followed suit.

The lifting of restrictions was studied by Kaminsky and Schmukler (2001). They selected six restrictions on the capital account and five

---

[5] Chile, Hong Kong SAR, Korea, Singapore, and Taiwan, have been christened the newly industrialized economies.

restrictions on the financial markets and made two indices: (i) financial restrictions on capital account, and (ii) restrictions on the domestic financial sector, and found that during 1973–2000 period these restrictions declined to the maximum extent in the industrial economies. In the Asian emerging market economies they declined significantly, although not as much as those in the industrial economies. Similarly, Latin American emerging market economies recorded a decline in these restrictions and controls but it was less than that in Asian economies. Despite a history of controls, industrial economies turned to liberal financial policies during the contemporary period. For certain, the NIEs and emerging market economies liberalized the restrictions but they were slow to do that. Also, unlike the industrial economies they suffered periods of policy reversals. During these periods, controls were first lifted and then re-imposed. The most notable periods of reversals were after the oil crisis of 1973, the debt crisis of 1982, in the mid-1990s in Latin America and after 1997 in the Asian economies.

There were several motivating factors behind liberalizing restrictions over the domestic financial sector and capital account. The World Bank (2001) argues that after prolonged application of the vast array of controls and restrictions, policy makers found that they are increasingly costly and difficult to maintain effectively. Besides, understanding this grew and analysts began to make distinctions between a government-led financial system and a market-led system, and saw that that the government-led, non-market system, consistently failed to achieve the desired economic objectives.

There was a change in the mindset of policy makers regarding the external capital. The experiences of the past two decades revealed that there are periods when external capital inflows help both government and corporate sectors. At times of crises, external capital is needed to re-capitalize banks that are in the financial doldrums. It is also needed to conduct financial restructuring of corporates in trouble. During the crises of the 1980s and the 1990s, many countries had to rely on external capital flows to tide over their crisis periods. Early in this period, foreign investors also provided capital for privatization of public sector enterprises in the emerging markets economies, which helped increase financial receipts of these enterprises. After a prolonged debate, at the beginning of the twenty-first century, policy makers seem more convinced and less skeptical than ever regarding a liberalized and deregulated financial system being more efficient. The majority seem increasingly convinced with regard to their contribution to growth and stability of the economy.

The other important group of economic agents supporting financial globalization is that of savers (investors) and borrowers, in the form of households and firms. By borrowing abroad households and firms can go beyond their immediate financial constraints and consume (or invest) according to their preferences. In particular, by raising capital abroad through bonds and equity issues, firms can reduce the cost of capital and expand their investor base. Additionally, it is well known that when external capital comes in the form of foreign direct investment (FDI), the recipient firms benefit by way of new technology, new management techniques, new norms of corporate governance and employee training. The benefit that investors look for include the more avenues of profitable investment that financial globalization provides. As the developing economies grow at a faster clip than the industrial economies, global investors can reasonably expect to have higher real returns on their investment.

In addition, investors benefit from cross-country risk diversion possibilities. With the liberalization and deregulation of the financial markets, institutions and individuals in the industrial economies can easily access the NIEs and the emerging markets by way of buying shares of international mutual funds. For over two decades mutual funds have provided a wide choice in channels of investment. These funds have differing coverage. For instance, they can be global, regional or country-specific. Other easy instruments are American Depository Receipts (ADRs) and Global Depository Receipts (GDRs) as well as international corporate and sovereign bonds.[6] All of these modes of global investment are currently in vogue (Obstfeld, 1995; Schmukler and Zoido-Lobaton, 2001).

Financial institutions are another important driving force behind the spread of financial globalization. They played a definitive role in deepening financial globalization through the spread of financial services. Advances in information and communication technology (ICT) assisted financial globalization by reducing the cost of communications, increasing power of computers, shrinking the globe and thereby making national boundaries less significant. Because of these advances in ICT, large financial institutions can serve several markets from one or two locations. These advances have succeeded in changing the face of the financial services industry by consolidating and restructuring it in the short span of two decades. They were instrumental in the creation of global banks and conglomerates that provide a large mix of financial

[6] Refer to section 11, on globalization of financial services, for the definitions of ADRs and GDRs.

products and services in several markets and countries (Crockett, 2000; IMF, 1995, 2000). As financial liberalization and deregulation spread among the NIEs and the emerging market economies, activities of global financial institutions spread to these economies as well.

3. Financial globalization in the nineteenth and early twentieth centuries

The United States was the largest debtor country of the New World during the nineteenth century. The French and Spanish monarchies and private investors from the Netherlands underwrote its War of Independence (1775–83). The financial reforms of 1790s in the United States were of vital historical significance and gave the new republic a new financial system. In modern parlance they established the United States as an emerging market economy of enormous promise. After these reforms were instituted, the US securities began to be considered high grade in European capital markets. Sustained ability to attract capital from global investors is considered the sine qua non of an emerging market economy. If this is true, the United States was the most successful emerging market economy of this period. The interest of global investors in the US economy persisted for almost two centuries.

Sylla *et al.* (2002) concluded that the transatlantic capital markets were fairly well integrated by 1815. Although during the quarter century before this time European capital did flow to the United States, the markets were far from integrated. The reason was that there was considerable turmoil in Europe before 1815.[7] Despite the turmoil, or perhaps due to it, European investors demonstrated considerable confidence in the young New World economy by purchasing US securities. The post-1815 financial integration proved that financial globalization could, and did, occur in the absence of the technological revolution of the much-celebrated post-1870 era. Transatlantic capital market was not deterred for the want of telegraphs, transatlantic cables, steamships, and adoption of classical gold standard by most countries. Price information moved across the Atlantic, although with a two-month lag. The post-1815 financial globalization contributed to the rapid growth of the US economy. Capital infusions from Europe raised the level of investment higher than what would have been feasible for the United States, had it relied on its own savings. The economy benefited from the external

---

[7] For instance, the intermittent Napoleonic wars were fought during 1796–1815. They were waged principally against England, Prussia, Austria, and Russia.

capital flows and during the nineteenth century it became the largest global economy.

During the nineteenth century, the British overwhelmingly dominated global financial operation by a wide margin and justly earned the sobriquet "the bankers of the world." According to Obstfeld and Taylor (2002), the British accounted for 80 percent of the total global capital flows during this period. The Dutch were the only initial challenger the British exporter of capital had. During the early part of the nineteenth century (1825), they held around 30 percent of global assets. This was no surprise because Amsterdam had developed as a large financial center in the eighteenth century, before London's rise to global financial dominance. As referred to briefly in section 1, towards the end of the nineteenth century, France and Germany also grew industrially and Paris and Berlin rose in importance as financial centers. Consequently, in relative terms the importance of Amsterdam declined.

There are different methods of measuring the volume of global capital flows or stocks consistent over time. One measure of capital flow could be the current account (CA) balance as a proportion of national income (Y). Thus, CA/Y is a germane and interesting ratio and can denote the capital inflow or outflow trends of an economy over a long period. Further, the national income identity tells us that current account equals the difference between savings (S) and domestic investment (I). It equals the net foreign investment. Alternatively, it equals the net foreign capital outflow. The sign and size of CA denote whether an economy is borrowing for investment from the global marketplace or lending abroad to support investment levels in other economies, and how much. Another measure could be total stock of overseas investment at varying points in time over a period. Normalization of investment stock data can be a problem, although not an insurmountable one. Investment stocks are commonly measured in nominal terms in dollars. In their endeavor to show how the global capital markets evolved, Obstfeld and Taylor (2002) adopted this approach and presented their estimates of investment stocks at various times.

Using the mean absolute value of CA, Taylor (1996) compiled long-term time series data for basic trends in global capital flows for a sample of 12 large economies.[8] The period chosen was 1870 through 1995. To make a long-term time series manageable, quinquennially averaged data

[8] The 12 sample countries selected by Taylor (1996) were Argentina, Australia, Great Britain, Canada, Denmark, France, Germany, Italy, Japan, Norway, Sweden and the United States.

were tabulated and used to denote the series. Using this measure, Taylor found that the average size of global capital flows in the 12 sample countries was between 4 percent and 5 percent of the national income before the First World War. There is consensus among economists that the period between 1870 and 1914 was the halcyon period of global mobility of capital. Technological developments of this era (steamships, telegraphs, trans-oceanic cables) supported the spread of economic liberalism and a virtual laissez-faire ambience. The first peak in global capital flows was reached in the boom period of the 1880s, when they reached 5.1 percent of the national income on an average. However, the next decade of 1890s registered a drop and the average capital flows dropped to 3 percent. Between 1910 and 1914, it again rose to 4 percent of the national income. The investment stock approach adopted by Obstfeld and Taylor (2002) demonstrates comparable results. According to their estimates, in 1870, foreign assets were 7 percent of global GDP. This figure soared to 20 percent for the 1900–14 period.

One of the most important characteristics of this period was that after 1870 an increasing number of countries adopted the classical gold standard (see section 1). The New World economies and peripheral countries also came into the fold of the classical gold standard, which left an indelible mark over this era. As all of the important currencies were pegged to gold, they implicitly maintained fixed exchange rates against every other major country's currency. This regime provided a stable and credible exchange rates system to the participating economies. Consequently interest rates across countries tended to converge. Under the gold standard, exchange transactions were free of any controls or restrictions, although infrequently central banks used moral persuasion over the domestic banking systems to support exchange rates.

To be sure, there were periods and countries where central banks failed to defend exchange rates through measures such as moral persuasion. On such occasions exchange rates were left free to float and find their own levels. This had to be done by several Latin American economies. London was the global financial hub and Britain enjoyed hegemony in the European financial system and helped bolster the credibility of exchange parities in Europe. Britain also promoted central bank co-operation in Europe and backed the unquestioned convertibility of gold at an unchanging par (Eichengreen, 1992a). Credibility in the global financial system promoted stability in capital movements. Thus, it is fair to infer that the classical gold standard regime had successfully promoted global capital flows. By reducing actual gold movements, financial flows in turn helped the system to function smoothly

(Obstfeld and Taylor, 1998). During 1870–1914, global integration progressed not only in the financial markets but also in goods and labor.

After 1900, the United States began to emerge as a capital exporting country. European borrowings during the First World War turned the United States into a major creditor country. The United States was getting ready to replace Britain and assume the mental of the "banker of the world." Under the burden of the war and recovery, Britain had to abdicate this hegemony during the 1920s (Bordo *et al.*, 1999). At the beginning of the Great Depression, the US economy had emerged as the dominant economic and financial power in the global markets and New York had replaced London in playing the pivotal role in the global financial world. Although the United States remained a creditor nation for much of the twentieth century, the financial hegemony of the United States was not complete, like that of Britain in the preceding century. The United States also did not display an eagerness to be a commensurate political leader of global stature or a superpower.

At the beginning of the twentieth century several institutional developments had taken place and a broad array of private debt and equity instruments were in use. Insurance activity and government bond markets were widening their activities and scope. Among the so-called core economies, bills of exchange, bond finance, and equity issues were common as was making FDI in selected core and peripheral economies. All major economic centers in Europe, North America and in the New World economies were using these instruments and so were a small number of financial centers in Asia, Africa and Latin America. The pound sterling was the domineering currency of this period. Use of key currencies and popular instruments underpinned expansion of global commercial network. The volume of world trade rose dramatically until the outbreak of the First World War.

This wave of globalization had run its course and ended on the eve of the First World War. Major technological innovation had supported this wave. Also, during this period major trading nations had adopted free trade as a policy. J.M. Keynes bemoaned the end of this era with the words, "What an extraordinary episode in the economic progress of man that age was which came to an end in August 1914."[9]

4. Financial globalization: the destructive phase

Progress in globalization and a smoothly functioning equilibrium in the global financial system was shattered by the First World War. Attempts

---

[9] See Keynes (1919), Ch. 2.

to return to globalization after the First World War failed because the economic structure of the combatants' economies had undergone a significant change due to the war. This failure led to erection of trade barriers and repeated devaluations of currencies in a competitive manner. This kind of competition turned out to be a destructive phase.

For appearances sake, countries maintained the gold standard – such as gold coinage, and exchange rate pegs – during the First World War but created obstacles in gold and capital movement and ignored the rules of the game. Patriotism supplanted all the considerations of having a smoothly functioning global financial system. The war years of 1915–19 recorded a sudden spurt in global financial movements – leading to a second peak of 5 percent. This capital movement reflected the wartime borrowings of the European economies (Taylor, 1996). Global capital flows began to diminish in volume in 1920. As the war had destroyed the global financial architecture, governments radically altered exchange rates and prices levels and also imposed exchange controls. In the early 1920s, European economies tried to re-peg their currencies to gold and after 1925 a fleeting gold-exchange standard was re-established. Many European economies relaxed foreign exchange controls for a short while. This was the period of the reconstituted gold standard, or the gold exchange standard.

Bordo and Eichengreen (1998) believe that the re-established gold exchange standard of 1925, with capital mobility, would have survived in the absence of the Great Depression, which in turn largely resulted from a disastrous error of the Federal Reserve Board in the United States. Their hypothesis was that the gold exchange standard could be suspended during the war years and restored at the end of the war at the original gold parity of $20.67. This system could have lasted until the early 1960s and then would have collapsed because of the Triffin dilemma.[10] Had this hypothetical scenario come true, the global economy would have shifted to the floating exchange rate much earlier than it did. Consequently, financial globalization would not have slowed as much as it did during the twentieth century.

The gold exchange standard finally collapsed in 1931 when the pound sterling – one of the most significant currencies of this period – departed from its gold peg.[11] The three major currency crises of 1931 led

[10] See Chapter 6, section 2, for definition and details regarding the Triffin dilemma.
[11] In June 1931, flight from the pound sterling began. The British government could not apply budgetary retrenchment measure to defend the currency because of the prevailing high rate of unemployment. The Bank of England did not carry

to flight from the Austrian schilling, Hungarian pengo, and the German mark. Increases in discount rates failed to produce the desired results. The grip of flight psychology was so strong that policy makers believed that exchange control was the only option left to them. Intervention in the foreign exchange markets did not work and the three economies continued to drain their gold reserves. After 1931, when both the classical gold standard and the gold-exchange standard had become irrelevant, foreign exchange controls returned and this caused economic turmoil. Financial instability promoted exchange controls all over the globe, in the core and periphery countries. Although they adopted controls with alacrity, thinking that they had found the appropriate solution to the problem of financial volatility, many governments found it difficult to manage these controls. Some of the exchange control policies were effective and successful, while others were difficult to implement and unsuccessful. Uncertainty in foreign exchange markets continued and large movements in exchange rates became common.

As the depression deepened, the Latin American economies not only depreciated their currencies but installed exchange controls like the other economies of this period. Many Latin American economies defaulted on their foreign loans, which made them a pariah. Global capital flows to this region virtually stopped (Alejandro, 1983). Given such uncertainties in global economic and financial environment, this turned out to be a lean period for global capital mobility. During the Great Depression era, financial flows shrank to a meager 1.5 percent of national income (Taylor, 1996). According to the investment stock approach adopted by Obstfeld and Taylor (2002), foreign assets were only 8 percent of global GDP in 1930, 11 percent in 1938 and a mere 5 percent in 1945.

The seeds of the Bretton Woods agreement of 1944 were sown by the domestic and global economic and financial chaos of the interwar period. After the Second World War, during the 1950s and the 1960s, global capital flows in the 12 sample countries[12] fell to the lowest levels recorded in Taylor's (1996) study, close to 1 percent of the national income. In 1960, the US share of global assets was 50 percent of total global foreign assets, the highest the United States ever held (Obstfeld and Taylor, 2002).

---

out an aggressive interest rate defense. The bank rate was raised shortly before the announcement of suspension of the gold standard in September 1931.

[12] See note 8 above.

Although Taylor's (1996) results and those of Obstfeld and Taylor (2002) emerged from simple long-term time-series analyses, they told a telling tale. They illustrated that global financial flows were far from smooth or uniform and that they suffered frequent dislocations and serious volatility. On the one hand, there were periods when global financial flows strengthened, such as in the late nineteenth century and in the early years of the twentieth century, immediately before the First World War, while on the other hand there were periods such as the Great Depression when they suffered a serious loss of momentum. More complex methodology can be adopted to study the global capital flow data. For instance, a study of current account identity is possible by focusing on the relationship between domestic savings and investment trends in the selected sample countries.[13]

5. Emerging financial architecture after the Second World War

After the Second World War, most currencies were not convertible. In addition, most countries had stringent restrictions over foreign investment. Restrictions existed from both sides – the receiving countries and the source countries. As most governments were concerned about exchange rate stability and autonomy in monetary policy, they had to abandon free capital movement as a priority policy option. In fact, there was not much of a choice involved. Given the restrictions and currency inconvertibility, trans-border capital movements could not take place. Therefore, cross-country capital movements reached and remained at their historical low levels in the 1950s and failed to pick up during the 1960s. The Bretton Woods era (1945–71) of fixed but adjustable exchange rates is known for limited capital mobility and autonomy in monetary policy.[14]

Before the end of the Second World War, a concerted attempt was made to reinvent a new global economic and financial order. Travails and disorder of the interwar period demonstrated the imperious need to create such an order. Finance ministry or treasury officials in the allied countries turned their attention to devising an efficient and functional postwar economic order.[15] Some of the best-known scholars of this

---

[13] To this end, several relevant studies are available. For instance, Eichengreen (1992b); Obstfeld (1995); and Taylor (1998).

[14] The complete breakdown of the Bretton Woods system took two years, during 1971–73.

[15] Four countries had prepared official plans for presentation and discussion: Canada, France, the United Kingdom and the United States.

period picked up the gauntlet. This included some towering figures of the twentieth century such as J.M. Keynes, who in 1941 circulated his proposal for the new international economic order. His paper (1982) was entitled *Shaping the Post-War World: The Clearing Union* and it attracted a great deal of scholarly attention.

In 1942, H.D. White made public his vision of institutions that were intended to maintain exchange rate stability, macroeconomic stability and non-discriminatory trade relations among the nations. After long debates, White's plan was accepted as the basis for the Bretton Woods agreement and the twin institutions, the International Monetary Fund (IMF) and the World Bank, were established, along with the subsequent establishment of the General Agreement on Tariffs and Trade (GATT). As these institutions had emerged subsequent to the economic and financial chaos between the two World Wars, one of their basic premises was that both variations in exchange rates and global capital movements should be closely watched, and if need be, controlled. Although this was the majority belief, there were serious dissents. Milton Friedman and Jacob Viner were among the most famous dissenters who opposed the consensus view and argued in favor of floating exchange rates and free short-term capital movements.

Countries participating in the Bretton Woods conference were attracted less by the Keynes concept of a new economic order because for all appearances it was found to be flirting with economic nationalism. His plan suffered from several excesses. It was premised on heavy governmental management of macroeconomic policies and exchange rates so that domestic stability can be attained. His proposition included extensive restrictions over foreign exchange transactions in general and capital movements in particular – something reminiscent of the interwar era. Exchange controls were its central feature, while the notion of floating exchange rates was considered a pariah. Open capital markets had no place in his vision of the global economy of the future. Keynes also proposed an International Clearing Union (ICU) to facilitate multilateral trade among member countries. Trade deficit and surpluses of the members were to be taken care of as claims on the ICU and liabilities to the ICU, respectively. Such credits and debits were to be settled with the help of "bancor," the new international currency whose value was to be fixed in gold.

The alternative plan suggested by White accepted capital movements and viewed periodic exchange rate adjustments as something more acceptable than did Keynes. As opposed to Keynes, White's proposal favored reduced capital and exchange rate controls. However, White's plan wanted some limits placed over capital mobility because it saw US funding of endless foreign imbalances in the balance of payments of the deficit countries. It proposed internationally agreed limits over capital flows for which speculators were responsible. In hindsight, White accepted the concept of global capital mobility but not without taking cautious measures against excesses in capital movements (Horsefield, 1969). Thus, Keynes and White in principle wanted some kind of a rein on capital movement – putatively Keynes far more than White. Both agreed on regulation of capital flight.

While there were serious disagreements in the views of the two principal proponents, there was partial similarity in ideas on capital account. It is reflected in the Articles of Agreement of the IMF. Article VIII set out that the principal systemic objective of the IMF is non-discriminatory multilateral convertibility on current account. There were no restrains on capital movements related to current account payments. However, Article XIV allowed restrictions over capital movements during a transitional period – countervailing Article VIII. This reflected the cautiousness in the views of the two principal proponents. At the same time Article VI(3) states that, "Members may exercise such controls as are necessary to regulate international capital movements. ... " Article VI(1) prohibits members from using the IMF resources "to meet a large or sustained outflow of capital. ... " It even empowers the Fund to request imposition of capital controls in such cases. It needs to be clarified that when the IMF accepted the notion of controlling capital movement, the underlying objective was to prevent currency crises and runs on currencies. This provided autonomy to governments to manage their monetary policy. In the background of the recent crises, the provisions under these Articles of Agreements have taken on new meaning and relevance.

Once the IMF commenced its operations, the shape of things that emerged was different from what was visualized by the founding fathers. Most member countries found it difficult to adhere to the Article VIII convertibility obligations. Although they were given a grace period of five years to prepare to commit to Article VIII, by 1957 only ten member countries had accepted its obligations.[16] Most other member countries were still following Byzantine foreign exchange controls. Flouting the IMF norms, some developed and developing member countries even turned to floating exchange rates. During the 1950s, Britain seriously considered switching to floating exchange rates, but after a prolonged

[16] The United States and Canada were among the first to adhere to Article XVIII. The other eight countries were Cuba, Dominican Republic, El Salvador, Guatemala, Haiti, Honduras, Mexico and Panama.

public debate it decided against it. Britain, France, Italy, and Germany did not accept their Article VIII obligations until 1961, while Japan followed suit in 1964. Germany had developed balance of payment surpluses since the early 1950s, and therefore, it went a step ahead and moved to full convertibility on capital account.

Along with recovery and reconstruction, economic and financial integration endeavors were underway among the European economies during the 1950s. Six large economies on the continent of Europe were trying to form the European Economic Community (EEC). Article 67(1) of the Treaty of Rome (1957) called on its signatories to eliminate all restrictions on capital movements between the member states.[17] This provision was a fundamental one because the ultimate objective of the Treaty was full financial and monetary integration and creating a single European market, which could not be achieved before this condition was squarely met. In 1959, Germany proposed and actively lobbied for complete liberalization of capital movement in the EEC member states as well as non-member states. To demonstrate the seriousness of its intent, Germany unilaterally abolished its own restrictions on capital import. In 1960, the economic and financial (ECOFIN) council of the EEC directed member countries to free the capital movements of short- and medium-term trade credits, FDI and listed shares. Although these policy moves prima facie were healthy for both the European and global economies, there was an unsuspecting downside. A new era of speculative capital flows was born and this bedeviled policy makers inside and outside of Europe. The next logical policy moves regarding capital account liberalization were stopped in their tracks by apprehensions of speculative attacks. Italy suffered a balance of payments crisis in 1964 and Britain in 1967, and this slowed the integration process.

One reason why Germany took initiative in promoting financial liberalization in the EEC was that the German economy had recorded relatively faster economic and productivity growth during the 1950s and the 1960s. Together they mandated a real currency appreciation, which meant a pressure for raising prices in Germany measured in dollars *vis-à-vis* that of the United States. This was going to be a politically unpopular move. Therefore, policy makers in Germany were not willing to accept this. However, once the German capital markets were liberalized, revaluation of the Deutschemark was inevitable. What policy makers were reluctant to do, market forces could easily achieve.

---

[17] Belgium, France, Germany, Italy, Luxembourg and the Netherlands signed the Treaty of Rome to create the European Economic Community (EEC).

Notwithstanding the two crises of the mid-1960s, some European economies did take liberalizing measures. As France was recording surpluses in its current and capital accounts, it unilaterally eased its controls on its capital account in 1967. The student movement of 1968 sparked capital flight from France, and the very next year capital controls were re-imposed in France. As Germany was the unwitting recipient of the French flight capital, it tightened its capital inflow regulations and had to impose capital controls. Speculation continued in 1969 and the French franc had to be devalued under speculative pressure. The counterbalancing speculative game went on in Germany, where speculators were expecting a currency revaluation for the reasons given in the preceding paragraph. Speculative pressure on the currency revaluation was strong and mounting. In response, first the government abandoned the official exchange rate parity and then the new government of Willy Brandt revalued the Deutschemark. In October 1969, it was revalued by 10 percent (Bakker, 1996).

During the 1950s and the 1960s, the members of the Organization for Economic Co-operation and Development (OECD) gradually became active participants in the financial globalization process. The slow growth of this process bears repeating. During these two decades the OECD countries were not only the dominant players in the global financial markets but also the few economies that participated in the global financial market place. The next group to successfully enter the global financial markets was that of the NIEs. This sub-group could be taken as being a limited market participant, whose credibility in the financial market and creditworthiness was on the rise for good reasons.

Towards the end of the 1950s, the global economy was facing the problem of dollar shortage, while growing US balance of payments deficits were causing alarm in their own right. The stock of short-term dollar claims on the United States had grown to acquire a disturbing high proportion. Some of these dollar claims were settled in gold while others were held despite mounting anxiety regarding sudden reduction in the gold content of the dollar – or an effective dollar devaluation. Conversions of dollar claims depleted US gold holdings, which at this time were the largest in the world. In an attempt to maintain its strength in terms of gold reserves, the United States took several regulatory measures to limit the outflow of gold. Some of the major restrictive policy measures were taken after 1961, and these included an escalating sequence of dividend and interest taxes, voluntary guidelines and mandatory limits (Bordo, 1993).

Although these restrictive and regulatory measures seemed rational when they were imposed, there were serious doubts regarding their effectiveness and outcome. The Eurodollar market was being created and this rendered these regulatory measures completely ineffective. When dollar outflows from the United States were being obstructed by regulations, the London or European subsidiaries of US banks could easily step in to fill the gap. In addition, European banks competed for dollar businesses. The ultimate impact of the regulations was sending dollars into the Eurodollar markets, and this led to a spectacular growth of these markets in a short time. The Eurodollar markets grew not only fast but also at the expense of onshore US banks. With regard to the global capital movements during the late 1960s, they had increased substantially, although they involved only the industrial economies.

In the early 1970s, market perception regarding the US dollar changed. Financial markets were not impressed with increased domestic and military spending in the United States. Consequently, the dollar came under speculative pressure. Capital flows grew more volatile and set the stage for the collapse of the pegged exchange rate system. Fearing imminent collapse, several industrial economies had floated their currencies before the Smithsonian agreement of December 1971. When speculators attacked the second set of Smithsonian parities of 1972, all of the large industrial economies except Britain raised their barriers to capital inflows. They placed quantitative restrictions on foreign borrowings as well as taxes on interest earnings. Soon the lira and the pound sterling came under selling pressure. Italy and Britain enforced restrictions on outflow of capital but the speculative pressures persisted. The collapse of the pegged exchange rate system came about in early 1973. By March 1973, the industrial country currencies were floating against the dollar. The five EEC currencies were jointly floating in the arrangement called "snake." The Italian lira was out of the "snake" and floating independently, while the Anglo-Irish currency union had its independent float.

Financial globalization slowed down significantly during the Bretton Woods period (1945–71). It also took place among a small number of industrial economies. Thus viewed, this was an era of slow and limited globalization. The Bretton Woods arrangement did not prove to be a viable global economic order. It failed to reconcile domestic policy objectives, pegged exchange rates, and a limited degree of capital mobility justified by an open trading system. During 1971–73, when an increasing number of industrial economies accepted "the floating exchange rate system as an open-ended interim regime," policy makers in many countries felt free to liberalize capital movements without sacrificing their domestic policy priorities.[18]

6. Financial globalization after the Bretton Woods failure

As set out in the preceding paragraph, during the Bretton Woods era only the OECD economies and to an extent the NIEs participated in the slowly developing global financial markets. Developing economies kept stringent control over their capital account throughout the Bretton Woods era. The only sources of external finance for them were official development assistance (ODA), which included official loans and grants and FDI. After the collapse of the Bretton Woods system, middle-income developing economies began to open up for greater capital mobility, while keeping an autonomous control over their monetary policy. Given the limiting conditions of the Mundellian trilemma (see section 1), fixed exchange rates could no longer be a popular policy option.

According to Mundell (2000), the contemporary era of financial globalization began with the oil shock of 1973 and the collapse of the Bretton Woods system. Both of these developments were momentous and were responsible for getting the global economy ready for the financial globalization that followed. The large current account surpluses earned by the members of Organization of Petroleum Exporting Countries (OPEC) could not be invested in these countries immediately, therefore, a good part of them was recycled to developing economies through the so-called money center banks. The recycled petrodollars went only to those developing countries that had access to capital markets. Also, a large majority of petrodollar loans were either sovereign loans or were guaranteed by governments.

By the early 1980s, several developing economies had accumulated large debts. Many of them, particularly those in Latin America, had overborrowed due to low interest rates in the 1970s. However, the 1980s began with a global downturn. Owing to weakened export revenues and historically rising interest rates, many Latin American developing countries failed to service their debt. A situation of generalized default emerged. Money center banks, which had over-lent, were unable and unwilling to rollover debts that were maturing. The debt crisis of 1982 started with Mexico declaring a moratorium in July on its external liability. Flagrant defaults were avoided by concerted efforts orchestrated

---

[18] This section draws on Obstfeld and Taylor (1998). For more detail, see this paper.

by the IMF. Towards the late 1980s, Brady Bonds were invented to resolve the debt crisis of the developing countries (Das, 1989). This subsequently helped in the development of bond markets for the emerging market economies.

Investors in the industrial countries found that deregulation, privatization, merger and acquisitions (M&As) and advances in the information and communications technology (ICT) coalesced to make FDI and equity investment in the emerging market economies more attractive than before. It was also made easy due to growth in global financial and banking markets. The result was an FDI and equity investment spike in the emerging market economies in the 1990s. The prime movers of the contemporary wave of globalization are governments, private investing and borrowing firms, financial institutions and to a limited extent households. However, the Asian crisis of 1997 adversely affected the capital flows to the emerging market economies, although the FDI flows remained unaffected.

During the contemporary period, gradually increasing amounts of private capital flows started going to the developing economies. Private capital did not go to all the developing economies. Only a sub-group of economies, namely, emerging markets, has succeeded in attracting capital and participated in the financial globalization process. As noted below, this condition is the sine qua non of the emerging market economies. They are somewhat imprecisely defined as the NIEs and middle-income developing countries in which governments and corporations have access to private international capital markets, or can attract institutional portfolio investment, or both. Different institutions include slightly different sets of countries in this category. For example, the Institute of International Finance (IIF) includes 29 countries from Asia, Africa, Europe, Latin America, and the Middle East. The IMF includes all of the NIEs and the middle-income developing countries in its definition of the emerging market economies. *The Economist* classifies 25 middle-income developing and transitional economies as the emerging market economies.

Domestic financial deregulation stimulated the financial globalization process. The most significant deregulation was that of the capital account. Full capital account liberalization movement began in Europe during the 1980s. As noted in section 5 above, the Treaty of Rome had aimed at achieving full financial and monetary integration. Encouraged by Germany, whose capital account was completely open in 1981, the members of the European Union (EU) began moving towards free intra-European capital mobility. France joined in these endeavors in 1983. The industrialized EU economies believed that a liberalized capital account would, *inter alia*, impose discipline over monetary and fiscal policies. The Netherlands opened its capital account completely in 1986, Denmark in 1989, Belgium, Luxemburg, and Italy in 1990, Spain, Portugal and Ireland in 1992, and Greece in 1994. Although Austria, Finland, and Sweden joined the EU in 1995, their capital account had been open for some time when they joined (Bakker, 1996).

Having witnessed the recent benefits of financial globalization, policy makers and economic agents in the emerging market economies are likely to work towards a more financially integrated world and towards achieving a deeper degree of financial integration. The newest developments in the ICT and effectiveness of public policy would further underpin cross-border financial flows.

However, despite the progress in financial globalization, the global financial system is far from being perfectly integrated. Several counter-globalization forces are still at work. Analysts have provided evidence of inadequate progress in financial integration, imperfections in the global capital markets, persistent capital market segmentation, home country bias, and correlation between domestic savings and investment.[19] Yet, a reversal of the recent trend is difficult to visualize, albeit it is not an impossibility. It is largely because of liberalization and deregulation of economies that have taken place, as well as technological advances in the financial services sector. Besides, the channels of financial globalization are so many and so diverse that a reversal of financial globalization would be difficult. This observation applies to both partially integrated and fully integrated economies. This is not to deny that during the slack periods of global growth, the progress towards globalization would not suffer.

7. Financial globalization and efficiency

One of the definitions of financial globalization is integration of domestic financial system of a country with the global financial markets and institutions. The enabling framework of financial globalization essentially includes liberalization and deregulation of the domestic financial sector as well as liberalization of the capital account, without which financial globalization cannot take place. As the trans-border capital flows begin, they integrate domestic and global financial markets. In a globalized financial environment domestic lenders and borrowers

[19] For evidence to this effect, refer to Frankel (2000); Obstfeld and Rogoff (2000); Tesar and Werner (1998) and Okina et al. (1999).

participate in the global markets, and utilize global financial intermediaries for borrowing and lending.

Financial globalization has definitive and obvious efficiency implications. For instance, when capital is free to move globally, its scope widens and it tends to be attracted toward the opportunities of highest return in the global economy. To be sure, it has long-term welfare implications. Second, increased integration and globalization of financial markets is essentially based on major technological and structural developments. They have lowered the costs of transactions, information and mobility. Third, in a world of globalized finances, the recipient economies can smooth their domestic consumption and investment curves with the help of global capital inflows. Fourth, it is well known that financial assets have variable and imperfectly correlated payoffs. Under these circumstances financial globalization provides and enhances opportunities for investors to diversify risk by allowing them to deploy capital in a wider array of global assets. Such risk diversification also improves returns on assets, enhancing systemic efficiency.

As set out in Chapter 1, financial globalization exposes private agents and economies to international competition. The competitive process is regarded as one that enhances efficiency both in the goods markets and those for the factors of production. One manifestation of enhanced international competition is the movement of capital to economies that promise highest risk-adjusted rate of return. In this kind of *mise-en-scène* there is a cost of maintaining inefficient and regulated market structures. As this kind of international competition rises, the cost to countries that maintain illiberal, regulation-ridden and inefficient financial market structures also rises.

However, there is a serious downside to global investment diversification. One lesson of the history, recent (the 1930s and the 1980s) and remote, is that capital-importing countries often enact capital controls laws and/or prevent repatriation of yields and profits. A benign view of capital controls followed the Great Depression and it was considered acceptable, but *only* under certain conditions for certain periods.[20] As these possibilities are real, they tend to make investors cautious; on occasions overly so. Eventually the apprehension of capital controls work as disincentives to financial globalization. Such apprehensions encourage misallocation of capital by keeping excessive amount of it

[20] When Malaysia imposed capital controls following the 1997–98 financial crisis, scholars such as Paul Krugman supported the move and provided several justifications.

in capital-abundant countries, while little capital flowing into capital-scarce emerging market and developing economies. They also bias domestic savings towards domestic investment activity (Feldstein and Horioka, 1980).

Immobility of capital, whatever the frictional factors, can adversely affect the cross-country pattern of economic growth (see section 8 below). For one, it will retard the convergence process among countries because capital would be confined to the capital-abundant economies. Such misallocation of capital will also have distributional implications. Inefficient allocation of capital would lead to low returns in the capital-abundant economies, while capital-scarce economies would perpetuate inefficiency of their own, which would be characterized by low wages. Such misallocation of productive resources would indeed have detrimental long-term welfare implications.[21]

Another potential advantage of open capital markets, which are mandatory under financial globalization, is that policy makers realize that there is an imperious need to have a high degree of market discipline. Following a logical and pragmatic set of macroeconomic policies and toeing the line in areas such as international financial regulatory and supervision norms become imperative policy targets. International accounting standards are known to follow financial globalization, which in turn lead to greater systemic transparency. This has both macroeconomic and institutional implications (Stiglitz, 2000). Unsound policies and poor financial regulatory environments are known to trigger quick capital outflows. This kind of cautiousness supplements the disciplining power, which is considered inherent in a commitment to an exchange rate peg. These advantages of financial globalization motivated its growth and expansion in various periods.

8. Financial globalization and growth nexus

If financial globalization, as mentioned in the preceding section, allocated global capital more efficiently, financial immobility naturally would yield the opposite results. It would have negative welfare implications. Economies that succeed in developing well-functioning domestic financial systems are able to do so by developing an adequate institutional base. One builds on the other in a symbiotic manner. Macroeconomic theory has developed sufficiently during the past decade and has analytically established that banks and other financial institutions endogenously

[21] Williamson (1996) provides a detailed and formal treatment of this issue.

improve the allocation of available credit. Total factor productivity (TFP) in the economy improves through the selection and funding of projects with high private and social returns (King and Levine, 1993). Furthermore, as soon as a sound financial and institutional base is created in an economy, global investors feel confident in investing in it. They promote a higher domestic rate of investment and therefore growth, eventually leading to financial globalization of the recipient economy. Two relationships are apparent here: first, the finance-growth nexus, and second, finance-growth-financial globalization nexus.[22]

Economic history provides evidence of support to the above hypothesis. Countries that developed a sound financial system, an adequate institutional base to underpin it and were financially innovative early in their growth process, also succeeded in growing rapidly. They easily attracted foreign capital and this served to bolster their growth endeavors. Three of the most conspicuous historical examples of such success are the Netherlands, Britain and the United States, in that historical order. Their economic history demonstrated that they first emerged as economic leaders in their own right, and then leaders in the export of capital. The Netherlands first, and Britain thereafter, led in developing a sound financial system and institutional base in the seventeenth century. The Netherlands was the political and economic power of the seventeenth century, and Britain in the eighteenth and the nineteenth centuries. At the end of the eighteenth century, after the declaration of independence, the United States developed its financial infrastructure on the same paradigm as did the two precursors. Section 6 of this chapter includes a discussion on the US financial reforms of 1790.

Following in the tracks of these three leaders, during the latter half of the nineteenth century, France and Germany in Europe and Japan in Asia, also became financial innovators. Like the three leaders, these three economies also grew first into rapidly growing economies and subsequently into substantial capital exporters. Financial development and trade expansion not only underpin the growth endeavors but also help in the convergence of interest rates among the globalizing economies. Rousseau and Sylla (2001) took a sample of 17 countries and long-term data series beginning at 1850 and used the well-known cross-country regression framework of Barro (1991) to study the finance-growth nexus. Their results supported the view that countries with well-developed and innovative financial systems engage in more trade and appear to be

---

[22] See Rousseau and Sylla (2001), and Jalilian and Kirkpatrick (2002), for a detailed discussion.

better integrated with the other economies. The 17 sample countries demonstrated an evidence of convergence of long-term interest rates. Economic growth and increasing globalization in the Atlantic economies (named above) and Japan may indeed have been finance-led.

9. Financial globalization and the domestic financial sector

Contagion and crisis are vexing and pernicious downsides of financial globalization. That being said, global integration can indeed have a strong influence on the development of the domestic financial sector in the developing economies. Two of the most important potential economic benefits of financial globalization are development and growth of the financial sector and greater availability of funds for productive investment. Globalization is responsible for improvement in the quality of financial infrastructure in the domestic economy, which in turn reduces the omnipresent problem of asymmetric information. Lenders in a developing economy confront the problem of asymmetric information much more than in an industrial economy. This is the prime cause of adverse selection and moral hazard in the developing economies.[23] By bringing about improvement in the asymmetric information scenario, financial globalization directly cures the twin malaise of adverse selection and moral hazard. This improves not only the quality of credit in the domestic financial markets but also its availability.

Globalizing financial markets benefit both savers (investors) and borrowers. In a financially integrated world capital movements easily and rapidly take place from where capital is to where it is needed. As referred to earlier, investors looking for better returns on their investments seek to invest in assets in the emerging markets and other developing economies where marginal return of capital is higher. That financial integration causes economy-wide benefits has been clarified in section 2. This kind of capital flow is reflected in the large current account deficits commonly seen in developing economies. With greater flows of capital, more capital becomes available to the economies that are well integrated with the global economy.

---

[23] Adverse selection implies resources going to low-quality projects, and moral hazard means borrower taking risky positions after borrowing funds and use of financial resources in a manner not beneficial to the lender. Adverse selection and moral hazard are the ongoing problems of a poorly developed financial market.

As more capital inflows take place with progress in financial integration, the depth and sophistication of domestic financial markets increase. Also, financial products, instruments and services expand, providing more financial opportunities to both borrowers and lenders. A larger number of instruments provide risk diversification opportunities to global lenders. Borrowers can also benefit by lowering their cost of capital. As global investors are more diversified by nature, they can consider paying higher prices for domestic bonds and equities. It was observed that with the expansion of capital inflows, emerging market economies were able to develop their stock and bond markets. Their financial services industry also expanded and strengthened.

An amber signal is warranted here. Although more equities and bonds are issued now in the emerging market economies, it cannot be taken to mean that all financial institutions have improved their operations and there is an all round improvement in the domestic financial markets. Due to competition with much larger international institutions, the opposite can also occur, that is, domestic financial markets can shrink or lose their importance for the domestic borrowers and lenders. Claessens *et al.* (2001) have provided evidence of shrinking domestic stock markets in several emerging market and developing economies as trading moved on to global bourses.

The malaise of asymmetric information can be effectively controlled and minimized by bringing about improvements in the financial infrastructure. As it improves with financial globalization, it creates a transparent, competitive and efficient domestic financial system and environment for the economic agents to operate. In such an environment asymmetric information cannot grow. As financial globalization ushers in greater competition in the domestic financial market, it can generate efficiency gains. As set out in section 2, it has been observed that financial globalization imposes stringent market discipline. By demonstration effect, international banks and other international institutions refine different areas of the domestic financial sector (e.g., accounting practices and supervision norms) and impel it towards the international frontier.

Eager to reduce risk exposure by diversifying their portfolios and to improve their profit performance, foreign banks and financial institutions enter the emerging market and developing economies and generally have a direct impact over financial sector development in the host economy. Foreign banks also promote adoption of best practices in the domestic financial sector. They provide know-how for better risk management practices as well as corporate governance techniques.

Corporate governance improves in the domestic financial sector because new global shareholders tend to monitor the management more closely. Foreign corporations bring with them state-of-the-art management techniques. When the International Finance Corporation (IFC) took a small stake in the Bank of Shanghai in the late 1990s, part foreign ownership led to significant changes in governance (Lardy, 2001).

10. Dimension of net capital flows to emerging market economies

Cross-country financial flows to emerging market economies were low, at a paltry $28 billion, during the mid-1970s. Net flows reached their peak level of $306 billion in 1997 in real terms, at the eve of the Asian financial crisis (Schmukler and Zoido-Lobaton, 2001; Das, 2003). They suffered a sharp decline after that because of the Asian and other financial and economic crises. The composition of external capital underwent a dramatic transformation during this period. Official flows or official development assistance (ODA) either stagnated or declined and as a result their relative significance in global capital flows declined. In their place, private capital flows became the major source of external finance for a good number of emerging market economies. FDI became an important and dependable source of finance for the emerging markets and other middle-income economies during the 1980s and the 1990s. Its growth was particularly strong during the 1990s. A large part of FDI to emerging market economies was in the form of mergers and acquisitions (M&As). Many large developing economies were privatizing public sector enterprises during this period and those that were rated as creditworthy by the financial markets succeeded in attracting FDI in the process (Lipsey, 1999).

While syndicated bank loans were a popular instrument during the 1970s, they gradually went out of use after the Latin American debt crisis of 1982. In the 1970s, developing countries hardly attracted portfolio investment in stocks and bond markets. They were as low as $100 million in 1970. Like FDI, they began to increase in the 1980s. Between 1983 and 1989, net portfolio investment to developing economies averaged $6.5 billion per annum. This average increased to $43.6 billion per annum during 1990–94 (IMF, 1995). Portfolio investment peaked at $103 billion in 1996 in real terms (Schmukler and Zoido-Lobaton, 2001; Das, 2003). Global institutional investors found this channel of investment functional and profitable. Mutual funds, insurance companies, and pension funds channeled large amounts through portfolio investment into the emerging market economies and in addition, a wide-ranging financial restructuring had taken place in the recipient economies making large portfolio investment possible. The Asian crisis of 1997 had a strong adverse influence over private capital flows to developing economies and they sharply declined after that.

The emerging market economies are defined above as those where governments and corporations have access to private international capital markets, or can attract institutional portfolio investment, or both. Not all of the emerging market economies have an equal access to the international capital markets. The access is directly related to their perceived creditworthiness in the global financial marketplace. Therefore, distribution of global capital among the recipient economies is highly uneven. Some economies such as those of China, East Asia and Latin America, have easy access and receive large amounts of global capital resources, while others such as those of South Asia (India being an exception in this group) have limited access. Many, such as the African economies, have not been able to attract any global capital.

Using the *Global Development Finance* database, Schmukler and Zoido-Lobaton (2001) have shown that low-income developing economies receive very little amounts of net global capital, while some does go to the middle-income developing economies. In accordance with the creditworthiness concept, the lion's share of global capital flows are attracted by the top 12 recipient countries.[24] All of these fall in the category of emerging market economies and as set out in Chapter 2, these economies are relatively more globalized than the others. During the 1990s, global capital flows to these 12 emerging market economies accelerated at a steep rate, and this affected the composition of the total global financial resources going to developing economies. The proportion of financial flows dedicated to the low- and middle-income developing economies decreased at the end of the 1990s. For all appearances, many economies in this group of rapidly financially globalizing economies are diverging from the rest of the developing economies.

11. Globalizing financial services

During the 1990s, the presence of international financial intermediaries has expanded considerably.[25] This applies more to international

---

[24] They are Argentina, Brazil, Chile, China, India, Indonesia, Korea (Republic of), Malaysia, Mexico, Russian Federation, Thailand, and Turkey.
[25] This section is based and draws on Schmukler and Zoido-Lobaton (2001), and Das (2003). The statistical data used here come from the same sources.

commercial banks than to investment banks, insurance companies and mutual funds. It is incorrect to say that the global expansion of financial intermediaries has been uniform because this has occurred fairly unevenly. Conversely, globalization of financial services also occurs when domestic savers (or lenders) and borrowers are able to make use of financial intermediaries located globally. For instance, financial services are said to be globalized when domestic stocks are traded on large international bourses abroad. During the 1990s, the presence of foreign banks increased in three regions – East Asia, Eastern Europe and Latin America.

Foreign bank ownership of assets increased rapidly during the 1990s. Total assets held by them increased mainly in the emerging market economies in Latin America, particularly in Argentina, Brazil, Mexico, Peru, and Venezuela. In the emerging market economies in Eastern European (Czech Republic, Hungary, and Poland) the share of total assets controlled by foreign banks crossed 50 percent of the total. When compared to these two regions, the activities of the foreign banks expanded less rapidly in the emerging markets of East Asia, such as Korea (Republic of), Malaysia, and Thailand (Schmukler and Zoido-Lobaton, 2001).

International bond issuance activity by emerging market economies recorded a sharp spurt in 1993, crossing $50 billion for the first time. It stabilized around this level until 1996 when it nearly doubled. Both 1993 and 1996 were the years of high global capital flows. In 1997, issuance activity by emerging market economies peaked at $120 billion. Due to the Asian financial crisis and its contagion effects, international bond issuance dropped to around $75 billion over the next three years (Schmukler and Zoido-Lobaton, 2001).

The ADRs and GDRs are negotiable certificates representing ownership of shares in a corporation in another country. They are held by a depository, which in turn issues a certificate that can be traded in another country, for example, the United States. Emerging market economies began using ADRs and GDRs for raising capital from the global capital markets in a small way in 1990. The middle-income developing countries began using them in 1992. Firms from both emerging market and middle-income developing economies increased their participation in the US equity markets using ADRs and GDRs. The top six emerging market economies that had the highest participation during the 1990s were Argentina, Brazil, China, India, Korea (Republic of), and Mexico. They accounted for most of the activity by developing countries in the US equity markets. In terms of capital flows, this group may be creating a divergence among the developing countries. This group benefits more from the global capital markets by way of lower cost of capital and longer maturity structure of its debt (Schmukler and Zoido-Lobaton, 2001).

12. Conclusions and summing-up

The evolution of global financial integration was not a record of ever-more-perfectly functioning markets with ever-lower transaction costs and ever-expanding scope. Long-term growth of global financial markets was far from linear. Vicissitudes in the volume of financial flows were more common than uncommon. Neither the concept nor the phenomenon of financial globalization can be considered novel. Cross-country capital movements have a long and well-documented history. Some of the earliest international banks among them were born in Venice. The Medici family of Venice was among the first wealthy families to successfully venture into international banking in a big way during the Renaissance period. From Italy, international banking expanded to the northern port cities of Bruges and Antwerp, and later to Amsterdam and London, essentially in that order. As economic activity expanded to the so-called New World offshoots of Western Europe, international financial transactions supported it and international financial centers developed in those parts of the New World. Using different measures and indicators, several analysts tried to establish that a greater degree of financial globalization existed in the previous epochs of globalization than in the contemporary period.

Economic agents that propel economies towards financial integration include governments, borrowers, investors, and financial institutions. Proactive endeavors of these four agents advanced financial globalization during the contemporary and other historic periods. The United States was the largest debtor country of the New World during the nineteenth century. The French and Spanish monarchies and private investors from the Netherlands underwrote its War of Independence (1775–83). The transatlantic capital markets were fairly well integrated by 1815. During the nineteenth century, the British overwhelmingly dominated global financial operation by a wide margin and justly earned the sobriquet "the bankers of the world." One of the most important characteristics of this period was that after 1870 an increasing number of countries adopted the classical gold standard. The New World economies and peripheral countries also came into the fold of the classical gold standard, which left an indelible mark over this era. The brisk phase of financial globalization that began in 1870 had run its course and ended on the eve of the First World War. After 1900, the United States began to emerge as a capital exporting country. European borrowings during the First World War turned the United States into a major creditor country. At the beginning of the twentieth century several institutional developments had taken place and a broad array of private debt and equity instruments were in use. Insurance activity and government bond markets were widening their activities and scope.

Progress in globalization and a smoothly functioning equilibrium in the global financial system was shattered by the First World War. Attempts to return to globalization after the war failed because the economic structure of the combatants' economies had undergone a significant change due to the war. This failure led to erection of trade barriers and repeated devaluations of currencies in a competitive manner. This kind of competition turned out to be a destructive phase.

After the Second World War, as most governments were concerned about exchange rates and autonomy in monetary policy, they abandoned free capital movement as a priority policy option. Cross-country capital movements reached their historical low level in the 1950s and failed to pick up during the 1960s. Before the end of the Second World War, a concerted attempt was made to reinvent a new global economic and financial order. While there were serious disagreements in the views of the two principal proponents, namely J.M. Keynes and H.D. White, there was partial similarity in ideas on capital account. It is reflected in the Articles of Agreement of the IMF. Along with recovery and reconstruction, economic and financial integration endeavors were underway among the European economies during the 1950s. Six large economies on the continent of Europe were trying to form the European Economic Community (EEC). Article 67(1) of the Treaty of Rome (1957) called on its signatories to eliminate all restrictions on capital movements between the member states. Germany took a good deal of initiative in promoting financial liberalization in the EEC was that the German economy had recorded relatively faster economic and productivity growth during the 1950s and 1960s. During the 1950s and the 1960s, the members of the Organization for Economic Co-operation and Development (OECD) gradually became active participants in the financial globalization process.

The Bretton Woods period (1945–71) is known for slow and limited financial globalization. The Bretton Woods arrangement did not prove to be a viable global economic order. It failed to reconcile domestic policy objectives, pegged exchange rates, and a limited degree of capital mobility justified by an open trading system.

Developing economies kept stringent control over their capital account throughout the Bretton Woods era. The only sources of external finance for them were official development assistance (ODA), which included official loans and grants and FDI. After the collapse of the Bretton Woods system, middle-income developing economies began to open up for greater capital mobility, while keeping autonomous control over monetary policy. Given the limiting conditions of the Mundellian trilemma, fixed exchange rates could no longer be a popular policy option for them. Awareness of benefits from financial globalization grew among the developing economies. Having witnessed the recent benefits of financial globalization, policy makers and economic agents in the emerging market economies began to work towards a more financially integrated world and towards achieving a deeper degree of financial integration. The newest developments in the ICT and effectiveness of public policy would further underpin cross-border financial flows. During the contemporary period, gradually increasing amounts of private capital flows started going to the developing economies.

Financial globalization has definitive and obvious efficiency implications. For instance, when capital is free to move globally, its scope widens and it tends to be attracted toward the opportunities of highest return in the global economy. To be sure, it has long-term welfare implications. Contagion and crisis are a vexing and pernicious downside of financial globalization.

Cross-country financial flows to the emerging market economies were low, at a paltry $28 billion, during the mid-1970s. Net flows reached their peak level of $306 billion in 1997 in real terms, at the eve of the Asian financial crisis. They suffered a sharp decline after that because of the Asian and other financial and economic crises. During the 1990s, presence of international financial intermediaries has expanded considerably. This applies more to international commercial banks than to investment banks, insurance companies and mutual funds. It is incorrect to say that the global expansion of financial intermediaries has been uniform because this has occurred fairly unevenly.

References

Bakker, A.F.P., 1996, *The Liberalization of Capital Movements in Europe 1958–1994*, Dordrecht: Kluwer Academic Publishers.

Baldwin, R.E. and P. Martin, 1999, "Two Waves of Globalization: Superficial Similarities, Fundamental Differences", Cambridge, Ma: National Bureau of Economic Research, Working Paper No. 6904.

Barro, R.J., 1991, "Economic Growth in a Cross-Section of Countries", *Quarterly Journal of Economics*, Vol. 106, No. 2, 407–43.

Bordo, M.D., 1993, "The Bretton Woods International Monetary System: A Historical Overview", in M.D. Bordo and B.J. Eichengreen (eds), *A Retrospective on the Bretton Woods System: Lessons for International Monetary Reform*, Chicago: University of Chicago Press, pp. 160–95.

Bordo, M.D., M. Edelstein and H. Rockoff, 1999, "Was Adherence to Gold Standard a "Good Housekeeping Seal of Approval" During the Interwar Period?", Cambridge, MA: National Bureau of Economic Research, Working Paper No. 7186, June.

Bordo, M.D. and B.J. Eichengreen, 1998, "Implications of the Great Depression for the Development of the International Monetary System", in M.D. Bordo, C. Goldin and E.N. White (eds), *The Defining Moment: The Great Depression and the American Economy in the Twentieth Century*, Chicago: University of Chicago Press, pp. 212–42.

Cameron, R.E., 1993, *A Concise Economic History of the World*, New York: Oxford University Press.

Claessens, S., D. Klingebiel and S. Schmukler, 2001, "The Future of Stock Markets in Emerging Economies", Washington, DC: World Bank (mimeo).

Crockett, A., 2000, "How Should Financial Market Regulators Respond to the New Challenges of Global Economic Integration?", in *Global Economic Integration: Opportunities and Challenges*, Kansas City, KA: Federal Reserve Bank of Kansas City, pp. 130–65.

Das, Dilip K., 1986, *Migration of Financial Resources to Developing Countries*, London: Macmillan.

Das, Dilip K., 1989, "Brady Plan and the International Banks: A Cautious Reception", *Business Standard*, Bombay, August 24, p. 6.

Das, Dilip K., 2003, *Financial Globalization and the Emerging Market Economies*, London and New York: Routledge (forthcoming).

Davis, L.E. and R.E. Gallman, 2001, *Evolving Financial Markets and Capital Flows: Britain, the Americas and Australia, 1870–1914*, Japan–US Center, Sanwa Monograph on International Financial Markets, Cambridge: Cambridge University Press.

Diaz-Alejandro, C.F., 1983, "Stories of the 1930s for the 1980s", in P. Aspe, R. Dornbusch and M. Obstfeld (eds), *Financial Policies and the World Capital Markets*, Chicago: University of Chicago Press.

Eichengreen, B.J., 1992a, *Golden Fetters: The Gold Standard and the Great Depression*, Oxford: Oxford University Press.

Eichengreen, B.J., 1992b, "Trends and Cycles in Foreign Lending", in H. Siebert (ed.), *Capital Flows in the World Economy*, Tübingen: Mohr.

Feldstein, M. and C. Horioka, 1980, "Domestic Savings and International Capital Flows", *Economic Journal*, Vol. 90, No. 2, 314–29.

Frankel, J., 2000, "Globalization of the Economy", Cambridge, MA: National Bureau of Economic Research, Working Paper No. 7858.

Horsefield, J.K., 1969, *The International Monetary Fund, 1945–65*, Vol. 3, Washington, DC: International Monetary Fund.

International Monetary Fund, 1995, *International Capital Markets: Developments, Prospects and Policy Issues*, Washington, DC: IMF.

International Monetary Fund, 2000, *International Capital Markets: Challenges, Prospects and Opportunities*, Washington, DC: IMF.

Jalilian, H. and C. Kirkpatrick, 2002, "Financial Development and Poverty Reduction in Developing Countries", *International Journal of Finance and Economics*, Vol. 37, No. 2, 98–108.

Kaminsky, G. and S. Schmukler, 2001, *On Financial Booms and Crashes: Regional Patterns, Time Patterns, and Financial Liberalization*, Washington, DC: World Bank.

Keynes, J.M., 1919, *Economic Consequences of the Peace*, available at <http://www.socsci.mcmaster.ca/~econ/ugcm/3ll3/keynes/peace.htm>.

Keynes, J.M., 1982, "Shaping the Post-War World: The Clearing Union", in D. Moggridge (ed.), *The Collected Writings of John Maynard Keynes*, Vol. 25, London, Macmillan.

King, R.G. and R. Levine, 1993, "Finance, Entrepreneurship and Growth: Theory and Evidence", *Journal of Monetary Economics*, Vol. 32, No. 3, 513–42.

Lardy, N.R., 2001, "Foreign Financial Firms in Asia", paper presented at a conference on *Open Doors: Foreign Participation in Financial Systems in Developing Countries*, jointly organized by the Brookings Institutions, the World Bank and the International Monetary Fund, Washington, DC, April 15.

Lipsey, R.E., 1999, "The Role of Foreign Direct Investment in International Capital Flows", Cambridge, MA: National Bureau of Economic Research, Working Paper No. 7094.

Mundell, R.A., 2000, "A Reconsideration of the Twentieth Century", *American Economic Review*, Vol. 90, No. 3, 327–40.

Neal, L., 1990, *The Rise of Financial Capitalism: International Capital Markets in the Age of Reason*, Cambridge: Cambridge University Press.

Obstfeld, M., 1995, "International Capital Mobility in the 1990s", in P.B. Kenen (ed.), *Understanding Interdependence: The Macroeconomics of the Open Economy*, Princeton, NJ: Princeton University Press.

Obstfeld, M. and K. Rogoff, 2000, "The Six Major Puzzles in International Macroeconomics: Is There a Common Cause?", in *The NBER Macroeconomic Annual*, Cambridge, MA: National Bureau of Economic Research, pp. 124–48.

Obstfeld, M. and A.M. Taylor, 1998, "The Great Depression as a Watershed: International Capital Mobility Over the Long Run", in M.D. Bordo, C. Goldin and N. White (eds), *The Defining Moment: The Great Depression and the American Economy in the Twentieth Century*, Chicago: University of Chicago Press, pp. 353–402.

Obstfeld, M. and A.M. Taylor, 2002, "Globalization and Capital Markets", Cambridge, MA: National Bureau of Economic Research, Working Paper No. 8846, March.

Okina, O., M. Shirakawa and S. Shiratsuka, 1999, "Financial Market Globalization: Present and Future", *Monetary and Economic Studies*, Bank of Japan, Institute for Monetary and Economic Studies, Vol. 17, No. 3, 48–82.

Rousseau, P.L. and R. Sylla, 2001, "Financial Systems, Economic Growth, and Globalization", Cambridge, MA: National Bureau of Economic Research, Working Paper No. 8323, June.

Schmukler, S.L. and P. Zoido-Lobaton, 2001, "Financial Globalization: Opportunities and Challenges for Developing Countries", Washington, DC: World Bank.

Stiglitz, J.E., 2000, "Capital Market Liberalization, Economic Growth and Instability", *World Development*, Vol. 28, No. 6, 1075–86.

Sylla, R., J.W. Wilson and R.E. Wright, 2002, "Trans-Atlantic Capital Market Integration: 1790–1845", paper presented at the high-level seminar on *Globalization in Historical Perspective*, organized by the International Monetary Fund, August 12–14, 2002, Washington, DC.

Taylor, A.M., 1996, "International Capital Mobility in History: Purchasing Power Parity in the Long-Run", Cambridge, MA: National Bureau of Economic Research, Working Paper No. 5742, August.

Taylor, A.M., 1998, "International Capital Mobility in History: The Saving-Investment Relationship", *Journal of Development Economics*, Vol. 57, No. 1, 147–84.

Tesar, L. and I. Werner, 1998, "Internalization of Securities Markets Since the 1987 Crash", in R.E. Litan and A. Santomero (eds), *Brookings-Wharton Papers on Financial Services*, Washington, DC: Brookings Institution Press, pp. 281–372.

Williamson, J.G., 1996, "Globalization, Convergence and History", *Journal of Economic History*, Vol. 56, No. 2, 277–306.

World Bank, 2001, *Finance for Growth: Policy Choices in a Volatile World*, Washington, DC: World Bank, Policy Research Report.

6
Global Financial Architecture and Financial and Regulatory Infrastructure

1. Global financial architecture

Some five years ago, Robert Rubin, the erstwhile US Treasury Secretary made a speech calling for measures to "strengthen the international financial architecture." The metaphor he used was adopted by the academic and policy-making communities and has since survived in the academic writings on this issue as a part of accepted jargon. But it was inapt because global financial system was not quite an architect's blueprint. If anything, it is an excellent example of what the Japanese call *kaizen*, meaning an incrementally evolving phenomenon, improving marginally but continuously, in stages, with time. Pressures from market participants and those from emerging market and Group of 7 (G-7) governments were responsible for this continual, marginal improvement in the global financial architecture.

While there is no widely agreed and tersely stated definition of what precisely constitutes global financial architecture, it refers broadly to the framework and set of institutions, structures and measures that can help prevent crises, or when faced with a crisis help manage it better in the more integrated international financial environment. The global financial system as it presently exists "is made up of a dense network of social, economic and financial institutions" (Eichengreen, 2003).

Terms such as global financial architecture or system are also used to describe institutions, structures and policies that influence and control global financial flows, including those to the emerging market economies. These institutions, structures and policies are also charged with predicting, managing, and preventing macroeconomic instability and crises in the global economy, including those in the emerging market economies. Any simple or elaborate plan of action for this purpose will necessarily have several facets or components. They would not only include crisis prevention and crisis resolution but also deal with weaknesses in the international financial system that contribute to propensity of global instability. The various facets are closely intertwined and putting one or some of them in place in isolation would not work, or would have a limited impact. Readers should be warned from the outset that the global financial architecture is too large a topic to be covered as a part of a chapter. This section only provides a small pen picture, which is selective and relevant to the title of this book. This treatment is far from exhaustive and complete.

2. Radical transformation

Over the past half century, since the creation of the Bretton Woods system, the principal characteristics of the global financial system have undergone radical, if somewhat gradual, transformation. There has been an inevitable and desirable evolution in it. Crockett (2003) called it a transformation "from an administered or *government-led* to a decentralized or *market-led* system." This transformation was desirable because for all of their flaws, markets are a more efficient mechanism for resource allocation than any of its conceivable alternative. This is true despite the presence of market imperfections.

When the Allied nations met in 1994 at Bretton Woods, New Hampshire, to design a mechanism for restoring back to health the shattered world economy, they created a "new" financial architecture for the postwar period, which covered a wide area including (i) exchange rate regime; (ii) trade and payments arrangements; (iii) the balance of payments adjustment process; (iv) international liquidity; and (v) financial market arrangements. The new financial order was based on clear rules laid down in the treaty establishing the International Monetary Fund (IMF) and the World Bank. The operating characteristics of the monetary system were well defined.[1] This "administered" system was logical and coherent and served its objective of facilitating the rehabilitation of war-ravaged postwar economies rather well.

By the end of the 1950s and the early 1960s, most industrial economies had started recording reasonably high rates of economic growth and they liberalized their current accounts. The capital account liberalization was slow to come. The administered system had to work

---

[1] See Chapters III–VIII of the Article of Agreement of the International Monetary Fund.

well because there were few possibilities of damage by financial market inefficiencies. As the global financial markets were not integrated, the contagion effect originating from problems in one country market to the other markets were limited. Also, as the financial institutions were essentially operating in a benign climate, they had little need to run high risks.

With the passage of time, and with the changing demands on the system, the administered system revealed its weaknesses. Also, with new developments in the global economy and financial markets, this system began to show its irrelevance in some areas. For instance, one of its much-discussed problems was that of international liquidity, which was considered a major systemic limitation. That is, it did not have any mechanism to increase the primary liquidity with growth in the global economy, particularly in keeping with rapid growth in world trade. Creation of an internationally controlled supply of liquidity in the form of Special Drawing Rights (SDRs) did not take place until the end of the 1960s. Second, as it was essentially a dollar-based system – holding of dollars reserves had an important role for the global economies. This provoked the ire of other countries, particularly the West Europeans. They begrudged the unique position of the United States in the global financial system. According to them the United States was absorbing the resources of the rest of the world and paying only in IOUs. Third, the IMF worried about the so-called Triffin dilemma, that is, if the accumulation of dollar balances by the treasuries of other countries becomes larger than the US gold reserves, the confidence in conversion of the dollars into gold at predetermined prices would be called into question, which in turn would undermine this system. Fourth, as world trade grew and an increasing number of countries liberalized their current and capital accounts, the number and size of current account disequilibria were increasing. Correction of these imbalances was a multilateral issue and was not possible without exchange-rate-related problems. Eventually, it was the relaxation of restrictions on capital movements on the one hand and growth and expansion of international financial markets on the other hand that weakened the administered system and made it look irrelevant.

During 1971–73, piece-by-piece the old administered or *government-led* financial system collapsed. Although the Smithsonian arrangement was created after 1971, it did not last for long. No attempts to mend or recreate the old system were made after the 1973 oil shock, when the price of crude oil quadrupled. With this, the global financial system passed a critical stage in its evolutionary phase. A decentralized or market-led system evolved in place of the old system. The principal characteristics of the global financial system were different under the new system. Unlike the old system, all the key features in the new financial system progressively became subject to market forces. This included, (i) the exchange rate mechanism; (ii) trade and payment arrangements; (iii) the current and capital account adjustment process; (iii) international liquidity provision; and (iii) the financial markets per se.[2] As the shift from government to market influence and control was more or less systemic and enveloped virtually all the aspects of the global financial operations, some referred to the new system as a "non-system," which was incorrect. The market-based system was not necessarily unsystematic. Classical economic theory has taught us that a market-based system is more efficient than any of its non-market alternatives but this theoretical dictum applies with an important proviso, that is, the conditions for markets to work efficiently are in place. Thus, for the new market-based system it was not as much the system or architecture that was of capital significance as the mechanism needed to make the system work efficiently.

For the market forces to make optimal allocation of resources it is a necessary precondition that markets are both complete and efficient. "Markets are complete if market participants are able to trade all conceivable claims, actual or contingent. And they are efficient if market prices contain all knowledge and information" and do not suffer from information asymmetry. Given these definitions, realistically markets can neither be fully complete nor completely efficient. Markets for contingent claims in all future states-of-the-world do not exist. Also, markets routinely suffer from varying degrees of information asymmetry or lack of vitally need information by the market participants (Crockett, 2003).

Under the new market-led system, the financial markets acted swiftly and imaginatively in creating new and a progressively wide range of instruments. This was their contribution to the completeness of the financial markets, indeed without making them fully complete. The wide range of derivative instruments that became available made it possible for the market participants to make contingent transactions on future outcomes of financial and economic variables. The flip side of this coin is that markets are prone to failure – both at national and global levels.

Advances in game theory have made it easy for us to comprehend why financial markets are so prone to disequilibrium. It happens partly

---

[2] For more detail of the transformation process, see Crockett (2003).

because the assets traded in them provide services over a certain length of time and also because fundamental value of the assets is difficult to assess absolutely correctly. As the return on assets depend on the future states-of-the-world and therefore has a strong element of uncertainty built into them, their value is difficult to assess correctly because of the endemic information asymmetries. As the asset values depend upon collective expectations of future outcomes, herd mentality and externalities can disturb them seriously. Crockett (2003) asserted that markets could not possibly be conceived to smoothly move to "socially optimal equilibria, even with rational private behavior and in the absence of mistakes of government policy." In a real life situation, bad policies and imprudent behavior of economic agents often compounds the problem of disequilibrium tendencies of the financial markets. It is no secret that unsustainable macroeconomic policies have been behind many recent crises.

3. Prevailing status

As set out in Chapter 5, and also as mentioned in the preceding section, market disequilibria and volatility have been and continue to be inherent to the functioning of post-Bretton Woods global financial markets. Information asymmetries frequently give rise to overshooting, sharp market corrections, and often crises. With rapid globalization of capital flows and portfolios, sophistication and dynamism of the financial world has increased enormously. However, an adequate and proper institutional and regulatory framework to regulate it is apparently not in place as yet. The existing framework is not adequate to deal with advancing financial globalization. Those who have studied the recent emerging market crises know that inadequacy and deficiency are not limited to one or two policy areas or institutions, but they are systemic. They extend to both national and supranational institutions. Shortcomings were conspicuous in the consistency of domestic macroeconomic policies, management of international liquidity, and particularly in the area of financial supervision and regulation.

Global financial architecture is a global public good. The global financial system is an organic whole; hence any reform plan would require collective action at the global level. There is a pressing need for fundamentally and comprehensively reforming the various facets of it. The basic objective of reforming the global monetary and financial order is to harness the potential of global private financial flows in such a way that they contribute to the stability and growth in the global economy.

Given the background of volatility, thoughtful, pragmatic and concerted action is required from the global community in this regard, particularly from the matured G-7 economies. The Group of 22 (G-22) is another important and relevant forum for this purpose, and which can make enormous long-term contribution.[3] That being said, reforms at the global level, while necessary, are not sufficient for attaining the basic objective noted above. There is widespread recognition that global financial stability and growth also rests on robust national systems and therefore requires enhanced measures and reforms at the domestic level.

There was never a shortage of proposals and novel ideas for reforms. They came thick and fast from both public and privates sources. The global financial architecture has been the focus of attention of policy mandarins and academics alike. The finance ministries of Canada, France, Germany, and the United Kingdom have proposed serious, well-structured, reform plans. The US Treasury has been actively involved in setting an agenda for reforms. After the Asian crisis, several Asian and other emerging market economies also joined in the debate with their additional agenda items. They were, *inter alia*, concerned with the social impact of the crises, which they believed, was being ignored by those charged with the management and resolution of financial and macro-economic crises. The G-22 has published many intensive reports with the help of academics active in this area. Several noted academic scholars and nonacademic experts (such as George Soros, Henry Kaufman, and Jeffrey Garten) suggested the creation of new institutions or tinkering with the role of the Bretton Woods twins. Think tanks and professional journals have made their especial contributions and there was wide variety in the emphases and profiles of the proposals. Many of the proposed plans were contradictory and mutually incompatible. Some rooted for further liberalization, while others plumped for the reimposition of capital controls. Some said that *nirvana* lies in greater exchange rate flexibility, while others insisted that global financial system would be dysfunctional until a stable or fixed exchange rates system is re-established (Eichengreen, 2003). Some thought that crisis resolution is the express duty of the global community, while other insisted that they should be left

---

[3] The Group of 22 (G-22) is a mixed ad hoc group, created by the United States in April 1998 and had its first meeting in Washington, DC. It was originally created to study the fallout from the Asian crisis and plan a "new international economic architecture." Its members are the G-7 economies plus Argentina, Australia, Brazil, China, Hong Kong (SAR), India, Indonesia, Korea (Republic of), Malaysia, Mexico, Poland, Russia, Singapore, South Africa, and Thailand. The Bretton Woods institutions were given observer status.

in their entirety to the market forces to resolve. Consequently, over the past decade a voluminous amount of literature has accumulated on the subject areas related to the global financial system.

In the wake of recent macroeconomic volatility and crises in the emerging market economies, particularly after the Asian crisis, the international community has attempted to devise a range of new initiatives to strengthen the global financial system. A good deal of action has been underway. For instance, Horst Kohler, the managing director of the IMF has made several speeches under the rubric of "international financial architecture" and sovereign debt restructuring mechanism (SDRM) was designed by the IMF in April 2002 (see to Chapter 4, section 3.2). The World Bank has published many policy and research papers on this and related themes but not all of the novel ideas were functional. They ranged from intellectually appealing to operationally impractical. Some of the proposals even verged on quixotic, such as the proposal regarding creating a new institution called the World Financial Authority.[4] In addition, there is a striking lack of consensus among those who presented new ideas or plans for systemic reforms. Many of the new plans and strategies for reforms affect different countries in different ways. Therefore, in the multipolar world of today, it is difficult to reach an agreement among the country-groups or countries on important financial and economic issues. The contemporary political and financial scenario greatly complicates the process of reaching an agreement. Besides, economic and financial decisions are made in a political environment. This is as true for domestic as global economic and financial decision-making processes. In such a *mise-en-scène,* is it at all possible for domestic and global policy makers (such as the IMF) to work in a non-partisan and apolitical manner?

Notwithstanding the obstacles, given the significance and far-reaching implications of the issue, the global community has not been passive about it. As noted, several initiatives to reform and strengthen the global financial architecture are presently underway. Professor Barry Eichengreen of the University of California, Berkeley, identified four immediate areas for strengthening the global financial system. He posited that it would be a realistic, feasible and attainable target for reforming and strengthening the global financial system. His so-called "four pillars" that would provide further systemic support are: (i) international standards; (ii) market friendly (or Chilean style) taxes on short-term capital inflow; (iii) greater exchange rate flexibility; and

---

[4] This was made jointly by Lord John Eatwell and Lane Taylor.

(iv) collective-action clauses in loan contracts to create an alternative to ever-bigger IMF bailouts. He contends that these reforms and improvements in these four areas could be a panacea for the crisis-prone global economy. Together they would strengthen crisis prevention mechanism, moderate the severity of crises, speed up the recovery of an emerging market economy after it has suffered a crisis, and contain moral hazard in the international financial markets.

4. Areas of immediate reforms

Several areas of the global financial system are in the need for reforms and call for global co-operation and collaboration. A brief discussion on these issues is provided below.

4.1. The Bretton Woods twins: a privileged position

Almost since their inception, the Bretton Woods twins have been active in creating a functional global financial architecture.[5] Taking the World Bank first, poverty alleviation is its principal mandate. Its familiarity and involvement with the developing and emerging market economies and its comparative strengths on social and structural issues has placed the World Bank in a privileged position in helping devise and implementing the global financial structure. In addition, it helps in bringing developing country experience and perspectives to the ongoing discussions, debates and negotiations on reforming the global financial architecture. In the recent past, the World Bank has also attempted to strengthen partnerships with the relevant standard-setting bodies and other institutions in the areas of corporate governance, accounting and auditing and insolvency regimes to forge a consensus and catalyze concerted actions (see section 1.2 below).

The *raison d'être* of the IMF was surveillance of monetary, fiscal and exchange rate policies of the member countries and its conditionality measures were essentially focused on these variables. The IMF has morphed its mission several times. In a financially globalized world, the original role of the IMF has expanded. In its present role it has evolved as a "global advice-and-rescue squad." According to Blinder (2003), it is "one part wealthy benefactor, one part stern schoolmarm and one part global firefighter. It lectures countries on economic orthodoxy, proffers financing in return for approved behavior and rides dramatically to rescue when

---

[5] The creation of the Bretton Woods twins is dealt with in Chapter 5, section 5.

countries fall prey to financial crises." The IMF has come to acquire a pivotal role in the global financial system. Being a pivotal institution, it needed to proactively push for reforms to create viable alternatives to ever-larger bailouts of the crisis-affected emerging markets. The crises and the following contagion effect have had a great deal of pernicious implications even for emerging economies that have sound fundamentals.

Managing international liquidity in such a manner that crises and contagions can be prevented would indeed reduce their adverse economic and social effects. Although this objective can be met by creating a lender of last resort or by making the IMF play this role, there are two reasons why existing institutional arrangements do not permit it. First, it would require surrendering economic autonomy by member countries of the IMF, a notion that is abhorrent to them so far. Second, the IMF is cash strapped. Its financial resources only make it feasible for it to arrange for or organize rescue packages for the crisis-affected emerging market economies. As of now, it cannot play the role of provider of required liquidity and prevent the march of contagions.

However, the IMF can play several salutary roles, both pre- and post-crisis. For one it can utilize its existing facilities to help those emerging markets that are – while not crisis stricken – facing macroeconomic difficulties that could at some later stage turn into crises through facilities such as the Compensatory and Contingency Financing Facility (CCFF). For instance, if an emerging market is facing an export price slump or export-demand-related problems, which could affect the whole economy if it remains unresolved, a facility such as CCFF can come to its rescue. Financial resources relative to this economy's quotas should be provided so that a potential crisis is stopped in its tracks. Second, by assisting an emerging market in this manner, the IMF can save it from falling a victim to a spreading contagion. The CCFF can be turned by the IMF into a low conditionality financing facility, which can be used at an early stage if the emerging market economy meets certain *ex ante* criteria. Whether or not these criteria are being met can be determined during the Article IV consultations. To dissuade economies to apply for low-conditionality loans without a pressing need, the IMF should make them available only at a higher interest rate than for the normal IMF resources and for a shorter term, which should be predetermined.

When a crisis situation develops in an emerging market that is otherwise following sound economic policies but is suffering from a short-term loss of investor confidence, the IMF can arrange for financial resources. As its own resources are limited, it will have to work in conjunction with the credit lines from creditor commercial banks.

This is the crisis aversion and resolution role of the IMF. While it cannot relinquish this task, it needs to strengthen its role as a monitor of economic management – or that of economic policeman. The IMF needs to closely monitor the operations of financial markets in the emerging market economies and ensure their conformity with the international financial norms. This would extend the role of the IMF to the private sector as well as to working with international committees of regulators. To this end, the following three initiatives in this area were underway in the IMF: (a) the preparation of the *Reports on the Observance of Standards and Codes*; (b) the preparation of the *Financial Sector Assessment Program*; and (c) the preparation of *Public Debt Management Guidelines* and a complementary *Practitioner's Manual* on the development of domestic markets for government debt.

The outcome of IMF's monitoring of the financial sector of the emerging market economy should be made public so that the policy makers in the economy and the global financial markets are aware of the progress or lack of it.

After a financial crisis strikes an emerging market economy, the IMF will need to take on the role of a proactive facilitator or co-ordinator of debt restructuring negotiations. This role is that of an "honest broker" between the creditors and debtors. Debt restructuring has been an inordinately onerous process for both the sides, which makes the honest broker's role highly significant. It would determine the success or failure of the negotiation process. If the IMF shows willingness to "lend into arrears," the two sides grow confident of coming to a reasonable agreement in a short time and the value of the assets of the emerging market economy does not hit rock-bottom after the crisis. Being a pivotal global financial institution, the IMF needs to be actively engaged in creating a standing committee of creditors as well as for "bailing in" of the lending banks. These endeavors seem to be a clear and viable alternative to the ever-larger bailouts.

Given the frequent episodes of instability on the one hand and the crucial role of the IMF in maintaining and enhancing the stability of the global financial system on the other hand, its resources need to be augmented. As the negotiations for quota increases are always protracted and painstaking, some rapid mechanisms need to be devised for this purpose. Three operations modes can be considered for this purpose. First, in a crisis situation the IMF should be able to access larger official resources than it can at present. Second, under the same set of circumstances it should be allowed to borrow from the financial markets. Third, under special circumstances and for special purpose it should also be allowed to create liquidity. This mechanism already exists. When more than one IMF member is suffering from a crisis or when there is a risk of a contagion or when there is systemic risk, the IMF should be able to create SDRs. As the creation of these SDRs is purpose specific, they should be cancelled as soon as borrowings are repaid to the IMF.

4.2. International codes of conduct

In a financially globalized world, a consensus on international codes of conduct in financial areas is indispensable. These international codes and standards cover corporate governance, accounting standards and financial supervision and regulation. Dissemination and transparency of financial information and data on financial affairs of governments, banks, and corporates are equally important for strengthening market discipline. Adherence to internally accepted disclosure norms influences financial allocation and channels capital flows away from borrowing entities that do not take adequate measures to preserve their financial stability. Adhering to international codes of conduct in these areas works as a preventive measure and minimizes the incidence of a crisis. As an old adage goes, "Prevention is the better part of cure." Some guidelines and regulations in these areas exist, which apparently were found to be inadequate during the spate of past crises. More comprehensive guidelines are being developed by several supranational institutions including the IMF, the World Bank, the Bank for International Settlements (BIS), the Organization for Economic Co-operation and Development (OECD), the International Organization of Securities Commissions (IOSCO) and other relevant institutions. Although some progress has been made in this task, much remains to be done.

It is easy to discern that all of the actionable areas enumerated in the preceding paragraph fall in the domestic domain of an emerging market economy. In section 1, I have stated that global financial stability and growth rests, *inter alia*, on robust national systems. When financial markets are integrated, global financial stability cannot be attained without domestic financial stability. The former is a precursor of the latter. Domestic financial stability can in turn be attained through the development and strengthening of appropriate institutional networks. In those cases where such a network is in place, it needs to be reformed to do its task effectively and efficiently. If these domestic institutions and arrangements are not supervised to maintain high standards of operations, to ensure a stable domestic financial environment would be difficult.

Likewise, the role of financial regulation and supervision in risk management in financial institutions is of crucial importance. Poorly managed banks and integration with the global financial market has been called a "combustible mix." Access to global financial resources inspires emerging market banks to take on excessive risk. For their part, the large foreign banks and investors feel enthused to provide capital because of the government guarantee given to these banks. Only proper risk-management practices and stringent prudential supervision can reduce this risk. Prudential supervision to compensate for shortcomings of banks' and corporates' risk-management practices are presupposed in a stable domestic financial system. Designing standards for financial regulation needs to go hand in hand with relevant global regulation and suprevision. To this end, there were recommendations for the creation of a new financial institution but this task can be managed cost-effectively without the creation of an excessive number of expensive international bodies. Supervision of adoption of international standards at the national level can be done by existing institutions such as the BIS and the IOSCO. However, creation of regional or sub-regional organizations for such supervision can indeed be considered.

In a financially integrated world where crises frequently turn contagious and create systemic shocks, the global community has a common interest and duty to each other in ensuring that all of the financially globalized economies adopt acceptable quality of domestic norms in these areas. Poor levels of adherence by some can cause serious problems for all of the members of the financially globalized community.

Can the international financial community see this as an intrusion into a country's internal affairs? Can the issue of sovereign rights be raised in this context? It has frequently been done in various quarters. However, Eichengreen (2003) disagrees with this line of logic and believes that the need for stability of global financial markets justifies ensuring that the domestic arrangements in all the enumerated areas are functional and maintain the required degree of efficiency. According to him, internationally recognized auditing and accounting practices, in whose absence global creditors will be unable to accurately assess the financial conditions of the banks and corporations to which they lend, should be extended to all of the emerging market economies. Also, adequate creditors' rights must be established in all of the emerging market economies so that creditors are able to monitor the economic and financial decisions of managers. Likewise, the international community needs to ensure that investor-protection laws have been enacted to prevent insider trading, market cornering and other financial malpractices. Different emerging market economies can satisfy "these desiderata in different ways, but in a world of capital market integration there is no avoiding the need to satisfy them."

The design of international codes and standards is as complex a process as the global financial system itself. The IMF took a good deal of initiative in this process. It conducted several studies of its own and those in collaboration with the Basel Committee, the BIS and the World Bank. This vindicates the earlier observation regarding the complexity of the process of devising international codes and standards. No one institution can claim to have the expertise or "human resources necessary to design and monitor compliance with detailed international standards in all the relevant areas" mentioned in this section. Also, the reform agenda is so large that no international organization has enough resources, knowledge or administrative capability to provide advice to the emerging market economies. Therefore, assistance of private sector bodies must also be sought in devising best practices and standards in these areas. The International Accounting Standards Committee (IASC), the International Federation of Accountants (IFA), the International Organization of Supreme Audit Institutions (IOSAI), the International Corporate Governance Network (ICGN) and the International Committee of National regulators or the Basel Committee can and should be called in to hold the hands of and collaborate with the international organization. These non-governmental bodies are essentially self-organizing and emerging market economies are members of most of them.

4.3. Autonomy of capital account

Capital account liberalization that took place in the emerging market economies was either done unilaterally or under the guidance of the Bretton Woods twins and the World Trade Organization (WTO). It is discussed at length in Chapter 3, particularly in sections 3 and 4. The hindsight is said to be 20/20 and in this case it reveals that capital account liberalization, when it is done abruptly and in a premature manner, without sufficiently reforming and strengthening the domestic financial system, can lead an emerging market economy into a crisis. Turning back to look at the experiences of the industrial economies, one observes that they had maintained considerably long periods of capital control after the Second World War, followed by gradual capital account liberalization. It is now widely recognized that having a strong domestic financial system, including an efficient regulatory and supervisory network, is a precondition for successful capital account liberalization.

As portfolio investment and short-term capital flows are characterized by instability, strong institutions and fundamentals are sometimes not enough to ward off a crisis when the maturity structure of borrowings is skewed towards the short term. Not only the magnitude but also the composition of inflows plays an essential role in determining the stability or vulnerability of the capital flows. Therefore, during the period of a surge in capital inflows, central banking authorities in emerging markets need to carefully watch (i) when to begin controlling the capital inflows, and (ii) what maturity of inflows should be discouraged. Chile-like reserve-requirements of short-term capital inflows has been greatly lauded by academics and policy mandarins alike. Such measures lengthen the maturity structure of the debt. In addition, they are considered to be market friendly measures, having least interference from the financial bureaucracy. Minimum-stay requirements or minimum-liquidity requirements can also be imposed on large investment banks, mutual funds and hedge funds during the periods of surge. Together they would dampen the volatility of trans-border capital flows. Based on this premise, a mechanism to ensure a reasonable maturity structure for external indebtedness, compatible with the export revenues, repatriated hard currency earnings and other macroeconomic variables, can be easily created as a complementary measure to ward off vulnerability.

4.4. Standstill provision

This is a post-crisis measure. After a crisis situation precipitates in an emerging market, in the past it helplessly faced financial chaos – such as capital flight, sharp exchange rate depreciation, and steep interest rate hike. Capital flight is exceedingly detrimental to the crisis-affected economy because it turns an illiquidity problem into an insolvency problem in a short period, exacerbating both the economic and the social cost of the crisis. Persistence of this situation is harmful for the global lenders as well because the probability of repayment of debt declines.

As this scenario has been observed frequently in the past, it is now believed that in a post-crisis situation, a standstill on external obligations and capital account convertibility would bring some order out of chaos. The next step is to bring the two sides, the creditors and debtor, to the negotiating table to reschedule the outstanding debt. Ideally, financial support to the crisis-affected economy should continue so that while negotiations for rescheduling are on, the economy continues to function. In this manner both the creditor and the debtor stand a better chance of resolving a difficult problem. The standstill provision works in favor of the creditors as well because it increases the probability of recovering a larger part of the value of their assets. To avoid the moral hazard on the part of the borrowers, the IMF should sanction the standstill exercise. It could then be combined with the IMF lending into arrears to make up for the liquidity needed by the economy during the debt-restructuring period.

4.5. Bailing-in the private sector

This is another post-crisis measure. In a financially globalizing world, something needs to be changed. In case of a financial crisis, global banks and other creditors should share in the burden of the crisis. It presently falls squarely on the shoulders of the taxpayers in the crisis-affected economy. Although it is difficult to ensure greater burden sharing by the creditors, efforts to do so have been underway for some time. So far no streamlined pattern has been designed for burden sharing, but there was no dearth of efforts in this regard and a case-by-case approach has been followed. It worked successfully in the cases of Korea, Pakistan and Ukraine in the past, but the three procedures were neither clear nor transparent. Therefore, these burden-sharing exercises earned low marks on international acceptability criterion. Consequently, the bailing-in approach is generally tried only in cases of small economies whose default is unlikely to threaten a systemic instability. It is indeed a prudent approach from a systemic point of view, but hardly an equitable approach. The global financial community needs more time and experience for developing minimum acceptable standards of clarity, transparency and equity in this regard.

5. Antidote for financial and macroeconomic instability

Faced with the potentially destabilizing effects of financial globalization, the emerging market economies have been trying to strengthen as well as harmonize their financial regulatory infrastructure in a concerted manner. As briefly referred to in the preceding chapter (see Chapter 5, section 5.2), financial and monetary authorities in the emerging market economies were aware of the need to import international best practices as well as to align domestic and international regulatory frameworks to avoid the destabilizing phenomenon of regulatory arbitrage. To this end, financial regulatory convergence was being undertaken – and is presently underway – in the emerging market economies.

It is set out in Chapter 4 (see section 5) that the entry of foreign banks and provision of financial services and products by them in the emerging market economies has not only increased market competition but also has had a disciplining effect over them. If the emerging market policy makers expect the entry of foreign banks, convergence in financial regulations across jurisdictions is essential for promoting integration with the global markets. The reverse is equally true; that is, convergence can also be a consequence of global financial integration. In the ultimate analysis it does not matter which way the causality works, as long as the convergence does take place. To attain the objectives of reduced systemic instability and for promoting financial integration with global markets, convergence in financial regulations is indispensable.

With acceleration in financial globalization during the past two decades, the relationship between financial integration and regulatory harmonization has become more intimate than ever before. So much so, that integration of financial products and services with financial regulatory frameworks is considered two different aspects of the same process – the ongoing globalization of finances. However, while the two aspects progress together, they do not generally have to move at the same pace. While market forces give a fillip to regulatory harmonization, this vitally important task should not be left to them alone because market forces and regulatory institutions often work at cross-purposes. "Coordination failures associated with market-led initiatives can generate negative systemic externalities, attracting capital towards regulated systems and institutions or generating forms of competition in laxity" that may eventually lead to financial and macroeconomic instability (Jordan and Majnoni, 2002).

Conventional wisdom is that development and diffusion of codes and standards of good practices begin in the real sector. The next stage is its spread to the financial sector. This implies that there is a relationship of diffusion and adoption of codes and standards of good practices with the level of development. At an early stage they apply to the real sector. Subsequently, as development proceeds they spread to the financial sector. This does not imply a shift of emphasis from the real to the financial sector. It is merely the result of considering the financial sector an instrument of economic integration.

The process of creation and diffusion of financial regulations has undergone discernible transformation over the past half century. Both governmental and non-governmental institutions conventionally set rules for the financial sector. The latter category includes technical bodies and supervisory authorities. Initially, governmental organizations and bodies laid down the regulations for co-operation among economies. This applied to both bilateral and multilateral co-operation. However, since the 1970s, non-governmental institutions began to lead the governmental institutions in the area of financial co-operation. Initiatives by technical and professional bodies increasingly began to pave the ground for action by the financial and monetary authorities. The first such initiative taken by a non-governmental technical body was the Basle Committee on Banking Supervisions (BCBS) created in 1975, in the aftermath of the Herstatt collapse in Germany. The basic objective of the BCBS was to underpin the supervision and co-ordination of banks that have widely spread international operations so that Herstatt-like crises did not recur.

The process of forging legal and regulatory instruments has also undergone a noticeable transformation. Initially, governments entered into treaties that entailed lengthy negotiations and ratification processes. This process was not only slow and inefficient but also incompatible with need of the world of finance, which moved at a rapid pace in developing new financial instruments. Necessity is the mother of invention. Non-governmental bodies were born to create codes, standards and rules of acceptable behavior. These regulations frameworks were different from the traditional treaties and were intended to shape the common behavior of the market participants without changing the legal frameworks. At the global level, since the mid-1980s several non-institutional informal groups such as G-3, G-5, G-7, G-10, G-20, G-22 and G-30 were created and functioned productively and efficiently. Of these, G-10 has remained continually and conspicuously active in formulating norms and putting forth financial regulations to bring the institutional and regulatory structure in line with the need of the financial world of the twenty-first century. The G-22 also responded to the needs of the time in an admirable manner and made valuable contribution when it was needed. The successful existence of these groups reflects the contributions they made to productive international co-operation in the area of international finance. During the contemporary period, the process of creation of new regulatory frameworks as well as harmonization took a markedly different route from that of the past.[6]

There are different modes of regulatory harmonization. Forming a monetary union is one oft-utilized government-induced mode. Regulatory harmonization has also worked in those parts of the globe where one or two large and successful economies have exerted gravitational pull for the neighboring economies. In such cases, the large

[6] See Jordan and Majnoni (2002), and Jordan and Lubrano (2002), for more detailed discussion of these issues.

economy works as a catalyst and initiates the process of regulatory alignment for the other neighboring economies to follow. The experiences of regions that have followed these modes demonstrated that adopting the principle of minimum harmonization reduced the difficulties of creating a top-down harmonization system. This principle has had immense utility for the global financial integration process in the recent past. In addition, market mechanism has made a great deal of contribution by successfully developing and enforcing financial standards through what is called the "reputational disciplines." These market-determined standards are set and maintained by large dominant institutions that have long-established reputations. The principle of minimum harmonization and the reputationally induced disciplines have been the most important pillars of the current episode of financial globalization. These two principles have played a greater role than the standards and codes of financial regulation (Jordan and Lubrano, 2002).

These two principles became instantly popular for three reasons. First, together these principles reflect both regulatory discipline and functionality of a market. Little wonder they appealed to both market regulators and market players. Second, their generality made them attractive to economies with different economic history and levels of economic growth. Third, the most important trait of these two principles was their conceptual simplicity and elegance.

However, it should be noted that they did not present a novel approach. They were part of a system of law that followed the practice of having norms that did not have the binding force of legislation.[7] Such conventions have been christened "soft law" due to a lack of a codified procedure for their definition and enforcement (Giovanoli, 2001). In national legal systems, soft law amounted to adoption of codes of best practices prevalent at an international level and accepted by a group of large countries. They are non-binding and voluntary in nature and referred to as "codes of conduct," "guidelines" or "recommendations" but their systemic acceptance is wide, effective and consequential.[8]

---

[7] The system of English Common Law is one of the best examples of this kind of legal arrangement. The Basle Committee on Banking Supervision (BCBS), or simply the Basle Committee, is a committee of central bankers and bank supervisors/regulators from the major industrialized countries that meets every three months at the Bank for International Settlements in Basle. It consists of senior supervisory representatives from Belgium, Canada, France, Germany, Italy, Japan, Luxembourg, the Netherlands, Sweden, Switzerland, the United Kingdom, and the United States.

[8] For a thorough discussion on these two principles, see Giovanoli (2001).

5.1. The new Basle Accord

In 1998, the BCBS created what became known as "the Basle 1988 Accord."[9] The business of banking, particularly risk management practices, supervisory approaches, and financial markets have undergone considerable expansion and transformation since then. To be sure, financial markets have become far more globalized since 1988. Therefore, the BCBS presented a proposal to replace the 1988 accord with a more flexible and risk-sensitive framework in January 2001. It has been called "the New Basle Capital Accord" (BCBS, 2001a).

It is perhaps the best example of developing a set of highly successful financial norms and standards during the recent period (Barth *et al.*, 2001; Powell, 2002). Although they were designed for the internationally active banks in the G-10 economies,[10] by early 2003 more than one hundred countries claimed adherence to the Basle 1988 Accord and now the New Basle Capital Accord has received the same reception from the central bankers and regulators/ supervisors. Some central banks apply these standards to all banks. The first set of proposals under the New Basle Accord was published in January 2001. Before developing the new framework and submitting these proposals, the BCBS consulted with banking supervisors all over the world. Several studies and surveys are planned. Their results are awaited. The final version of the Accord is scheduled to be completed by the fourth quarter of 2003, allowing for adoption of the new accord framework in 2004 (BCBS, 2002).

The 1988 Accord focused on the total amount of bank capital, which is vital in reducing the risk of bank insolvency and the potential cost of a bank's failure for depositors. The new framework essentially builds on this premise, but it takes into account the current developments in the global banking services industry. It endeavors to improve safety and soundness in the financial system by "placing more emphasis on banks' own internal control and management, the supervisory review process and market discipline." In addition, the 1988 Accord provided only one

---

[9] The Basle Committee on Banking Supervision (BCBS), or simply the Basle Committee, is a committee of central bankers and bank supervisors/regulators from 12 industrialized countries that meets every three months at the Bank for International Settlements in Basle. It consists of senior supervisory representatives from Belgium, Canada, France, Germany, Italy, Japan, Luxembourg, the Netherlands, Sweden, Switzerland, the United Kingdom, and the United States.

[10] The Group of Ten or G-10 presently (in 2003) has 11 members, although the name G-10 persists. These 11 members are Belgium, Canada, France, Germany, Italy, Japan, the Netherlands, Sweden, Switzerland, the United Kingdom and the United States.

option for measuring the appropriate regulatory capital level of internationally active banks. However, the best ways to measure, manage and mitigate risks, vary from bank to bank. Therefore, banks need to be provided with flexibility on this count. An amendment in this area was introduced in 1996, and this focused on trading risks and allowed some banks to use their own system to measure their market risks for the first time. The new framework proposals go a step further than the 1996 amendment, and include a spectrum of approaches. They range from simple to advanced methodologies for the measurement of both credit risk and operational risk in determining regulatory capital levels. They also link risk andregulatory capital for internationally active banks (BCBS, 2001a; 2001b).

The New Basle Capital Accord essentially takes an internal rating-based (IRB) approach. It raises the question whether or not the IRB approach would lead to significant changes in regulatory capital requirements and affect the spreads for the banks that lend to the emerging market economies. The answer to this concern is that banks with a greater than average risk appetite would find their capital requirements increasing, and vice versa. The intention of the Accord is to leave broadly unchanged the capital requirement for an average risk portfolio. It is expected that the Accord will enhance the soundness of the financial system by aligning regulatory capital requirements to the underlying risks in the banking business as well as by encouraging better risk management by banks. The overall impact of the new Accord is expected to enhance market discipline. It has been proposed that for the purpose of sovereign lending, internationally active banks should develop internal ratings according to an S&P or Moody's scale and capital charges should be levied according to the corresponding weights assigned by the standard approach. Although denied by the BCBS, there is a possibility that implementation of the new Accord in the G-10 economies could affect the cost of capital in the emerging market economies.

The new framework of proposals rests on three "pillars." The first pillar sets out minimum regulatory capital requirements. It maintains both the existing definition of regulatory capital and minimum requirement of 8 percent of capital to risk-weighted assets. The revised version of the Accord focuses on improvements in the measurement of risks. The credit risk measurements in the new Accord are more elaborate than those in the current version. For the first time, the new framework proposes a measure for operation risk, while the market risk measure remains unchanged. For the measurement of credit risk, two principal options have been proposed. The first is the standard approach, and the second the IRB approach, referred to above.

The supervisory review process is the second pillar of the new framework. It requires supervisors to ensure that each bank has sound internal processes in place to assess the adequacy of its capital based on thorough evaluation of its risks. The new framework stresses the importance of bank management developing an internal capital assessment process and setting targets for capital that are commensurate with the bank's particular risk profile. Supervisors' responsibility is to evaluate how well banks are assessing their regulatory capital adequacy needs *relative to their risks*. There is emphasis on the risk profile of the lending banks and the supervision process should ensure that it is being taken into account while computing the adequacy of capital. The implementation of the new set of proposals will require a much more detailed dialogue between supervisors and banks.

The third pillar of the new framework aims at bolstering market discipline through enhanced disclosure by banks. Effective disclosure is essential to ensure that market participants can better understand banks' risk profiles and the adequacy of their capital positions. The new framework sets out disclosure requirements in several areas, including the way a bank calculates its capital adequacy and its risk management methods (BCBS, 2001a; 2001b).

6. Exchange rate policies and financial globalization

The exchange rate regime is an important facet of global financial architecture. The choice of an exchange rate regime is vital in determining the stability of an emerging market economy in a globalized financial market. As textbooks report, the Mundellian trilemma or "impossible trinity" has three policy strands: (i) free capital mobility; (ii) a fixed or stable nominal exchange rate; and (iii) an autonomous monetary policy – only two of which could coexist.[11] During the Bretton Woods period (1945–71) the economic and political environment was not conducive to rapid trans-border capital flows. During this period, the large economies of Europe were engrossed in postwar reconstruction with the help of the Marshall Plan formulated by the United States.[12] They

---

[11] Obstfeld and Taylor (2002) have tried to interpret the various periods of globalization in terms of the Mundellian "impossible trinity."

[12] The Truman Administration announced the Marshall Plan for European Recovery in June 1947. It covered almost all of the European nations outside of the Soviet bloc. The two exceptions were Franco's Spain, and Germany. It has gone down as the most successful economic assistance program ever formulated or implemented. Many European economies had returned to the prewar levels of production, or near it, by the end of 1950.

needed the autonomy of monetary policy to achieve their domestic reconstruction objective. As capital flows did not start until quite late during this period, the other policy strand that came to these economies, as a residual, was adoption of the stability in exchange rates. However, the strategic priorities of the post-Bretton Woods era were different. Of the three Mundellian conditions, autonomous monetary policy to achieve domestic objectives and free capital mobility were the favored choices of this period. Therefore, exchange rate stability had to be given up in favor of capital mobility and when this received affirmation from the policy makers, financial globalization began to progress during the post-Bretton Woods era.

The process of financial globalization created many exchange-rate-related problems for the emerging market economies.[13] Many of these were based on the fact that financial markets, both domestic and international, in general are far from perfect. Financial market imperfections include incomplete markets, asymmetric information, noise trading, bubbles, herding behavior, multiple equilibria, moral hazard and contagion. Together they make an impressive (or unimpressive) litany of malaise. Problems such as incomplete markets apply more to the domestic financial markets, while those such as asymmetric information plague the global financial system more.

While the post-Bretton Woods pursuance of autonomy in the domestic monetary policy and free capital mobility worked reasonably well for the industrial economies, the same cannot be said about the emerging markets, which frequently faced torrid conditions in this arena. They tried adopting a range of exchange rate arrangements but in many cases it was with only limited success. Consequently, these economies were bruised by frequent crises. The range of exchange rate arrangements they covered included soft peg, hard peg, crawls, stationary bands, moving banks, flexible exchange rate system, currency boards and dollarization. Of late, several emerging market economies have demonstrated a preference for the flexible exchange rate system. Although the popularity of this arrangement has been on the rise, the emerging market economies that adopted it have displayed an overly cautious attitude in practising it. These economies have shown that even after opting for a flexible exchange rate, they want to restrict the currency value movements in practice. Consequently, they are not able to benefit from an autonomous monetary policy (Larrain and Velasco, 2001; Calvo and Reinhart, 2002).

---

[13] See, for instance, Chang and Velasco (2000); Bordo *et al.* (2001); Aghion *et al.*(2001); Calvo (2002); and Calvo and Reinhart (2002).

The emerging market economies not only did not benefit from all the possible advantages of financial globalization but also were bruised by currency, banking and debt crises, or the so-called triple crises. The recent (2002–03) crises in Ecuador and Argentina had all three elements (Bordo *et al.*, 2001). Global market financial flows into the emerging market economies were far from steady. They were not able to follow counter-cyclical monetary policy, and could not take advantage of consumption smoothening, deepening and diversification of their domestic financial markets, discernable reduction in the cost of capital, and significant augmentation of capital and domestic investment. Thus, the benefits of financial globalization to emerging markets have so far been far from optimal (Mishkin, 2001).

Eichengreen (2003) believed that in a rapidly globalizing economy, the pursuit of a flexible exchange rate policy is helpful for an emerging market economy. This regime encourages banks and corporates not to rely excessively on short-term unhedged foreign debts. In a flexible exchange rate regime, economic agents remain eager to hedge their foreign currency exposures. Conversely, a pegged exchange rate provides an incentive to economic agents for accumulating unhedged foreign currency debts. To defend the peg, the central bank is forced to carry on the drumbeat that the status quo will be maintained and that the peg will not change. Given this background, hedging becomes an expensive and redundant measure. As opposed to this, when the exchange rate is flexible and financial transactions involving foreign currency are hedged, large and unexpected variations in exchange rate do not create financial havoc for the banks and corporates by increasing the cost of servicing of short-term debts. A sharp currency depreciation would not become a financial crash as it did for some of the Asian economies during the period of the Asian crisis.

De la Torre *et al.* (2002) take this argument a step farther than Eichengreen (2003) and posit that in the contemporary era of financial globalization emerging market economies need the "blessed trinity" to ward off the triple crises (see Chapter 3, section 1.1 also). Their concept of the blessed trinity includes: (i) a strong currency, if possible international; (ii) flexible exchange rate; and (iii) sound institutions. If the "blessed trinity" is achieved, the economies can integrate well with the global capital markets and take advantage of all of the potential benefits. The reverse of the "blessed trinity" apparently is having a weak currency, an overly cautious floating system and weak institutions. When this combination exists, economies not only are not able to integrate well with the global financial markets but also become vulnerable to the triple crises.

Of the three characteristics of the blessed trinity, the first is the most onerous and time-consuming to achieve. While a flexible exchange rate having a credible float and sound institutions is achievable in a relatively shorter period by a set of knowledgeable policy makers who know their job, the process of creating a strong currency which has an international stature – one that is accepted as a store of value both at home and abroad – takes time and constant endeavors. Credible macro-economic policies contribute to and support the international stature of a currency. In particular, the fiscal policy of the currency issuing country has to be balanced and devoid of any shade of profligacy, so that issuer solvency is never called into question. An emerging market that has succeeded in achieving the blessed trinity can integrate successfully into imperfect global financial markets without difficulty because "the component of the trinity interact in virtuous ways to control the risks of financial globalization while maximizing its benefits."

7. Conclusions and summing-up

Robert Rubin first used the inapt metaphor "international financial architecture." It was subsequently adopted by the academic and policy-making community and has since survived in the academic writings on this issue as a part of accepted jargon. It was inapt because the global financial system was not quite an architect's blueprint. If anything, it is an excellent example of what the Japanese call *kaizen*. There is no widely agreed definition of what precisely constitutes global financial architecture. It refers broadly to the framework and set of institutions, structures and measures that can help prevent crises, or when faced with one help manage them better in the more integrated international financial environment.

Over the past half-century, the principal characteristics of the global financial system have undergone radical, if somewhat gradual, transformation. There has been an inevitable and desirable evolution in it, a transformation "from an administered or *government-led* to a decentralized or *market-led system.*" However, with the passage of time, and with the changing demands on the system, the administered system revealed its weaknesses. During 1971–73, piece-by-piece the old administered or *government-led* financial system collapsed. No attempts were made to mend or recreate the old system after the 1973 oil shock, when the price of crude oil quadrupled. With this, the global financial system passed a critical stage in its evolutionary phase – decentralized or market-led system evolved in place of the old system. Under the new system, the financial markets acted swiftly and imaginatively to create new and a progressively wide range of instruments. This was their contribution to the completeness of the financial markets, indeed without making them fully complete.

Market disequilibria and volatility have been and continue to be inherent to the functioning of post-Bretton Woods global financial markets. Information asymmetries frequently give rise to overshooting, sharp market corrections, and often crises. With rapid globalization of capital flows and portfolios, sophistication and dynamism of the finan-cial world has increased enormously. The institutional and regulatory machinery was not able to keep pace with it, resulting in frequent mal-functioning in the global financial system, which manifested itself in volatility.

The global financial system is an organic whole. Hence, any reform plan would require collective action at the global level. There is a press-ing need for fundamental and comprehensive reform of its the various facets. The basic objective of reform is for the global monetary and financial order to harness the potential of global private financial flows in such a way that they contribute to the stability and growth in the global economy. Given the background of volatility, thoughtful, prag-matic and concerted action is required from the global community in this regard, particularly from the matured G-7 economies. The G-22 is another important and relevant forum for this purpose, and which can make enormous long-term contribution.

There was never a shortage of proposals and novel ideas for the reforms of the global financial system. They came thick and fast from both public and private sources. Notwithstanding the obstacles, given the significance and far-reaching implications of the issue, the global community has not been passive about it. Several initiatives to reform and strengthen the global financial architecture are presently underway. One thoughtful scheme identified four immediate areas for strengthen-ing the global financial system – (i) international standards; (ii) market-friendly (or Chilean style) taxes on short-term capital inflow; (iii) greater exchange rate flexibility; and (iv) collective-action clauses in loan contracts to create an alternative to ever-bigger IMF bailouts.

The areas that call for immediate attention are the role of the Bretton Woods twins, particularly that of the IMF, and the international codes of conduct. In a financially globalized world, a consensus on interna-tional codes of conduct in financial areas is indispensable. These international codes and standards cover corporate governance, account-ing standards and financial supervision and regulation. The third important area is capital account liberalization. Hindsight reveals that capital account liberalization, when it is done abruptly and in a premature manner, without sufficiently reforming and strengthening the domestic financial system, can lead an emerging market economy to a crisis. Fourth, is adoption of post-crisis measures such as standstill provisions and bailing in the private sector. In a financially globalizing world, something needs to be changed. When a financial crisis strikes, the global banks and other creditors should share in the burden of the crisis. It presently falls squarely on the shoulders of taxpayers in the crisis-affected economy.

Faced with the potentially destabilizing effects of financial globalization, the emerging market economies have tried to strengthen as well as harmonize their financial regulatory infrastructure in a concerted manner. This could be an antidote to a crisis. Financial and monetary authorities in the emerging market economies were aware of the need to import international best practices as well as align domestic and international regulatory frameworks to avoid the destabilizing phenomenon of regulatory arbitrage. The process of creation per se and diffusion of financial regulations has undergone discernible transformation over the past half century. Both governmental and non-governmental institutions conventionally set rules for the financial sector. The role of the latter category expanded during the 1990s.

The process of creation and diffusion of financial regulations has undergone discernible transformation over the past half century; particularly many new developments took place in this area during the past two decades. The same observation applies to the process of forging legal and regulatory instruments. Non-governmental bodies were born to create codes, standards and rules of acceptable behavior. They took over what was considered the domain of the governments in the past. Two of the modes of convergence of regulatory harmonization that came into vogue during the past two decades were: the principle of minimum harmonization and the reputationally induced disciplines. They have been the most important pillars of the current episode of financial globalization.

The BCBS created what became known as "the Basle 1988 Accord." The business of banking, particularly risk management practices, supervisory approaches, and financial markets have undergone considerable expansion and transformation since then. To be sure, financial markets have become far more globalized since 1988. Therefore, the BCBS presented a proposal to replace the 1988 Accord with a more flexible and risk-sensitive framework in January 2001. It has been called "the New Basle Capital Accord." It is perhaps the best example of the development of a set of highly successful financial norms and standards during the recent period. Although designed for the internationally active banks in the G-10 economies, by early 2003 more than one hundred countries claimed adherence to the Basle Accord.

The exchange rate regime is an important facet of global financial architecture. The choice of an exchange rate regime is vital for the determination of the stability of an emerging market economy in a globalized financial market. During the post-Bretton Woods era, emerging market economies have been unable to benefit optimally from financial globalization because the process of financial globalization created many exchange rate-related problems. Many of these problems came about because financial markets, both domestic and international, are far from perfect. Although emerging markets tried to adopt a range of exchange rate arrangements, in many cases it was with only limited success and these economies continued to be bruised by crises. Flexible exchange rate arrangements have become popular among these economies. However, monetary authorities in the emerging markets tended to apply it in an overly cautious manner in practice and therefore are unable to benefit from the autonomy of monetary policy. The concept of the "blessed trinity" promises improvements in their exchange rate arrangements. It entails having (i) a strong international currency; (ii) flexible exchange rate; and (iii) sound institutions. If the "blessed trinity" is achieved, the emerging markets can integrate well with the global capital markets and take advantage of all the potential benefits, without falling prey to the triple crises. Of the three characteristics of the blessed trinity, the first is the most onerous and time-consuming to achieve.

References

Aghion, P., P. Bachetta and A. Banergee, 2001, "Currency Crises and Monetary Policy in an Economy with Credit Constraints," *European Economic Review*, Vol. 45, No. 7, 1121–50.

Barth, J.R., G. Caprio and R. Levine, 2001, "The Regulation and Supervision of Banks around the World: A New Database," Washington, DC: World Bank, February (mimeo).

Basle Committee on Banking Supervision (BCBS), 2001a, "The New Basle Capital Accord: An Explanatory Note", Basle: Bank for International Settlements, January.

Basle Committee on Banking Supervision (BCBS), 2001b, "Consultative Document: The New Basle Capital Accord", Basle: Bank for International Settlements, January.

Basle Committee on Banking Supervision (BCBS), 2002, "An Overview of the New Basle Capital Accord", Basle: Bank for International Settlements, July.

Blinder, A.S., 2003, A New Global Financial Order: The Art of the Possible", in Dilip K. Das (ed.), *An International Finance Reader*, London and New York. Routledge, pp. 104–13.

Bordo, M., B. Eichengreen, D. Klingebiel and M.S. Martinez-Peria, 2001, Financial Crises: Lessons from the Past 120 Years", *Economic Policy*, Vol., No. 110–36.

Calvo, G.A., 2002, "Globalization Hazard and Weak Government in Emerging Markets", Washington, DC: Inter-American Development Bank, working paper, February.

Calvo, G.A. and C. Reinhart, 2002, "Fear of Floating", *Quarterly Journal of Economics*, Vol. 117, No. 379–408.

Chang, R. and A. Velasco, 2000, "Liquidity Crises in Emerging Markets: Theory and Policy", Cambridge, MA: National Bureau of Economic Research, Working Paper No. 7272.

Crockett, A., 2003, "Strengthening the International Financial Architecture", in Dilip K. Das (ed.), *An International Finance Reader*, London and New York: Routledge, pp. 87–103.

De la Torre, A., E.L. Yeyati and S.L. Schmukler, 2002, "Financial Globalization: Unequal Blessings", Washington, DC: World Bank, Policy Research Working Paper No. 2903, October.

Eichengreen, B., 2003, "Strengthening the International Financial Architecture", in Dilip K. Das (ed.), *An International Finance Reader*, London and New York: Routledge, pp. 65–86.

Giovanoli, M., 2001, "A New Architecture for the Global Financial Market: Legal Aspects of International financial Standard Setting", Basle: International Monetary Law Association.

Jordan, C. and M. Labrano, 2002, "Strengthening Financial Sector Governance in Emerging Market Economies", Washington, DC: Brookings Institution, Policy Brief No. 12.

Jordan, C. and G. Majnoni, 2002, "Financial Regulatory Harmonization and the Globalization of Finance", Washington, DC: World Bank, Policy Research Working Paper No. 2919, October.

Larrain, P. and A. Velasco, 2001, "Exchange Rate Policy in Emerging Markets: The Case for Floating", *Essays in International Economics*, No. 224, December.

Mishkin, F., 2001, "Financial Policies and Prevention of Financial Crises", in M. Feldstein (ed.), *Economic and Financial Crises in Emerging Market Countries*, Chicago: University of Chicago Press, pp. 134–60.

Obstfeld, M. and A.M. Taylor, 2002, "Globalization and Capital Markets", Cambridge, MA: National Bureau of Economic Research, Working Paper No. 8846, March.

Powell, A., 2002, "A Capital Accord for Emerging Economies?", March, available at <http://econ.worldbank.org/files/13169_wps2808.pdf.>

Bibliography

Abreu, M., 1996, "Trade in Manufactures: the Outcome of the Uruguay Round and Developing Country Interests", in W. Martin and L.A. Winters (eds), *The Uruguay Round and the Developing Countries*, Cambridge: Cambridge University Press.

Abu-Lughod, J., 1989, *Before European Hegemony: The World System AD 1250–1350*, Oxford and New York: Oxford University Press.

Agenor, P.R., 2002, "Benefits and Costs of International Financial Integration: Theory and Facts", Washington, DC: World Bank, Policy Research Working, Paper No. 2788, February.

Agenor, P.R., 2003, "Does Globalization Hurt the Poor?", January 7 (unpublished paper).

Aghion, P., P. Bachetta and A. Banergee, 2001, "Currency Crises and Monetary Policy in an Economy with Credit Constraints", *European Economic Review*, Vol. 45, No. 7, 1121–50.

Anderson, J.E. and E. van Wincoop, 2001, "Gravity with Gravitas: A Solution to the Border Puzzle", Cambridge, MA: National Bureau of Economic Research, Working Paper No. 8079. Revised version available at <www.virginia.edu./~econ/vanwincoopx.htm>.

Anderson, K., J. Francois, T. Hertel, B. Hoekman and W. Martin, 2001, "Potential Gains from Trade Reforms in the New Millennium", Washington, DC: World Bank.

Andrea, G. and J. Court, 2002, "Inequality, Growth and Poverty in the Era of Liberalization and Globalization", Helsinki: United Nations University, World Institute for Development Economic Research, Policy Brief No. 4.

Bakker, A.F.P., 1996, *The Liberalization of Capital Movements in Europe 1958–94*, Dordrecht: Kluwer Academic Publishers.

Baldwin, R.E. and P. Martin, 1999, "Two Waves of Globalization: Superficial Similarities, Fundamental Differences", Cambridge, MA: National Bureau of Economic Research, Working Paper No. 6904.

Baldwin, R.E. and A.J. Venables, 1995, "Regional Economic Integration", in G. Grossman and K. Rogoff (eds), *Handbook of International Economics*, Amsterdam: Elsevier Science, pp. 1597–1634.

Ball, L., 2000, "Policy Rules and External Shocks", Cambridge, MA: National Bureau of Economic Research, Working Paper No. 7910.

Barquet, N. and P. Domingo, 1997, "Smallpox: The Triumph Over the Most Terrible of the Ministers of Death", *Annals of Internal Medicines*, October 15, 636–8.

Barro, R.J., 1991, "Economic Growth in Cross-Section of Countries", *Quarterly Journal of Economics*, Vol. 106, No. 2, 407–43.

Barth, J.R., G. Caprio and R. Levine, 2001, "The Regulation and Supervision of Banks around the World: A New Database", Washington, DC: World Bank, February (mimeo).

Basle Committee on Banking Supervision (BCBS), 2001, "The New Basle Capital Accord: An Explanatory Note", Basle: Bank for International Settlements, January.

Basle Committee on Banking Supervision (BCBS), 2001, "Consultative Document: The New Basle Capital Accord", Basle: Bank for International Settlements, January.

Basle Committee on Banking Supervision (BCBS), 2002, "An Overview of the New Basle Capital Accord", Basle: Bank for International Settlements, July.

Beine, M., F. Docquier and H. Rapoport, 2001, "Brain Drain and Economic Growth: Theory and Evidence", *Journal of Development Economics*, Vol. 64, No. 1, 275–89.

Blinder, A.S., 2003, A New Global Financial Order: "The Art of the Possible", in Dilip K. Das (ed.), *An International Finance Reader*, London and New York: Routledge, pp. 104–13.

Bordo, M.D., 1993, "The Bretton Woods International Monetary System: A Historical Overview", in M.D. Bordo and B.J. Eichengreen (eds), *A Retrospective on the Bretton Woods System: Lessons for International Monetary Reforms*, Chicago: University of Chicago Press, pp. 160–95.

Bordo, M.D., M. Edelstein and H. Rockoff, 1999, "Was Adherence to Gold Standard a 'Good Housekeeping Seal of Approval' During the Interwar Period?", Cambridge, MA: National Bureau of Economic Research, Working Paper No. 7186, June.

Bordo, M.D., B. Eichengreen, D. Klingebiel and M.S. Martinez-Peria, 2001, "Financial Crises: Lessons from the Past 120 Years", *Economic Policy*, April, Vol. 45, No. 4, 110–36.

Bordo, M.D. and B.J. Eichengreen, 1998, "Implications of the Great Depression for the Development of the International Monetary System", in M.D. Bordo, C. Goldin and E.N. White (eds), *The Defining Moment: The Great Depression and the American Economy in the Twentieth Century*, Chicago: University of Chicago Press, pp. 212–42.

Bourguignon, F. and C. Morrisson, 2001, "Inequality Among World Citizens: 1820–1992", Working Paper No. 2001–25, Paris: THEMA et DELTA.

Brash, D.T., 2000, "How Should Monetary Policy Makers Respond to the New Challenges of Global Economic Integration?", paper presented at the symposium on *Global Economic Integration: Opportunities and Challenges*, sponsored by the Federal Reserve Bank of Kansas, at Jackson Hole, Wyoming, August 24–26.

Buiter, W.H., 2000, "The New Economy and Old Monetary Economics", London: Bank of England, discussion paper.

Calvo, G.A., 2002, "Globalization Hazard and Weak Government in Emerging Markets", Washington, DC: Inter-American Development Bank, working paper, February.

Calvo, G.A. and C. Reinhart, 2002, "Fear of Floating", *Quarterly Journal of Economics*, Vol. 117, No. 2, 379–408.

Cameron, R.E., 1993, *A Concise Economic History of the World*, New York: Oxford University Press.

Cannadine, D., 1990, *Decline and Fall of the British Aristocracy*, New Haven, CT: Yale University Press.

Centre for International Economics (CIE), 2001, *Globalization and Poverty: Turning the Corner*, Canberra: CIE.

Chang, R. and A. Velasco, 2000, "Liquidity Crises in Emerging Markets: Theory and Policy", Cambridge, MA: National Bureau of Economic Research, Working Paper No. 7272.

Citrin, D. and S. Fischer, 2000, "Meeting the Challenges of Globalization in the Advanced Economies", in H. Wagner (ed.), *Globalization and Unemployment*, Berlin: Springer, pp. 19–35.

Claessens, S., D. Klingebiel and S. Schmukler, 2001, "The Future of Stock Markets in Emerging Economies", Washington, DC: World Bank (mimeo).

Clarida, R., J. Gali and M. Gertler, 1999, "The Science of Monetary Policy: A New Keynesian Perspective", *Journal of Economic Literature*, Vol. 37, No. 2, 1661–1707.

Clark, X., D. Dollar and A. Kraay, 2001, "Decomposing Global Inequality, 1960–99", Washington, DC: World Bank.

Coe, T.D., A. Subramanian and N.T. Tamirisa, 2002, "The Missing Globalization Puzzle", Washington, DC: International Monetary Fund, Working Paper No. WP/02/171.

Collier, P. and J.W. Gunning, 1999, "Explaining African Economic Performance", *Journal of Economic Literature*, Vol. 37, No. 2, 64–111.

Cordell, T. and I. Grilo, 1998, "Globalization and Relocation in a Vertically Differentiated Industry", Washington, DC: International Monetary Fund, Working Paper No. WP/98/48, April.

Crafts, N.F.R., 1985, *British Economic Growth During the Industrial Revolution*, Oxford: Clarendon Press.

Crafts, N.F.R., 2000, "Globalization and Growth in the Twentieth Century", Washington, DC: International Monetary Fund, Working Paper No. WP/00/44. March.

Crockett, A., 2000, "How should Financial Market Regulators Respond to the New Challenges of Global Economic Integration?", in *Global Economic Integration: Opportunities and Challenges*, Kansas City, KA: Federal Reserve Bank of Kansas City, pp. 130–65.

Crockett, A., 2003, "Strengthening the International Financial Architecture", in Dilip K. Das (ed.), *An International Finance Reader*, London and New York: Routledge, pp. 87–103.

Crosby, A., 1972, *The Columbian Exchange: Biological and Cultural Consequences of 1492*, London: Greenwood Press.

Daianu, D., 2002, "Is Catching-Up Possible in Europe?", Warsaw: Leon Kozminski Academy of Entrepreneurship and Management, Transformation Integration and Globalization Economic Research (TIGER), Working Paper Series No. 19, May.

Daly. M. and H. Kuwahara, 1998, "The Impact of the Uruguay Round on Tariff and Non-Tariff Barriers to trade in the Quad", *World Economy*, Vol. 21, No. 2, 207–34.

Das, Dilip K., 1986, *Migration of Financial Resources to Developing Countries*, London: Macmillan.

Das, Dilip K., 1989, "Brady Plan and the International Banks: A Cautious Reception", *Business Standard*, Bombay, August 24, p. 6.

Das, Dilip K., 1990, *International Trade Policy*, London: Macmillan.

Das, Dilip K., 1991, *Korean Economic Dynamism*, London: Macmillan.

Das, Dilip K., 1991, *Import Canalisation*, London: Sage.

Das, Dilip K., 1996, *The Asia-Pacific Economy*, London: Macmillan and New York: St Martin's Press.

Das, Dilip K., 2000, "Portfolio Investment in Emerging Market Economies: Trends, Dimensions and Issues", *Journal of Asset Management*, September, Vol. 3, No. 3, 144–82.

Das, Dilip K., 2001, "Stimulants to Capital Inflows into Emerging Markets and the Recent Role of Speculators", *Journal of International Development*, January, Vol. 18, No. 1, 32–64.

Das, Dilip K., 2001, "Liberalization Efforts in China and Accession to the World Trade Organization", *Journal of World Investment*, Vol. 2, No. 4, 761–89.

Das, Dilip K., 2001, *China's Accession to the World Trade Organization: Issues and Implications*, Canberra: Australian National University, Asia Pacific School of Economics and Management, Working Paper No. EA01–1; available at <http://ncdsnet.anu.edu.au>, July 2001, 41 pp.

Das, Dilip K., 2001, *Global Trading System at the Crossroads: A Post-Seattle Perspective*, London and New York: Routledge.

Das, Dilip K., 2003, *Financial Globalization and Emerging Market Economies*, London and New York: Routledge (forth coming)

Davidson, C. and S. Matusz, 2001, "Globalization, Employment and Income: Analyzing the Adjustment Process", Nottingham: University of Nottingham, Leverhulme Centre for Research on Globalization and Economic Policy, Research Paper 2001/04.

Davis, L.E. and R.E. Gallman, 2001, *Evolving Financial Markets and Capital Flows: Britain, the Americas and Australia, 1870–1914*, Japan–US Center, Sanwa Monograph on International Financial Markets, Cambridge: Cambridge University Press.

De la Torre, A., E.L. Yeyati and S.L. Schmukler, 2002, "Financial Globalization: Unequal Blessings", Washington, DC: World Bank, Policy Research Working Paper No. 2903, October.

Diaz-Alejandro, C.F., 1983, "Stories of the 1930 for the 1980s", in P. Aspe, R. Dornbusch and M. Obstfeld (eds), *Financial Policies and the World Capital Markets*, Chicago: University of Chicago Press.

Dollar, D. and A. Kraay, 2001, "Trade, Growth and Poverty", Washington, DC: World Bank, Policy Research Working Paper No. 2199.

The Economist, 2001, "Enter the Dragon", March 10, pp. 21–24.

The Economist, 2002, "Survey on E-Commerce: Shopping Around the Web", February 26.

Eichengreen, B.J., 1992, *Golden Fetters: The Gold Standard and the Great Depression*, Oxford: Oxford University Press.

Eichengreen, B.J., 1992, "Trends and Cycles in Foreign Lending", in H. Siebert (ed.), *Capital Flows in the World Economy*, Tübingen: Mohr.

Eichengreen, B., 2003, "Strengthening the International Financial Architecture", in Dilip K. Das (ed.), *An International Finance Reader*, London and New York: Routledge, pp. 65–86.

Engel, C. and J.H.Rogers, 2001, "Deviations from Purchasing Power Parity: Causes and Welfare Costs", *Journal of International Economics*, Vol. 55, No. 10, 29–57.

Environics, 2001, "Poll Findings Suggest Trouble Ahead for Global Agenda: Survey of 20,000"; available at <http://environicsinternational.com>, September.

Faini, R., J. de Melo and K. Zimmermann, 1999, *Migration: The Controversies and the Evidence*, Cambridge: Cambridge University Press.

Feenstra, R.C., 1998, "Integration of Trade and Disintegration of Production in the Global Economy", *Journal of Economic Perspective*, Vol. 12, No. 4, 31–50.

Feldstein, M. and C. Horioka, 1980, "Domestic Savings and International Capital Flows", *Economic Journal*, Vol. 90, No. 2, pp. 314–29.

Fernandez, R. and J. Portes, 1998, "Returns to Regionalism: An Analysis of Non-Traditional Gains from Regional Trade Agreements", *World Bank Economic Review*, Vol. 12, No. 2, 197–200.

Financial Times, 2002, "Middle Classes in China's Long March to Prosperity", December 29, p. 3.

Findlay, R., 1996, "The Emergence of the World Economy: Towards A Historical Perspective", New York: Columbia University, Columbia University Economics Discussion Paper No. 9596, April.

Findlay, R. and K.H. O'Rourke, 2001, "Commodity Market Integration, 1500–2000", paper presented at the NBER Conference on *Globalization in Historical Perspective*, Santa Barbara, CA, May 2002.

Fischer, S., 1999, "Reforming the International Financial System", *Economic Journal*, Vol. 109, No. 3, 557–76.

Fletcher, M.E., 1958, "The Suez Canal and the World of Shipping; 1869–1914", *Journal of Economic History*, Vol. 18, No. 3, 556–73.

Flynn, D.O. and A. Giraldez., 1995, "Born with a Silver Spoon: The Origin of World Trade in 1571", *Journal of World History*, Vol. 6, No. 2, 201–220.

Frankel, J.A., 1997, *Regional Trading Blocs in the World Economic System*, Washington, DC: Institute of International Economics.

Frankel, J., 2000, "Globalization of the Economy", Cambridge, MA: National Bureau of Economic Research, Working Paper No. 7858.

Frankel, J.A., 2001, "Globalization and the Economy", in J. Nye and J. Donahue (eds), *Governance in a Globalizing World*, Washington, DC, Brookings Institution Press, pp. 132–58.

Frankel, J.A. and D. Romer, 1999, "Does Trade Cause Growth?", *American Economic Review*, Vol. 89, No. 2, 379–99.

Friedman, T.L., 1999, "Dueling Globalization: A Debate Between Thomas Friedman and Ignacio Ramonet", *Foreign Policy*, Fall, 110–19.

Fujita, M., P.R. Krugman and A.J. Venables, 1999, *The Spatial Economy: Cities, Regions and International Trade*, Cambridge, MA: MIT Press.

Gamber, E.N. and J.H. Hung, 2001, "Has the Rise in Globalization Reduced US Inflation the 1990s?", *Economic Enquiry*, Vol. 39, No. 1, 58–73.

Giovanoli, M., 2001, "A New Architecture for the Global Financial Market: Legal Aspects of International financial Standard Setting", Basle: International Monetary Law Association.

Goklany, I.M., 2002, "The Globalization of Human Well-Being", Washington, DC: Cato Institute, Policy Analysis Paper No. 447, August 22.

Grubel, H.G., 2000, "The Merit of a Canada-US Monetary Union", *North American Journal of Economics and Finance*, Vol. 11, No. 19–40.

Hatton, T. and J.G. Williamson, 1998, *The Age of Mass Migration: Causes and Economic Impact*, Oxford: Oxford University Press.

Hatton, T. and J.G. Williamson, 2001, "Demographic and Economic Pressure on Immigration Out of Africa", Cambridge, MA: National Bureau of Economic Research, Working Paper No. 8124.

Held, D., A.G. McGrew, D. Goldblatt and J. Perraton, 1999, *Global Transformations: Politics, Economics and Culture*, Stanford: Stanford University Press, p. 16.

Hertel, T. and W. Martin, 2001, "Liberalizing Agriculture and Manufactures in a Millennium Round: Implications for Developing Countries", in B. Hoekman and W. Martin (eds), *Developing Countries and the WTO: A Pro-Active Agenda*, Oxford: Blackwell, pp. 110–42.

Hicks, J., 1959, *Essays in World Economics*, Oxford: Clarendon Press.

Hoekman, B.M. and M.M. Kostecki, 2001, *The Political Economy of the World Trading System*, Oxford: Oxford University Press.

Horsefield, J.K., 1969, *The International Monetary Fund, 1945–65*, Vol. 3, Washington, DC: International Monetary Fund.

Hufbauer, G., E. Wada and T. Warren, 2002, *The Benefits of Price Convergence: Speculative Calculations*, Washington, DC: Institute for International Economics, Policy Analysis in Economics. Paper No. 65.

Hummels, D., 1999, "Have International Transportation Costs Declined?", Chicago: University of Chicago (mimeo).

International Monetary Fund, 1995, "International Capital Markets: Developments, Prospects and Policy Issues", Washington, DC: IMF.

International Monetary Fund, 2000, "International Capital Markets: Challenges, Prospects and Opportunities", Washington, DC: IMF.

International Monetary Fund, 2002, *World Economic Outlook*, October. Washington, DC: IMF.

Irwin, D.A., 1998, "From Smoot-Hawley to Reciprocal Trade Agreements: Changing the Course of U.S. Trade Policy in the 1930s", in M.D. Boro, C. Goldin and E. White (eds), *The Defining Moment: The Great Depression and the American Economy in the Twentieth Century*, Chicago: University of Chicago Press.

Jalilian, H. and C. Kirkpatrick, 2002, "Financial Development and Poverty Reduction", *International Journal of Finance and Economics*, Vol. 7, No. 1, 97–108.

Jordan, C. and M. Lubrano, 2002, "Strengthening Financial Sector Governance in Emerging Market Economies", Washington, DC: Brookings Institution, Policy Brief No. 12.

Jordan, C. and G. Majnoni, 2002, "Financial Regulatory Harmonization and the Globalization of Finance", Washington, DC: World Bank, Policy Research Working Paper No. 2919, October.

Kalaitzidakis, P., 2001, "Measures of Human Capital and Nonlinearities in Economic Growth", *Journal of Economic Growth*, Vol. 6, No. 3, 229–54.

Kaminsky, G. and S. Schmukler, 2001, *On Financial Booms and Crashes: Regional Patterns, Time Patterns, and Financial Liberalization*, Washington, DC: World Bank.

Kenwood, A.G. and A.L. Lougheed, 1983, *The Growth of International Economy 1820–1980: An Introductory Text*, 2nd edn, London: Unwin Hyman.

Keohane, R.O. and J.S. Nye, 2001, "Introduction", in Keohane and Nye (eds), *Governance in a Globalizing World*, Washington, DC: Brookings Institution Press, pp. 1–41.

Keynes, J.M., 1919, *Economic Consequences of the Peace*, available at <http://www.socsci.mcmaster.ca/~econ/ugcm/3ll3/keynes/peace.htm>.

Keynes, J.M., 1982, "Shaping the Post-War World: The Clearing Union", in D. Moggridge (ed.), *The Collected Writings of John Maynard Keynes*, Vol. 25, London: Macmillan.

Khan, A.R. and C. Riskin, 1998, "Income Inequality in China: Composition, Distribution, and Growth of Household Income, 1988–1995", *China Quarterly*, Vol. 31, No. 2, 221–53.

Khan, A.R. and C. Riskin, 2001, *Inequality and Poverty in China in the Age of Globalization*, New York: Oxford University Press.

Kindleberger, C.P., 1989, "Commercial Policy Between the Wars", in P. Mathias and S. Pollard (eds), *The Cambridge Economic History of Europe*, Vol. III, Cambridge: Cambridge University Press.

King, M., 1999, "Challenges for Monetary Policy: New and Old", in *New Challenges for Monetary Policy*, Kansas City, KA: Federal Reserve Bank of Kansas City.

King, R.G. and R. Levine, 1993, "Finance, Entrepreneurship and Growth: Theory and Evidence", *Journal of Monetary Economics*, Vol. 32, No. 3, 513–42.

Kolodko, G.W., 2000, *From Shock to Therapy: The Political Economy of Post-Socialist Transformation*, Oxford. Oxford University Press.

Kolodko, G.W., 2001, "Globalization and Transformation: Illusions and Reality", Paris: OECD Development Center, Technical Paper No. 176, May.

Kolodko, G.W., 2002, "Globalization and Catching-Up in Emerging Market Economies", Helsinki: United Nations University, World Institute for Development Economic Research, WIRER Discussion Paper WDP/2002/51, May.

Krueger, A.O., 1980, "Trade Policy as an Input to Development", *American Economic Review*, Vol. 70, No. 2, 288–92.

Krueger, A.O., 2000, "Factors Affecting Export Growth and Performance", in Dilip K. Das (ed.), *Asian Exports*, Oxford: Oxford University Press, pp. 25–74.

Krueger, A.O., 2003, "Promoting International Financial Stability: Sovereign Debt Restructuring", in Dilip K. Das (ed.), *An International Finance Reader*, London and New York: Routledge, pp. 114–41.

Krugman, P., 1997, "What Should Trade Negotiators Negotiate About", *Journal of Economic Literature*, Vol. 35, March, 113–20.

Laird, S., 2002, "Multilateral Market Access Negotiations in Goods and Services", in C. Milner and R. Read (eds), *Trade Liberalization, Competition and the WTO*, Cheltenham: Edward Elgar, pp. 23–58.

Laird, S., 2002, "The WTO Agenda and the Developing Countries", in C. Milner and R. Read (eds) *Trade Liberalization, Competition and the WTO*, Cheltenham: Edward Elgar, pp. 227–52.

Lamartine Yates, P., 1959, *Forty Years of Foreign Trade*, New York: Macmillan.

Lane, P.R., 1997, "Inflation in Open Economies", *Journal of International Economics*, Vol. 42, No. 2, 327–47.

Langlois, J.D., 1981, *China Under Mongol Rule*, Princeton, NJ: Princeton University Press.

Lardy, N.R., 2001, "Foreign Financial Firms in Asia", paper presented at a conference on *Open Doors: Foreign Participation in Financial Systems in Developing Countries*, jointly organized by the Brookings Institution, the World Bank and the International Monetary Fund, Washington, DC, April 15.

Larrain, P. and A. Velasco, 2001, "Exchange Rate Policies in Emerging Market Economies: The Case for Floating", *Essays in International Economics*, No. 224, December.

Lejour, A.M. and P.J.G. Tang, 1999, "Globalization and Wage Inequality", Rotterdam: CPB Netherlands Bureau of Economic Policy and Analysis (mimeo).

Limao, N. and A.J. Venables, 2000, "Infrastructure, Geographical Disadvantage, and Transport Costs", Washington, DC: World Bank.

Limao, N. and A.J. Venables, 2000, *Infrastructure, Geographical Disadvantage and Transport Costs*, Washington, DC: World Bank.

Lindert, P. and J. Williamson, 2001, "Does Globalization Make the world More Equal", Cambridge, MA: National Bureau of Economic Research, Working Paper No. 8228.

Lindert, P. and J. Williamson, 2001, "Globalization : A Long History", paper presented at the annual conference on Development Economics – Europe Conference, Barcelona, World Bank, June 25–27.

Lindsey, B., 2000. "Globalization in the Streets Again", Washington, DC: Cato Institute, Center for Trade Policy Studies, May 27. Available at <freetrade.org/pubs/articles/bl-4-15-00.html>.

Lipsey, R.E., 1999, "The Role of Foreign Direct Investment in International Capital Flows", Cambridge, MA: National Bureau of Economic Research, Working Paper No. 7094.

Maddison, A., 1995, *Monitoring the World Economy 1820–1992*, Paris: OECD.

Maddison, A., 2001, *The World Economy: A Millennial Perspective*, Paris: OECD.

Marshall, R., 1993, *Storm from the East: From Genghis Khan to Khubilai Khan*, Los Angeles: University of California Press.

Martin, W., 2001, *Trade Policies, Developing Countries and Globalization*, Washington, DC: World Bank.

Martin, W. and L.A. Winters, 1996, "The Uruguay Round: A Milestone for the Developing Countries", in W. Martin and L.A. Winters (eds), *The Uruguay Round and the Developing Countries*, Cambridge: Cambridge University Press, pp. 1–29.

Matusz, S.J. and D. Tarr, 2000, "Adjusting to Trade Policy Reforms", in A.O. Krueger (ed.), *Economic Policy Reform: The Second Stage*, Chicago: University of Chicago Press, pp. 130–64.

Melchior, A., K. Telle and H. Wiig, 2000, "Globalization and Inequality: World Income Distribution and Living Standards 1960–98", Oslo: Royal Norwegian Ministry of Foreign Affairs, Report No. 68, September.

Meyer, L.H., 2000, "Structural Changes and Monetary Policy", presentation made before the Joint Conference of Federal Bank of San Francisco and the Stanford Institute of Economic Policy Research, San Francisco, March 3. Available at <http://www.frbsf. org/economics/conferences/000303/agenda/html>.

Micklethwait, J. and A. Wooldridge, 2000, *A Future Perfect*, New York: Random House.

Milanovic, B., 2002, "Can We Discern the Effects of Globalization on Income Distribution?", Washington, DC: World Bank, Policy Research Working Paper No. 2876, April.

Milner, C. and R. Read, 2002, "Introduction: The GATT Uruguay Round, Trade Liberalization and the WTO", in C. Milner and R. Read (eds), *Trade Liberalization, Competition and the WTO*, Cheltenham: Edward Elgar, pp. 1–22.

Mishkin, F. 2001, "Financial Policies and Prevention of Financial Crises", in M. Feldstein (ed.), *Economic and Financial Crises in Emerging Market Countries*, Chicago: University of Chicago Press, pp. 134–60.

Mote, F.W., 1999, *Imperial China: 900–1800*, Cambridge, MA: Harvard University Press.

Mundell, R.A., 2000, "A Reconsideration of the Twentieth Century", *American Economic Review*, Vol. 90, No. 3, 327–40.

Mussa, M., 1998, "Trade Liberalization", in Z. Iqbal and M.S. Khan (eds), *Trade Reform and Regional Integration in Africa*, Washington, DC: International Monetary Fund, pp. 19–65.

Neal, L., 1990, *The Rise of Financial Capitalism: International Capital Markets in the Age of Reason*, Cambridge: Cambridge University Press.

Needham, J., 1954, *Science and Civilization in China*, Vol. I, Cambridge: Cambridge University Press.

Obstfeld, M., 1995, "International Capital Mobility in the 1990s", in P.B. Kenen (ed.), *Understanding Interdependence: The Macroeconomics of Open Economy*, Princeton, NJ: Princeton University Press.

Obstfeld, M., 2000, "Globalization and Macroeconomics", *NBER Reporter*, Cambridge, MA: National Bureau of Economic Research, Fall, 18–23.

Obstfeld, M. and K. Rogoff, 2001, "The Six Major Puzzles in International Macroeconomics: Is There A Common Cause?", Cambridge, MA: National Bureau of Economic Research, Working Paper No. 7777.

Obstfeld, M. and A.M. Taylor, 1998, "The Great Depression as a Watershed: International Capital Mobility Over the Long Run", in M.D. Bordo, C. Goldin and N. White (eds), *The Defining Moment: The Great Depression and the American Economy in the Twentieth Century*, Chicago: University of Chicago Press, pp. 353–402.

Obstfeld, M. and A.M. Taylor, 2002, "Globalization and Capital Markets", Cambridge, MA: National Bureau of Economic Research, Working Paper No. 8846, March.

Okina, O., M. Shirakawa and S. Shiratsuka, 1999, "Financial Market Globalization: Present and Future", *Monetary and Economic Studies*, Bank of Japan, Institute for Monetary and Economic Studies, Vol. 17, No. 3, 48–82.

Organization for Economic Co-operation and Development (OECD), 1997, *Economic Globalization and the Environment*, Paris: OECD.

Organization for Economic Co-operation and Development (OECD), 2002, *Revenue Statistics*, Paris: OECD, October.

O'Rourke, K.H. and J.G. Williamson, 2000, "When Did Globalization Begin?", Cambridge MA: National Bureau of Economic Research, Working Paper No. 7632, April.

Parsley, D.C. and S.J. Wei, 2001, "Limiting Currency Volatility to Stimulate Goods Market Integration: A Price-Based Approach", Cambridge, MA: National Bureau of Economic Research, Working Paper No. 8468.

Phillips, E.D., 1969, *The Mongols*, New York: Praeger.

Powell, A., 2002, "A Capital Accord for Emerging Economies?", March, available at <http://econ.worldbank.org/files/13169_wps2808.pdf>.

Rapoport, H., 2001, "Who is Afraid of the Brain Drain? Human Capital Flight and Growth in Developing Countries", Stanford, CA: Stanford University, Stanford institute for Economic Policy Research, Economic Policy Brief.

Razin, A. and E. Sadka (eds), 1999, *The Economics of Globalization*, Cambridge: Cambridge University Press.

Robertson, R., 2000, "Trade Liberalization and Wage Inequality: Lessons from Mexican Experience", *World Economy*, Vol. 23, No. 6, June, 827–49.

Rodrik, D., 1997, *Has Globalization Gone Too Far?*, Washington, DC: Institute of International Economics.

Rogers, J.H., 2002, "Price Level Convergence, Relative Prices, and Inflation in Europe", Washington, DC: Board of Governors of the Federal Reserve System, International Finance Discussion Paper No. 699.

Rogoff, K., 1999, "Economic Institutions for Reducing Global Financial Instability", *Journal of Economic Perspectives*, Vol. 13, No. 1, 21–42.

Rose, A.K., 2002, "Estimating Protectionism from the Gravity Model", Washington DC: International Monetary Fund (mimeo).

Rossabi, M. 1988, *Khubilai Khan: His Life and Times*, Los Angeles: University of California Press.

Rousseau, P.L. and R. Sylla, 2001, "Financial Systems, Economic Growth, and Globalization", Cambridge, MA: National Bureau of Economic Research, Working Paper No. 8323, June.

Rugman, A.M., 2002, "New Rules for International Investment: the Case for a Multilateral Agreement on Investment (MAI) at the WTO", in C. Milner and R. Read (eds), *Trade Liberalization, Competition and the WTO*, Cheltenham Edward Elgar, pp. 176–89.

Sab, R. and S.C. Smith, 2001, "Human Capital Convergence: International Evidence", Washington, DC: International Monetary Fund, Working Paper No. WP/01/32.

Sampson, G.P., 2000, *Trade, Environment and the WTO: the Post-Seattle Agenda*, Baltimore, MD: Johns Hopkins University Press.

Schmukler, S. and P. Zoido-Lobaton, 2001, "Financial Globalization: Opportunities and Challenges for Developing Countries", Washington, DC: World Bank.

Schulze, G.G. and H.W. Ursprung, 1999, "Globalization of Economy and Nation State", *World Economy*, Vol. 22, No. 2, 295–352.

Slaughter, M., 1999, "Globalization and Wages: A Tale of Two Perspectives", *World Economy*, Vol. 22, No. 3, 609–29.

Solimano, A., 2001, "International Migration and the Global Economic Order: An Overview", Washington, DC: World Bank, Policy Research Working Paper No. 2720, November.

Srinivasan, T.N., 2002, "Globalization: Is it Good or Bad?", Stanford, CA: Stanford Institute for Economic Policy Research, Economic Policy Brief, December 23.

Stiglitz, J., 1998, "Towards A New Paradigm for Development: Strategies, Policies, and Processes", Raul Prebisch Lecture, delivered at the UNCTAD Secretariat, Geneva, October 19.

Stiglitz, J.E., 2000, "Capital Market Liberalization, Economic Growth and Instability", *World Development*, Vol. 28, No. 6, 1075–86.

Sutton, J., 2000, "Rich Trade, Scarce Capabilities: Industrial Development Revisited", Discussion Paper No. E1/28, London: London School of Economics and Political Science, September.

Sylla, R., J.W. Wilson and R.E. Wright, 2002, "Trans-Atlantic Capital Market Integration: 1790–1845", paper presented at the high-level seminar on

Globalization in Historical Perspective, organized by the International Monetary Fund, August 12–14, 2002, Washington, DC.

Tanzi, V., 2000, "Globalization, Technological Developments, and the Work of Fiscal Termites", Washington, DC: International Monetary Fund, Working Paper No. WP/00/181.

Taylor, A.M., 1996, "International Capital Mobility in History: Purchasing Power Parity in the Long-Run", Cambridge, MA: National Bureau of Economic Research, Working Paper No. 5742. August.

Taylor, A.M., 1998, "International Capital Mobility in History: The Saving-Investment Relationship", *Journal of Development Economics*, Vol. 57, No. 1, 147–84.

Tesar, L. and I. Werner, 1998, "Internalization of Securities Markets Since the 1987 Crash", in R.E. Litan and A. Santomero (eds), *Brookings-Wharton Papers on Financial Services*, Washington, DC: Brookings Institution Press, pp. 281–372.

United Nations Conference on Trade and Development (UNCTAD), 2002, *World Investment Report 2001*, Geneva: UNCTAD.

Wagner, H., 2000, "Which Exchange Rate Regime in an Era of High Capital Mobility?", *North American Journal of Economics and Finance*, Vol. 11, No. 1, 191–203.

Wagner, H., 2000, "Globalization and Inflation", in H. Wagner (ed.), *Globalization and Unemployment*, Berlin, Springer, pp. 345–90.

Wagner, H., 2001, "Implications of Globalization for Monetary Policy", Washington, DC: International Monetary Fund. Working Paper No. WP/01/184, November.

Wei, S.J. and Y. Wu, 2002, "*Globalization and Inequality Without Differences in Data Definition, Legal System, and Other Institution*", Cambridge, MA: National Bureau of Economic Research, Working Paper No. 8611.

Williamson, J.G., 1996, "Globalization, Convergence and History", *Journal of Economic History*, Vol. 56, No. 2, 277–306.

Winters, L.A., 2002, "Trade Policies for Poverty Alleviation", in B. Hoekman, A. Mattoo and P. English (eds), *Trade, Development, and the WTO*, Washington, DC: World Bank.

World Bank, 1997, *Sharing Rising Incomes: Disparities in China*, Washington, DC: World Bank.

World Bank, 1998, *Assessing Aid: What Works? What Doesn't and Why?*, New York: Oxford University Press for World Bank.

World Bank, 2000, *Global Economic Prospects and Developing Countries*, Washington, DC: World Bank.

World Bank, 2001, *World Development Report 2000/2001*, New York: Oxford University Press.

World Bank, 2001, *World Development Indicators*, Washington, DC: World Bank.

World Bank, 2001, *Global Economic Prospects and the Developing Economies*, Washington, DC: World Bank.

World Bank, 2001, *Finance for Growth: Policy Choices in a Volatile World*. Washington, DC: World Bank Policy Research Report.

World Bank, 2002, *Globalization, Growth and Poverty*, New York: Oxford University Press.

World Development Report, 2000, Washington, DC: Oxford University Press for World Bank.

World Trade Organization (WTO), 1994, "Developing Countries and the Uruguay round: An Overview", Geneva: Committee on Trade and Development, 77th Session, November 25.

World Trade Organization (WTO), 1998, "Tariffs: More Binding and Closer to Zero", available at <http://www.wto.org/about/agmnts2.htm>.

World Trade Organization (WTO), 1999, *The Legal Texts: the Results of the Uruguay Round of Multilateral Trade Negotiations*, Cambridge: Cambridge University Press.

World Trade Organization (WTO), 2001, "Doha WTO Ministerial: Briefing Notes: 52 Years of GATT/WTO", Geneva: available at <http://www-heva.wto-ministerial.org/english/the wto_e/minist_e/min01_e/brief_e/brief21_e.htm>.

Ziegler, D., 2003, "The Weakest Link: A Survey of Asian Finance", *The Economist*, February 13, p. 5.

Index